James Madison's Religion

Minneapolis
FIRST EDITION 2025

James Madison's Religion
Copyright © 2025 by Stephen J. Vicchio.
All rights reserved.

No part of this book may be used or reproduced in any manner whatsoever without written permission except in the case of brief quotations used in critical articles and reviews. For information, write to Calumet Editions, 6800 France Avenue South, Suite 370, Edina, MN 55435

Printed in the United States of America.
10 9 8 7 6 5 4 3 2 1

Cover and interior design: Gary Lindberg

ISBN: 978-1-962834-59-9

Alexander Hamilton's Religion

Stephen J. Vicchio, Ph.D.

Wisdom Editions
Minneapolis

Also by Stephen J. Vicchio

PLAYS

Hannah and Martin: Some Ontological and Moral Puzzles

The Unnamed Play

Ivan and Adolf: The Last Man in Hell

Executioner's Hill

OTHER WORKS

Hell: A Detailed History of an Idea

Estevanico: The First Black Man in America

Evil in World Religion

From Vladimir to Vladimir: A History of Russian-Ukraine Relations

Hamilton's Religion

Mala'ika: Angels in Islam

Evil and Suffering in the Bible

Muslim Slaves in the Chesapeake 1634–1865

The Akedah, or Sacrifice of Isaac

The Idea of the Demonic

Limbo: The History of an Idea

Contents

Introduction 1
Chapter One: Madison's Earliest Religious Life 9
hapter Two: Madison on God and Jesus Christ. 31
Chapter Three: Madison on the Bible. 55
Chapter Four: Madison on Ethics 79
Chapter Five: Madison on Religious Freedom
 and Religious Toleration 105
Chapter Six: Madison on Church and State. 127
Chapter Seven: Madison on Immortality
 and Survival After Death 149
Chapter Eight: Madison on Human Nature and Democracy. 171
Chapter Nine: Madison on Religions Other Than His Own 193
Chapter Ten: Madison on Slavery. 217
Chapter Eleven: Conclusions of this Study
 on James Madison's Religion 241
Appendix A: Foreign Words and Expressions. 273
Appendix B: Madison and the
 Scottish Philosophy of Common Sense. 277
Appendix C: Madison and the Federalist Papers. 287
Appendix D: Madison's Philosophical Foundations 297
Appendix E: Madison as Father of the Constitution 299
About the Author 307

.

Introduction

The Study to follow is an examination of the religious beliefs of the fourth President of the United States, James Madison. This Study consists of ten chapters and an 11th chapter that serves as a Conclusive Chapter in which we will describe the major conclusions of this Study.

There is also an Appendix to this work where we catalogue the Foreign Words and Phrases employed in this Study. The purpose of this Introduction is to describe what will follow in the next ten chapters of this Study. The subject-matter of Chapter One is Mr. Madison's earliest religious life beginning with his baptism by the Rector of St. Thomas Episcopal Church, by the Rev. William Davis, on March 1, 1751. We also have indicated that James Madison Sr., the President's father took his family to worship at that same church.

We also will give an account in Chapter One to the early education of James Madison Jr, from lessons with his maternal grandmother to the fourth President's attendance at a school run by Scotsman Donald Robertson in the second half of the 18th Century, some distance from the Madison home at Montpelier.

In Chapter One, we also mentioned the tutoring that Mr. Madison received at the hands of Anglican cleric, Rev. Thomas Martin, who resided at Montpelier for two years while tutoring the fourth president.

In the First Chapter, we also have given a description of Mr. Madison's college mentor, Dr. John Witherspoon, the President of the College of New Jersey who instructed the young Madison in classical Hebrew and Moral Philosophy. We also have pointed to the influence on Mr. Madison of the Scottish Common Sense School of Philosophy while a student of Mr. Witherspoon.

In Chapter One of this Study, we also have explored some of the ways that the subject of Religion may be found in the letters of Mr. Madison, most of these from the 1770s and 1780s. Among these letters, as we shall see in Chapter One were missives to his college roommate, William Bradford, one to Rabbi Jacob de la Motta, and one to Mr. Madison's friend and judge, Edward Livingston.

At the end of the First Chapter, we made six conclusions about these letters of Mr. Madison's. These may be summarized this way:

1. Mr. Madison believed that God was the Architect of the Universe.
2. Mr. Madison preferred a Republican Government.
3. Mr. Madison was dedicated to the idea of the free exercise of Religion.
4. Mr. Madison was persuaded by the Scottish Common Sense School of Philosophy in matters of Religion and Conscience.
5. Mr. Madison was fond of expressions like 'equal rights under the law."
6. Mr. Madison's writings have the traces of an influence of Hebrew poetic forms he learned from Mr. Witherspoon.

The subject-matter of Chapter Two of this Study will be dedicated entirely to what Mr. Madison said and wrote about the existence and activities of God. We will begin the Chapter by pointing to several places where the fourth President commented about the Divine. Among these sources, as we shall see, will be the 1776 Virginia "Declaration of Rights," Mr. Madison's "Essay on Property," and a letter to his friend, William Bradford.

We also will indicate in Chapter Two that James Madison held views in his College Senior Thesis much like those of English philosopher, John Stuart Mill in his 1859 word. *On Liberty*, on the issues of Freedom of Religion and Religious Toleration.

We also will show in Chapter Two that like many of the other American Founding Fathers, James Madison had a penchant for avoiding the use of the word "God," and substituted instead a variety of synonyms for that word. In fact, as we shall see, Mr. Madison employed fourteen separate substitute names for the Divine.

In a Third Section of Chapter Two, we shall explore what James Madison said and wrote about the Christian Faith and in a Fourth Section what he believed about the person of Jesus of Nazareth. At the very end of Chapter Two, we will provide a catalogue of ten beliefs that Mr. Madison had about the existence of and activity of God in the Judeo-Christian tradition.

The central concern with Chapter Three of this Study shall be on James Madison's perspectives on Holy Scripture. The Chapter will be divided into three, main Sections. In the first of these we will give an account of the major sources that may have influenced Mr. Madison's views on the Bible. Among those sources, as we shall see, are Donald Robertson, the Rev. Thomas Martin, and John Witherspoon from whom Mr. Madison learned classical Hebrew.

In the Second Section of Chapter Three we will explore what Mr. Madison said and wrote, as well as quoted from, the Old Testament. The chief source is this Section will be the Madison family Bible, an edition of William Burkitt's *Expository Notes on the Bible*. We also will claim that James Madison was influenced by John Witherspoon's *Collected Sermons*.

We also will give a list and discussion of the many Old Testament passages upon which Mr. Madison commented, including sections of the Psalms, the Book of Job, Proverbs, Isaiah, and the Book of Daniel.

James Madison's views on the New Testament will be the focus of the next Section of Chapter Three. In that section we will provide a catalogue of New Testament perspectives made by the fourth President, mostly in a document entitled, "Notes on a Commentary on the Bible," which was completed between 1770 and 1773, when Mr. Madison was in college and graduate school studying with Mr. Witherspoon.

The two main goals of Chapter Four of this Study, as we shall soon see, is to give an account of what the fourth President believed and had to say about Ethics and the Conscience. We will begin Chapter Four by giving an account of some of the main sources of James Madison's views on Ethics and Conscience. Among these, we will list five: the

Scottish Common Sense School; Witherspoon's *Sermons* and *Lectures on Moral philosophy*; Aristotle's *Ethics*; Seneca's *Letters on Virtue*; and Cicero's *Essay on Virtue*.

After discussing the contribution that each of these five sources may have had on the early, intellect life of James Madison, we will follow that Section with an analysis of twelve of the other American Founding Fathers on the idea of Conscience. Among these, as we shall see, are Roger Williams, George Washington, John Adams, Thomas Jefferson, John Jay, Benjamin Rush, and many others.

The next and central Section of Chapter Four of this Study will be entirely dedicated to what James Madison believed and wrote about Ethics and Conscience. Indeed, at the end of Chapter Four, we will provide a list of four conclusions that James Madison believed about the notion of Conscience. These four conclusions may be summarized this way:

1. The idea of Conscience is an innate and universal sense of the Good.
2. Conscience is a Gift, or Grace, from God.
3. No man has a right to interfere in the Conscience of another.
4. The Right to Conscience is more fundamental than any Civil Rights.

The main foci of Chapter Five of this Study on James Madison's Religion will be on the ideas of Religious Freedom and Religious Toleration. Chapter Five of this Study will be divided into three main Sections. The first of these will be about what Mr. Madison believed and wrote about Religious Liberty; the Second Section will describe what the fourth President thought and observed about Religious Toleration; and the Third Section of Chapter Five will consist of some very general comments about what James Madison thought about other religions other than his own.

The idea of Separation of Church and State and what James Madison believed and wrote about that phenomenon will be the focus of Chapter Six of this Study on James Madison's Religion. Before dealing with Mr. Madison's views on the matter in Chapter Six, we will first provide a short history in the West that have dealt with the idea of Religion and Government being two separate realms. Among the items in that history shall be the perspectives of Augustine, Jean Calvin, Roger Williams, the Rev. James Burgh, and Thomas Jefferson's letter to the Danbury Baptists.

The remainder of Chapter Six, as we shall see, will be an analyses of what the fourth President of the United States, James Madison, believed and wrote about the phenomenon of the Separation of Church and State. In that material we will find an undaunting support of Thomas Jefferson's ideas about the matter.

The ideas on Survival After Death, and what James Madison believed and wrote about them, will be the primary focus of Chapter Seven of this Study. We will begin the Chapter by making the distinction between the ideas of Resurrection of the Body and Immortality of the Soul. The former a Jewish idea and the latter a Greek idea.

In order to compare and contrast these two ideas we will employ the grave markers of an 19th Century, Presbyterian couple, one of whom is now "sleeping in the dust," while his wife has "gone to her eternal reward.'

In the Second Section of Chapter Seven, we will introduce two main ideas that existed in the 17th and 18th Century about the issue of Immortality. On the one side, we will see that David Hume was skeptical about the matter at hand, while German, Immanuel Kant proposed that Immortality can be proved through what he called "Practical Reason."

James Madison would have been fully aware of these two 18th Century, philosophical points of view. In the remainder of the Chapter, we shall sketch out the few references to Immortality that may be found in the *Collected Works* of James Madison. In fact, as we shall see, the few references to Survival After Death in the works of the fourth President all come in his essays of the *Federalist Papers*.

Indeed, as we shall see in Chapter Seven, these references to "Soul" and "Spirit," come in *Federalists* 10, 17, 18, 46, 51, and 55. And in each of these examples of James Madison, he employed the words 'Spirit' and 'Soul,' but not in a theological or metaphysical context. But the number of these examples, as we shall see, are few and far between.

The notions of what James Madison thought and wrote about Human Nature and the idea of Democracy will be the foci of Chapter Eight of this Study. We will begin that Chapter by rehearsing several 18th Century perspectives on human nature, including those of Thomas Hobbes, Jean-Jacques Rousseau, John Locke, and David Hume. This will be followed by an analysis of what James Madison believed and wrote about human nature. The most important answer to that question is that, like the other authors of the *Federalist Papers*—Alexander Hamilton and John Jay—Mr. Madison had a pessimistic view of human nature, not all that different from Thomas Hobbes or Augustine of Hippo.

The remainder of Chapter Eight will be taken up with the question of Democracy and what James Madison thought and wrote about the matter. As we shall see, the fourth President was fearful that what he called the "dangers of Factions," may create what he called a "Tyranny of the Majority."

In the Final Section of Chapter Eight, we will attempt to bring together the two topics of the Chapter, human nature and democracy and suggesting how in the mind of James Madison these two phenomena are connected.

The central focus of Chapter Nine of this Study on James Madison's Religion shall be on what the fourth President believed and wrote about other religions other than his own Episcopal Faith. Indeed, in that Chapter we will explore the fourth President's dealings with the Baptists, the Presbyterians, the America Jewish Community, the Catholics, and to the practitioners of the Faith of Islam.

The major Conclusion we shall make about these six Sections of Chapter Nine is that James Madison was in full support of the Religious Liberties of the members of each of these Faiths. We also will indicate in Chapter Nine that James Madison was not a Deist because he believed that God acts in history.

Finally, the major focus of Chapter Ten of this Study on James Madison's Religion shall be on the fourth President's complicated attitudes toward the practice of Slavery in America. We will begin Chapter Ten with some general comments about Slavery and the American Presidency. This will be followed by a discussion of several prominent slaves at the Madison family Montpelier home. We also will discuss in Chapter Ten a short account of Slavery in Virginia, as well as the two major Slave Rebellions in that region in the early 19th Century.

In the Central Section of Chapter Ten, we will discuss the "Ambivalent Attitudes of James Madison on Slavery." In that Section we will show that Mr. Madison was pulled in two directions when it came to the issue of human captivity. On the one hand, he grew up in a slave-holding family and profited from the work of slaves his whole life. On the other hand, he was in favor of Freed America Slaves being established on the West Coast of Africa and was President for a while of the American Colonization Society.

In short, James Madison was quite ambivalent about the practice of Slavery in America. One may to see that ambivalence directly is to look at the many comments that James Madison, the fourth President of the United States, made in his essays in the *Federalist Papers*, as we shall see in Chapter Ten of this Study on James Madison's Religion. This brings us to Chapter One and some observations about Mr. Madison's Earliest Religious Beliefs.

Before we get to the First Chapter, however, we must point out that throughout this Study we will use the "great American statesman" and the "fourth President," to indicate when we are speaking about James Madison Jr.

A Note on Sources

Both the primary and the secondary sources of this Study are related to six works on the fourth President of the United States, James Madison. We will list these sources here, upfront, so when we get to the Notes of this Study, we will already have provided a record of those sources. After this note, we will move to Chapter One of this Study on Jams Madison's Religion.

- Robert S. Alley. *James Madison on Religious Liberty*. (New York: Prometheus Books, 1985.)
- Lenni Brenner (Ed.) *Jefferson and Madison: On Separation of Church and State*. (Fort Lee, New Jersey: Barricade Books, 2004.)

- Richard Brookhiser. *James Madison*. (New York: Basic Books, 2011.)
- Ralph Ketcham. *James Madison*. (Charlottesville: University of Virginia Press, 1990.)
- Burt Neuborne. *Madison's Music: On Reading the First Amendment*. (New York: the New Press, 2015.)
- Rodney K. Smith. *James Madison: The Father of Religious Liberty*. (Springville, Utah: Plain Sight Publishing, 2019.)

Chapter One:
James Madison's Earliest Religious Life

Henry Lee is the greatest at the ability to persuade, but Madison is the greatest at the ability to convince.

—John Marshall. "On Madison."

If God were in the details, Madison would be there to greet you upon arrival.

—Joseph Ellis. *James Madison*

If men were angels, there would be no need for government. If angels were to govern men, neither external nor internal controls on government would be necessary. In framing a government which is to be administered of men over men. The great difficulty lies in this: You must first enable the Government to control the governed; and in the next place, oblige it to control itself.

—James Madison. *Federalist Papers* number 51.

Introduction

The purpose of this First Chapter is to explore and to discuss the phenomenon of the fourth President of the United States, James Madison, in regard to his earliest religious life, from the time of his birth in 1751 until his graduation from the College of New Jersey, now Princeton University, in 1722. This purpose will be accomplished by dividing the Chapter into the following parts. First, we shall discuss the sources of James Madison's earliest Religious life.

Second, we will examine the roles played by what was known as the "Brick Church" that was established in 1740.[1] Third,, we will discuss the education of James Madison and the effects it seems to have had on his religious views. And finally, we will point to many of James Madison's early letters that point to his religious views, particularly after College.

The Sources for Madison's Early Religious life

In 1624, the Anglican Church, or the Church of England, became the established Church of the American Virginia Colony that had begun in 1607 in the Tidewater Region of the Colony. From 1624, then, the Anglican Church was the established Church in the Colony. All Virginians at the time were mandated to pay taxes to support this established Church. The General Assembly, early on in the Colony, protected this established Church in law and penalized dissenters with fines or even arrest.

The Virginia General Assembly also required all office holders of the Colony to be members of the Anglican Church and the Assembly also saw itself as the authority that established the creation of parishes, as well as the setting of the salaries of its Ministers.

By the birth of James Madison in March of 1751, the Virginia Colony had become more accepting of dissenters and non-Anglican Protestant Sects. In 1776, the Virginia "Declaration of Rights" said, "All men are equally entitled to the free exercise of religion, according to the dictates of conscience."[2] Three years later, in 1779, Thomas Jefferson introduced a bill entitled, "Statute for Establishing Religious Freedom."[3]

---

1 Most of the notes in this chapter can be found in Ketcham's biography of James Madison. Pp. 12–13

2 Virginia Declaration of Rights. [1776.] This document was drawn upon by Thomas Jefferson for the opening paragraph of the Declaration of Independence. It was widely copied by other colonies and became the basis for the Bill of Rights written by George Mason. It was adopted by the Virginia Constitutional Convention on June 12, 1776

3 Thomas Jefferson. 'Statute for Establishing Religious Freedom." [1779.] Mr. Jefferson's proposal was defeated and then finally passed on January 16, 1786

This bill advocated for complete religious freedom, but it was thought to be too radical at the time so Jefferson's 'Statute' did not pass at that time. Eventually, however, the third President's bill on Freedom of Religion did pass on January 16, 1786. It became the forerunner of the first amendment of the U.S. Constitution.

Before the American Revolution, the Church of England was the established Church in Colonial Virginia, which meant that colonists were legally required to attend its services and, through taxation to support the Church's ministers financially. The Church's lay vestries, of which James Sr. was a member, controlled a number of the governmental functions, including relief for the poor and the supervision and housing of orphans.

The first important source for understanding the early religious life of James Madison, then, is something that can be pointed to from ten years before his birth, that is, the establishment of an Anglican Church, as the established Church, in the American Colony of Virginia. In the year 1740 a Church of England congregation was established about seven miles from the home of James Hamilton Sr., the statesman's father who was a vestryman at that Church.

This original church was called Saint Mark's or the Brick Church, for it was constructed of brick and mortar. Later, the Church was renamed Saint Thomas. It had that name when James Madison was born in 1751. We know very little about the life of the St. Thomas Church, beyond the following facts. It originally consisted of about thirty families or 100 people in the congregation. James Madison Sr. served as a Vestryman at St. Thomas, and he attended weekly Sunday services with his family at the Anglican Church.[4]

We also know that James Madison Jr. was baptized at St. Thomas by the Rev. Mr. William Davis, on March 31, 1751 and he had two Godfathers and two Godmothers.[5] Mr. Madison had been born two weeks earlier on March 16, 1751 in the home of his maternal grandmother, Mrs. John Moore, about 55 miles East of the Madison's Plantation.[6] The Rev. Davis was Rector of St. Thomas until 1758.

---

4   Ketcham, p. 389
5   Ibid., pp. 8–9
6   Ibid

When the American Revolution began, St. Thomas Parish had two "Chapels of Ease," that were bult to serve members of the Church in the outlying regions of Virginia, while those nearer to town worshipped at the brick 'Mother Church' located on the property of Col. James Taylor II. Two of Col. Taylor's great grandsons—James Madison and Zachary Taylor—would serve as Presidents of the United States.

Shortly after the beginning of the Revolution, both Chapels of Ease were abandoned and the mother Church was torn down. All that remained of it were a few scattered bricks that later were placed in the porch floor of the new Church. Another relic of the old Brick Church was the London-made silver communion ware donated to the Church by James Madison's grandmother.

A second source for Mr. Madison's early religious life was his paternal great grandmother, a woman named Frances Taylor Madison, James Sr.'s mother. She was a devout Christian and had made the contributions to the Parish's communion plate. Religion also played an important part in the life of her son, James Sr., whose library at home contained about a hundred volumes, mostly works on Religion and medicine. By all accounts, Frances Madison was among the early religious teachers of Mr. Madison.

Among the volumes of James Sr.'s library, in addition to the King James Version of the Bible, could also be found:

- The Episcopal *Book of Common Prayer*. [1549.]
- Walter Marshall's The Gospel Mystery of Sanctification. [1692.]
- Henry Scougal's The Life of Man in the Soul of God. [1677.][7]

James Madison was called "Jemmy" by his family. He was a sickly child suffering many ailments that often confined him to his home. One effect is that he became devoted to reading and he delved into his father's library at a very early age.[8]

Like George Washington, Alexander Hamilton, and Benjamin Franklin, another great influence in the life of Mr. Madison was the

---

7   Ibid., p. 17

8   Ibid

periodical called the *Spectator*, started by Joseph Addison, and the Fourth President's grandmother had it delivered to the Montpelier Mansion.[9]

The final issue of the *Spectator* appeared in 1713, but its back issues were frequently read by members of the Virginia gentry and discussed for many years. Mr. Madison was so impressed with the *Spectator* that he sent several issues to his eleven year old nephew, Richard D. Cutts. In a letter that accompanied the gifts, Mr. Madison wrote:

When I was at an age that will soon be yours, a book fell into my hands which I read, as, I believe, with particular advantage… The work I speak of is the *Spectator*, well known by that title. It had several authors, and at the head of them was Mr. Addison.[10]

The *Spectator* was a daily newspaper founded by Joseph Addison and Richard Steele in England that lasted from 1711 until 1713. Each 'paper' or number was approximately 2500 words long beginning on March 1, 1711. These were collected into seven volumes and was revived a year later in 1714 with no success.

In the same letter to his nephew, Madison called Addison "of the first rank among fine writers of his age, and the fourth President added that Mr. Addison had "sentiment that are natural without being obvious." Madison also indicated to his nephew that 'Jonathan Swift counted Addison as one of his favorite authors.' These years at home, under the tutelage of his father and grandmother, were the youngest years of his education from age seven until age twelve. When Jemmy was twelve, his father enrolled him in a small school seventy miles away on the plantation home of the Rev. Robert Innes. The children boarded at the Rev. Innes home and the school was led by a Mr. Donald Robertson, a Scottish school master who had been educated at Aberdeen and Edinburgh.

The five years of study with Mr. Roberson began in 1763, when the future- statesman was twelve years old. Robertson introduced his student to ancient and modern languages (Greek, Latin, French, and Italian), the Bible with a Calvinistic bent including the Westminster Confession.

---

9 Ibid., p 41.
10 Ibid., p. 477

Greek and Roman historians and philosophers, and more Contemporary Enlightenment thinkers like John Locke and the Baron Montesquieu.

Mr. Robertson was an Anglican Pastor, a College of New Jersey (later Princeton) graduate, as was Mr. Madison. The fourth President's low-Church family did not send young James to William and Mary, Jefferson's College, with High-Church leanings. They sent him to study instead under John Witherspoon who became the College of New Jersey's President in 1768.

Mr. Robertson in 1752, at the age of thirty-five, had come to America where at first he worked as a private tutor for the children of John Baylor of Caroline County in Walkerton, Virginia. After the five years of tutoring, Mr. Robertson was encouraged to open a school of his 150 acre farm in the upper part of King and Queen County. Between 1758 and 1773, the school had thirty to forty pupils each year that provided a broad liberal arts education to the sons of the Virginia elite.

Mr. Hamilton remained under the tutelage of Mr. Robertson for five years. The first of those years may have been the most important for Robertson concentrated on Madison's proficiency with the English language, honing the soon to be statesman's use of the written word. Madison learned from Mr. Robertson that sloppy reading and sloppy writing often obscure very simple ideas. Mr. Madison later would be known for the lucidity, depth, and breadth of his prose.

We will say more about Donald Robertson, as well as a second teacher of James Madison, the Rev. Thomas Martin, in the next Section of this Chapter One of this Study on James Madison's Religion. This brings us to the Second Section of Chapter One, in which we will say more about the early education of James Madison Jr., our next topic in this First Chapter.

The Early Education of James Madison.

Ralph Ketchem in his biography of Mr. Madison gives us a flavor of the formal education of the sons of elite, Virginian landowners in the late 18th Century. He relates: 'Nearly all formal educated men in the Western world between the Renaissance and the beginning of the 20th Century, had its foundation in the lore and history and wisdom of

Greece and Rome.[11]

Ketchem goes on to speak of the Greco-Roman writers that Madison as well as others like him in his class, were expected to master. These included Plato, Aristotle, Thucydides, Plutarch, Cicero, Virgil, and Livy's 'idealized account of the Roman Republic.'[12]

James Madison began studying with Donald Robertson in 1762 at the age of eleven and continued to study with the Scotsman until the American was sixteen in 1767. With Mr. Robertson, Mr. Madison studied Latin, Greek, and French, as well as algebra, geography, and literature. A knowledge of Greek was thought necessary so that one could read the New Testament in the original language. It was also required for entrance into most of the prestigious colleges in the late 18th Century such as Harvard, Yale, and Columbia, for examples.

In later years, Mr. Madison described Donald Robertson as "a man of extensive learning and a distinguished teacher. "[13] In this small, school setting on Mr. Innes' plantation Jemmy doubtless received the attention he needed, which, together with his natural talents, enabled Madison to make rapid progress in his academics.

Donald Robertson also introduced Mr. Madison to many Classical and Enlightenment thinkers such as Justinian's *Institutes*, Michel Montaigne's *Essays,* works by Englishman, John Locke, as well as Montesquieu's *The Spirit of Laws*, David Smollet's *History of England*, and Thomas A Kempis' book, The *Imitation of Christ*. **11** Among the works of John Locke's that Madison studied with Mr. Robertson were his *Essay on Human Understanding* and his *Essay on Toleration* about which we will speak extensively in Chapter Five of this Study on James Madison's Religion.[14]

Documents related to Donald Robertson also show that the teacher owned copies of Robert Dodsley's *The Preceptor; Containing a General Course of Education*, which was one of the first texts related to teaching skills in the American Colonies.

---

11   Ibid., pp. 39–50
12   Ibid., pp. 42–43
13   Ibid., pp. 19–21
14   Ibid., pp. 86–87

Mr. Madison at around age eleven found a second family which he kept lose for the rest of his life, the world of books. In 1762, he was sent seventy miles away to Caroline County Virginia to study with Donald Robertson, a Scottish school master. Mr. Madison went home for vacations and holidays, but otherwise he boarded with Mr. Robertson for the next five years.

From 1762 on, Mr. Madison also began to keep extensive notebooks on his studies in which he made many references to Astronomy, Mathematics, and the writings of Locke, Fontenelle, Plato, and Euclid. The keeping of notebooks was a common practice among the academic elite in the Colonies, not only in their school days but throughout their lives. Teachers like Mr. Robertson knew well the value of notebooks as an educational tool. John Adams, for example, once explained to his son, John Quincy Adams about the value of keeping notebooks:

> One develops a fondness for writing by use. We learn to write readily and what is of more importance, we think, and improve our judgments by committing our thought to paper.[15] By nearly all accounts, Mr. Robertson inspired Jemmy Madison to work diligently on his Latin which he mastered so well that in later years, he corrected many English translations of many Latin works by some of the great Jurists of his day such as Hugo Grotius, Emmerich Vattel, and Samuel Von Puffendorf.[16]

When James Madison Jr. turned sixteen, James Sr., placed Jemmy's education into the hands of a man named the Rev. Thomas Martin, a man who was twenty-five at the time. The Scots-Irish Martin had attended the College of New Jersey and after graduation, he was assigned to be the Rector of the Madison Parish Church, Saint Thomas.[17] Thomas Bryan Martin (1731–1798), was an English-American tutor, land agent, legislator, and planter in what today would be a portion of West Virginia.[18]

---

15   Ibid., p. 21
16   Ibid., p. 17
17   Ibid
18   Ibid., p. 212

The Rev. Thomas Martin (1724–1770) graduated from the College of New Jersey in 1762. His brilliant career as a teacher and Episcopal clergyman included two years while living at the Madison estate, Montpelier. In fact, the Rev. Martin came to live in the Madison home of Montpelier while he tutored Jemmy and his younger brothers, Francis [then fourteen] and Ambrose who was twelve when Martin arrived at the Madison Plantation. Additionally, the Rev. Martin may also have tutored seven year old sister, Nelly. Since James Jr. was the eldest son, the Rev. Martin took great pains to assist the boy in his College endeavors, beginning at the age of sixteen.[19] Indeed, after two-and-a-half years of tutoring from the Rev. Mr. Martin, it was time for the tutor to assist James Madison in his college applications.

The Rev. Martin had originally came to the Virginia Colony when he was appointed Rector of the Brick Church that later became St. Thomas Parish. It is likely the Mr. Martin also tutored James' brothers Francis and Ambrose, their sister, Nelly, five year old William and some neighbor children as well, at least according to Ralph Ketchem.[20] Mr. Ketchem goes on in his first chapter on James Madison's "Boyhood and Early Education," to relate that Joseph Addison's *Spectator,* as one of the chief literary sources that went into the early education of James Madison Jr.[21]

Among the *James Madison Papers* can be found several letters between the fourth President and the Rev. Thomas Martin, including one from the American statesman dated August 10, 1769 in which Madison tells his mentor how he was getting along in his new college environment.

What was surprising about Madison' choice for college is that he did not apply to William & Mary, the usual choice among the Virginia gentry. Instead, James Madison chose the College of New Jersey, the alma mater of the Rev. Martin. It is not clear, however, how much influence the Scotch-Irish scholar had exerted on his pupil.[22]

James Madison was considerably less effusive about the teaching of Rev. Martin than he was about that of Mr. Robertson. During his two

---

19　Ibid
20　Ibid
21　Ibid., p. 41
22　Ibid., pp. 22–24

years with the Rev. Martin. Mr. Hamilton continued to approach his studies with vigor and with independence, as evidence by his success in his College pursuits. Because of his preparations with Robertson and Martin, this allowed Madison to pass the entrance exam at the College of New Jersey so much so that the statesman entered the college as a sophomore that also facilitated his graduation in only two years.

At any rate, on a fine summer day in 1769, the 18 year old Jemmy Madison left his family's plantation to attend college three hundred miles away in New Jersey. In those days, such a trip took nearly two weeks to complete. The boy was accompanied by his tutor, the Rev. Martin and the preacher's brother, Alexander Martin. They made the journey on horseback. One of the Madison family's most trusted black servants, a man named Sawney, accompanied his master on the trip.[23]

It is likely that the route taken by the Madison party ran through the Low Country to Fredericksburg, then on to Annapolis, in Maryland, New Castle in Delaware, and Philadelphia, then the largest city in America with a population of 30,000 people. After Philadelphia, the Madison party crossed the Delaware and on to the building with the tall tower known as Nassau Hall, a large stone building whose four floor ten housed the College of New Jersey.

In this one building there were classrooms, student dormitory, dining hall, library and the chapel, where students and faculty worshipped together every morning and heard the President John Witherspoon preach from the pulpit of the chapel. Soon after settling in, Mr. Madison wrote to the Rev. Martin on August 10, 1769. In the letter to his academic mentor, Jemmy Madison spoke of his curriculum and how he had already "read over half of Horace and made me pretty well acquainted with prosody, both of which will be almost neglected the two succeeding years."[24]

John Witherspoon had arrived in Princeton, the city where the College of New Jersey was located, in 1768, just a year before the arrival of James Madison. The College was in great financial straits

---

23   Ibid., p. 25
24   James Madison to Thomas Martin. August 10, 1769

and could not even pay Mr. Witherspoon's salary. He soon resolved, however, to get the institution out of debt by raising money in places as far away as New England and England.[25] President Witherspoon also introduced new courses to the curriculum including history, French, and oratory.[26]

Mr. Witherspoon was an adherent of the Scottish Common Sense School that included such figures as Thomas Reid (1710–1796) and Francis Hutcheson (1694–1746.), as a movement to counter-act the radical-Idealism of George Berkeley. The Common Sense School held the view that human beings have an innate sense of morality, or conscience, which teaches men to distinguish good from evil, as well as the idea that religion springs from certain first principles that humans are able to grasp intuitively.[27]

Scholar Lawrence Cremin writes about these first principles of the Common Sense School when he indicates:

> It is these first principles, abstracted into a faculty called the moral sense, that Mr. Witherspoon explicates, giving attention not only to the traditional concerns of practical Divinity. i.e., the duties to God, self & others, but also in unusual measure to politics, economics, and jurisprudence.[28]

Indeed, of particular importance to Madison and his fellow students was Mr. Witherspoon's expansion of his course on Moral Philosophy to include, "the general principles of public law and politics."[29] John Witherspoon was also the only active Clergyman to

---

25   Ketcham, pp. 32 and 35

26   Ibid., p. 35

27   Thomas Reid. *An Inquiry into the Human Mind.* (Collegeville: Penn State University Press, 2002.), p. 32. Mr. Reid was one of the founders of the Scottish Common Sense School of Philosophy, along with Dugald Stewart (1753–1828), Sir William Hamilton (1788–1856), and Aberdeen scholar, James Beattie (1735–1803

28   Lawrence Cremin. *The Transformation of the School.* (New York: Knopf, 1961.), p. 17

29   The Declaration was primarily signed by the fifty-six delegates of the Continental Congress, in Philadelphia on August 2, 1776. Mr. Witherspoon was the only

sign the U.S. Declaration of Independence. He was also a leader in the American Great Awakening Movement and established the College of New Jersey as a Presbyterian Institution.

The curriculum at the College also included Latin, Greek, theology, and the works of many Classical and Enlightenment thinkers. Great emphasis was placed on speech and debate. Mr. Madison became a leader in the College's Whig Party. While at the College, Madison' closest friend was classmate, William Bradford, a future Attorney General of the United States.[30]

The daily schedule at the College of New Jersey in Madison's day was closely regulated and prescribed. The day began at 5:00 with a morning bell. At 6:00 there was a chapel service where President Witherspoon often preached. The next hour was reserved for study, followed by breakfast. At 9:00 there was recitation, followed by more study until 1;00 p.m. when lunch or dinner was served.

After the noonday meal, there was another period of recitation and study. At 5:00 p.m.

there was evening prayers, followed by Supper at 7:00, and to bed at 9:00 p.m. only to follow exactly the same schedule six days a week. Scholar Garrett Ward Sheldon, in his 2001 book, *The Political Philosophy of James Madison,* observed, 'This is a regimen I am sure resembles that conducted by Princeton students today."[31]

James Madison was able to finish the three year College curriculum in two years, graduating in 1771. At the time, he contemplated entering the ministry but instead he remained at Princeton to study Hebrew and Moral Theology with the College's President, John Witherspoon. Mr. Madison then returned to Montpelier in the winter of 1772. [32]

Perhaps the most influential text in Mr. Madison's college days was Mr. Witherspoon's *Lectures on Moral philosophy*, required reading in the President of the College's required Ethics Class for all senior

---

active clergyman to sign the document

30   Ketchem, pp. 18 and 27

31   Garrett Ward Sheldon. *The Political Philosophy of James Madison.* (Baltimore: Johns Hopkins Press, 2001.), p. 132

32   Ketcham, p. 34

students at the College of New Jersey. We will say more about this book of Mr. Witherspoon and his moral theory in Chapter Four of this Study on James Madison's Religion.

Mr. Madison's ideas on Philosophy and Morality were strongly shaped by President Witherspoon who also taught the young statesman how to read Classical Hebrew so he could read the Old Testament in its original language. Madison biographer, Terence Ball wrote about he relation of Madison to Witherspoon suggesting the young student was:

> Immersed in the liberalism of the Enlightenment and converted to eighteenth-century political radicalism. From then on James Madison's theories would advance the rights of the happiness of man and his most active efforts would serve devotedly the cause of civil and political liberty.[33]

Another influence on Mr. Madison in his college days was another classmate named Philip Freneau (1752–1832), American poet, nationalist, polemicist, and, for a while, Sea Captain and newspaper editor. Mr. Freneau was called the "Poet of the American Revolution," but through his newspaper the *National Gazette,* he was a strong critic of George Washington and a proponent of Thomas Jefferson's anti-Federalist policies.[34] Philip Freneau was James Madison's college roommate on the fourth floor of Nassau Hall.[35]

Philip Freneau was a serious student of theology and a stern moralist his entire life. He had originally planned to enter the ministry but in college found his true calling in literature. James Madison recognized very early on Freneau's wit and verbal skills that made him a powerful adversary with the pen. A number of letters are extant between James Madison and Philip Freneau, including one from the

---

33 Terence Ball. *James Madison.* (London: Routledge, 2017.), p. 111

34 The *National Gazette* was a Democratic-Republican partisan newspaper that was first published on October 31, 1791. It was edited and published bi-weekly by poet and printer, and friend of James Madison, Philip Freneau until October 23, 1793

35 Ketchem, pp. 34–36

latter to the former on November 22, 1772, after Madison had returned to Montpelier.[36]

In the letter, Mr. Freneau complains that he had not seen Mr. Madison since the previous April, which would have been seven months. Freneau also indicates to his future President friend that he had just "completed a little poem of about 400 lines entitled a "Journey to Maryland.' Freneau ends the letter cordially calling himself, "Your humble servant and friend."[37]

When James Madison graduated from the College of New Jersey in 1771, he received 'Honor' grades in Greek and Latin, as well as in Mathematics, Rhetoric, Geography, and Philosophy. Not satisfied, he went on to become the College's first graduate school student when he studied Hebrew and Moral Philosophy with John Witherspoon in the Fall of 1772.

John Witherspoon, as we shall see throughout this Study on James Madison's Religion was a theological and philosophical influence on the fourth President's views on Conscience and the Moral Good, as well as Survival After Death, as we shall see in Chapters Four and Seven. One way to measure the effectiveness of President John Witherspoon's tenure at the Princeton, New Jersey college over which he presided is that of the 478 graduates from the College in his years as President. 86 of those became active in civil government; one became an American President [Madison.]; one a Vice-President [Aaron Burr.] in addition to 10 cabinet members, 21 U.S. Senators, 39 Congressmen, 12 Governors, a Supreme Court Justice [Brockholst Livingston]; and one Attorney General, James Madison's good friend from Philadelphia, William Bradford.[38]

It is also significant that 20 percent of the Signers of the Declaration of Independence, one-sixth of the delegates to the Constitutional Convention, and one-fifth of the First Congress under that Constitution were graduates of the College of New Jersey, or Princeton University.[39]

In his newly constituted classes on Literature, President Witherspoon related:

---

36 Philip Freneau to James Madison. November 22, 1772
37 Ibid
38 Ketchem, pp. 41–45
39 Ibid

> In this course, we endeavor to unite together piety and literature—to show their relation to and their influence on each other and to guard against anything that may seem to separate them and set them into opposition one to another.[40]

There was nothing that was narrow about the selections of texts for Mr. Witherspoon's Literature course. In fact, the President's list included a number of distinguished works by French, Roman Catholic writers and scholars. In addition to a changed curriculum at the College level, John Witherspoon also brought new life to the grammar school that was run by the College in the basement of Nassau Hall. All of the students on campus learned the importance of the kind of discipline that comes with a mind of diligence.

John Witherspoon was also a great influence in James Madison's views and understanding of the Bible, as we shall see in Chapter Three of this Study on James Madison's Religion. It is enough now, however, to also point out that Mr. Witherspoon taught Mr. Madison how to read the Hebrew Bible, or Old Testament, in its original classical Hebrew language.

Ralph Ketchem, in his biography of James Madison, gives this summary of the statesman's time at the College of New Jersey. He relates:

> In summary, Madison's education at Princeton furnished from the wisdom of Greece and Rome, a lifelong realism about human nature, a comprehensive concept of the political obligation and an instinctive admiration of patience, prudence, and moderation. From the Christian tradition, he inherited a sense of the prime importance of Conscience, a strict personal morality, and an understanding of human dignity as well as depravity.[41]

We will say much more in Chapter Four, on James Madison's Views on Ethics and Conscience. It is enough now, however, to

---

40   Ibid., p. 44
41   Ibid., pp. 28–29

indicate that for the America statesman the idea of Conscience was a central moral category, influenced by the Common Sense School and John Witherspoon. This brings us to an analysis of James Madison's religious life after his time in College and Graduate School, the topic of Section Three of this First Chapter.

Madison and Religion After College

Although there is ample evidence that James Madison attended Church as a child and while in College and Graduate School, there is very little evidence of the fourth President's religiosity in the remainder of his life, with the exception of one fact. That is, that in his years as President of the United States, 1809–1817, Madison attended Sunday services at the St. John's Episcopal Church on 16th and H street in Washington.[42]

The Greek revival building was designed by Benjamin Latrobe and is adjacent to Lafayette Square, one block from the White House. This is why St. John's is sometimes referred to as the 'Church of the Presidents.' Every sitting President has attended St. John's at least once since its construction in 1816, starting with James Madison. Every U.S. president since Franklin D. Roosevelt, has attended spiritual services on Inauguration Day, many at St. John's, with exception of Richard Nixon. Saint John's was designated as a national historic a landmark in 1960.[43]

Beyond the fact about James Madison's Church attendance while the fourth President was in office, little else can be said. As historian, Alf J. Mapp puts the matter, "Back home in Virginia he pursued on his own further studies in both theology and law. Nevertheless, he believed that, even if his health problems should ease, his weak voice would prevent him from both the bar and the pulpit.[44]

Religion scholar David L. Holmes agrees. He observes, "Once he embarked on his legal and political career, Madison rarely wrote or spoke

---

42   Ibid., p. 29

43   Ibid

44   Alf J. Mapp. *The Faiths of Our Fathers*. (New York: Rowman and Littlefield, 2005.), p. 118–119

about religious subjects. Yet, religion remained one of his lifelong interests.[45] In another part of the same essay mentioned above, Alf Mapp wrote:

> Not only did he have an intense interests in religion as an unbroken thread running through his life, a perpetual strand of that thread was his devotion to religious liberty.[46]

Again, quoting David L. Holmes. He concludes about Mr. Madison, "Like so many other founding fathers, James Madison seems to have ended up in the camp affirming the existence of a Deistic God."[47]

In a rare comment about religion in his public life, James Madison wrote in 1826 that, "religious belief is so essential to be moral order of the world and to the happiness of man tat arguments which enforce it cannot be adequately draw from too many sources."[48] The bottom line on James Madison and religion in his life after college is that the fourth President of the United States rarely said, or wrote, anything about the phenomena of God and religious belief.

One final way that James Madison's earliest religious views might be seen is in many of his letters in the period from his return from College in 1772 well into the 1780s, as we shall see in the Fourth and Final Section of Chapter One.

Madison and Religion in His Letters

From the period from 1773 until well into the 1780s, we may see gleans of James Madison's views on religion in his letters from the period. Consider a November 9, 1772 letter to his College friend, William Bradford in which the fourth President observed, "A watchful eye must be kept on ourselves lest while we are building ideal monuments of Renown and Bliss here, we neglect to have our names enrolled in the Annals of Heaven."[49] In this letter the American statesman asserts his

---

45 David. L. Holmes. *The Faith of the Founding Fathers*. (Oxford: Oxford University Press, 2006.), p. 187
46 Mapp, p. 119
47 Holmes, p. 188
48 James Madison to John Adams. October 11, 1826
49 James Madison to William Bradford. November 9, 1772

obvious belief in survival after death, as well as the tendency among many of the Founding Fathers to avoid the use of the word "God," in favor of synonyms like "Heaven."[50]

In another letter to William Bradford from September, 1773, Mr. Madison again turns his attention to Religion when he wrote:

> I have sometimes though that there could be no stranger testimony in favor of Religion or against temporal Enjoyments even the most rational and manly than for men who occupy the most honorable and gainful departments and are rising in reputation and wealth, publicly to declare their unsatisfaction by becoming fervent Advocates in the cause of Christ & I wish you may give in your Evidence in this way. Such incidents have seldom occurred therefore they would be more striking and would be instead a 'Cloud of Witnesses.'[51]

At the close of this passage, Mr. Madison refers to a line from Saint Paul's Letter to the Hebrews 12: 1 that speaks of being "surrounded by such a great cloud of witnesses and let us throw off everything that hinders and the sin that so easily entangles. And let us un with perseverance the race marked out for us."[52]

Mr. Madison also casts moral doubts on the idea that the political elite are the best exemplars of advocating the cause of Jesus. He even indicates that such a situation in actuality rarely occurs.[53] In another letter to Mr. Bradford written on April 1, 1774, Mr. Madison again speaks about some of his basic religious beliefs and their relation to Ethics when the American statesman observed:

---

50   Ibid

51   James Madison to William Bradford. September 19, 1773

52   Hebrews 12: 1. [King James Version.] Jacob de la Motta (1789–1845) was a member of the South Carolina Medical Society and he served as a surgeon in the U.S. Army during the War of 1812. He also gave the eulogy at the funeral of Rabbi Gershom Mendes Seixas, the most famous Jew in America at the time and he established and dedicated the Mikva Israel Congregation in Savannah in 1820. We say much more about Rabbi Jacob de la Motta in Chapter Nine of this Study

53   James Madison to William Bradford. September 19, 1773

> That Religion or the duty we owe to our Creator, and the manner of discharging it, being under the direction of Reason and conviction only, not of violence or compulsion, all men are equally entitled to the full and free exercise of it according to the dictates of Conscience.[54]

Here in this letter, James Madison refers back to the moral theory he had learned from his College mentor, President John Witherspoon and his dedication to the Scottish Common Sense School of the innateness of ethical provisions in human beings, as well as the notion that these moral principles are known through Reason. We will say far more about Mr. Madison's views on Ethics in Chapter Four of this Study on James Madison's Religion. It is enough now, however, to give this 'coming attraction,' if you will.[55]

In another letter to Jacob de la Motta, from August of 1820, a few years after he had left the White House, James Madison wrote:

> We are teaching the world the great truth that Government do better without Kings and Nobles than with them. The merit will be doubled by the other lesson that Religion Flourishes in greater purity, without than with the aid of Government.[56]

Jacob de la Motta (1789–1845) was an early Jewish physician mostly in South Carolina. In 1816, he delivered the eulogy on Rabbi Gershom Mendes Seixas and in 1820, he delivered a discourse at the consecration of the Synagogue of the Mikva Israel Congregation in Savannah, Georgia. This published discourse attracted the attention of both Thomas Jefferson and James Madison, both of whom wrote appreciative letters, of which the above quotation is an excerpt of Mr. Madison's letter.

Mr. Madison speaks of preferring a rule by a Republic rather than a monarchy, and he suggests that in a Republic it is far easier for citizens to express their varied religious points of view. We will say more about

---

54 William Bradford to James Madison. April 1, 1774
55 Ketchem, p. 68
56 James Madison to Jacob de la Motta. August 17, 1820

James Madison and Judaism in Chapter Eight of this Study. For now, it is sufficient to say that he was friendly to a number of prominent Jews in the late 18th Century.

Finally, on July 10, 1822, in a letter to his friend, Edward Livingston, the fourth President related that, "Among the features peculiar to the political system of the United States is the perfect equality of rights which it secures to every religious sect."[57] Again, we will say much more about this idea of 'securing religious rights' in Chapter Five of this Study on James Madison's Religion. Edward Livingston (1764–1836) was an American statesman and Jurist. He drafted the Louisiana Civil Code of 1825 based mostly on the Napoleonic Code. Livingston represented both Louisiana and New York in the U.S. Congress.

This brings us to the major Conclusions we have made in this First Chapter, followed by the Notes of the same. The central foci of Chapter Two will be what James Madison, the fourth President of the United States, believed and wrote about the phenomena of God, as well as the Religion of Christianity and the person of Jesus Christ.

Conclusions of Chapter One

We have begun this First Chapter of this Study on James Madison's Religion by suggesting that the overall goal of the Chapter has been to explore the earliest and most sustaining beliefs of James Madison in regard to Religion. We then suggested that Chapter One will unfold in four Section by which we will explore these goals.

In the first of these Sections, we have concentrated our attention on the sources that went into the making of Mr. Madison's earliest religious life. These included his parents, his

maternal grandmother, the Brick Church at Saint Thomas in Virginia, as well as the books in Mr. Hamilton's father's library, including some classical and Enlightenment volumes, like Joseph Addison's *Spectator*.

---

57   James Madison to Edward Livingston. July 10, 1822. Livingston was the Minister to France under President Andrew Jackson; his Secretary of State from 1831 to 1833; U.S. Senator for the state of Louisiana, 1829 to 1831; and was a member of the U.S. House of Representatives from 1823 to 1829

In the Second Section of the First Chapter, we turned our attention to the early education of James Madison from lessons with his grandmother, to the attendance of classes with Scotsman Donald Robertson, to the tutoring Mr. Madison received from the Reverend Thomas Martin at Montpelier in preparation for the fourth president's study in College, and, after graduation from the College of New Jersey in Princeton. His study of Hebrew and Moral Philosophy with his College mentor, President John Witherspoon.

We have indicated in Chapter One the major influence that President John Witherspoon and his Scottish Common Sense School philosophy appears to have had on the ethics of James Madison, as well as Witherspoon's teaching of classical Hebrew to the man who will become the fourth President of the United States. We also have indicated that along the way in College, some of Mr. Madison's most important intellectual influences were those of some of his fellow classmates, including William Bradford and Philip Freneau.

In the Section on the Early Education of James Madison, we also have shown the long-lasting effects on the life of James Madison that may be seen in the contributions of Donald Robertson and the Rev. Thomas Martin in the education of James Madison jr. In fact, as we have shown, the Rev. Martin came to live at the Madison Montpelier estate while tutoring the young Jemmy Madison and accompanied the young scholar to the College of New Jersey when Jemmy began College in Princeton, New Jersey.

In the same Section of Chapter One, we also have indicated the strict schedule that John Witherspoon had outlined for his chargers from the 5:00 a.m. morning bell to the 9:00 p.m. lights out. We also have shown the amazing societal effects that can be seen in President Witherspoon's time as president of the College.

In the Third Section of the First Chapter, we have explored and discussed the phenomenon of Religion in the life of James Madison after college. In this Section we made two major conclusions. First, while president, Mr. Madison attended Sunday services at the Saint John's Episcopal Church in Washington, D.C. And secondly, that the fourth President of the United States rarely said, or wrote, anything about Religion.

In the Fourth and Final Section of Chapter One, we have shown some of the ways in which the subject of religion may be found in the letters of James Madison, mostly from the 1770s and 1780s. Among these letters we have analyzed were missives to Mr. William Bradford, one to Rabbi Jacob de la Motta, and one to James Madison's friend, Judge Edward Livingston.

In each of these several letters, we have seen the following conclusions. First, that James Madison believed in God and as the Architect of the Universe. Second, that he preferred a Republican Government overruled by a Monarch and Upper Class. Third, that James Madison was dedicated to the idea of the free expression of Religion, 'according to one's Conscience.' Fourth, that James Madison was persuaded by the Scottish Common Sense School of thought in regard to the nature and practice of moral principles. Fifth, we have indicated Mr. James Madison's penchant for utilizing expressions like 'equal rights under the law,' and the 'securing' of those rights. And finally, we have shown the emphasis in the words and speeches of James Madison that put reliance on Reason, with very little emphasis on Revelation.

This bring us to the Notes of this First Chapter of this Study on James Madison's Religion, followed by Chapter Two in which we will emphasize what the fourth President of the United States said and wrote about the phenomena of God and Jesu Christ.

Chapter Two:
James Madison on God, Christianity, and Jesus.

James Madison is the greatest man of our age.

—Thomas Jefferson. Letter to George Mason

The Founding Father were...skeptical men of the Enlightenment who questioned each and every received idea they had been taught.

—Brooke Allen. "The Moral Minority"

It is the mutual duty of all to practice Christian forbearance, love, and charity toward each other.

—James Madison. Virginia Bill of Rights [1776]

Introduction

The major goal of the Chapter Two of this Study on James Madison's Religion is to describe and to discuss what the American statesman believed and wrote about God. We will accomplish this goal by dividing the Chapter into four separate parts. In the First part, we will point to some very general comments that the Fourth President made about the Divine.

In the Second Part of Chapter Two, we will examine fourteen different terms that James Madison employed as substitutes for the word "God." Like many of the other Founding Fathers—like George Washington and Thomas Jefferson, for examples—Madison used many synonyms for "God" instead of the actual word "God."

Many of the places in James Madison's works where he discussed Christianity will be the focus of the Third Section of Chapter Two; and in the Fourth and Final Part of Chapter Two we will identify and then discuss what the Fourth President of the United States has said, or has written, about the person of Jesus Christ.

In our examination of the *Papers of James Madison*, published by the University of Chicago Press between 1962 and 1977, we have discovered in these ten volumes 156 references to the word God, its substitutes, or to the Divine. In only about 36 of those is the word "God" employed. In the remaining 120 examples, as we shall see in Section Two of this Chapter, we find seventeen different substitutes for the word "God," including 'Nature's God,' the 'Governor of the Universe,' the 'Supreme Law-Giver,' among many other synonyms.[58]

In the Third Section of this Second Chapter we will examine what James Madison had to say about the Christian Religion and in the Fourth, and Final Section, we will identify and discuss what the fourth President more specifically had to say about the person of Jesus of Nazareth.

This brings us to many of the most General comments that James Madison, the fourth President, made about God, the subject-matter of the First Section of Chapter Two of this Study on James Madison's Religion.

Madison's General Comments About God

Of the dozens of comments that James Madison made in his Collected Papers most of them are like this remark that he made in an April 1, 1774 letter to his College friend William Bradford, 'That Religion or the duty we owe to our Creator, and the manner of discharging it, being under the direction of reason and conviction only, not of violence or compulsion…"[59]

Here Mr. Madison asserts a belief in God, that humans have duties to that God, and that the best tool for ascertaining the activities of God, in

---

58 For more on the number of names that George Washington employed for "God," see Chapter two of Stephen Vicchio's *George Washington's Religion*. (Eugene: Wipf and Stock, 2019.)

59 James Madison to William Bradford. April 1, 1774

typical Enlightenment language, is the use of Reason. Mr. Madison again speaks in a very general way of the obligation we owe to God when in Article XVI of the Virginia Declaration of Rights of 1776, he wrote, "To God, therefore, not to man, must an account be rendered..."[60]

In a letter to Frederick Beasley on November 20, 1825, James Madison made a number of comments about the Divine, beginning the letter with these words: I have duly read the copy of your little tract on the proofs of the Being & Attributes of God.[61]

Mr. Madison goes on in the same letter to speak of the views of Cambridge philosopher Samuel Clarke (1675–1729) who was a great proponent of the Argument From Design, or the Teleological Argument for God's existence. Mr. Madison observed:

> The reasoning that could satisfy such a mind as that of Clarke ought certainly not to be slighted in the discussion. And his belief in a God All Powerful. Wise, and Good is so essential to the moral order of the world...[62] The fourth President's use of the word "order" suggests on the part of Mr. Madison's an assent to the Argument From Design, in which the Universe is made by a God Who is All-Good, All-Knowing, and All-Powerful.

In the same letter to Mr. Beasley, James Madison also hints at a belief in what is known as the First Cause Argument for God's existence, also known as the Cosmological Argument, which argues against the existence of an infinite causal chain of cause and effect and in favor of a First Cause or Prime Mover.

In the 1825 letter to Mr. Beasley, Mr. Madison also speaks of the "finiteness of human understanding, another indication of the belief of the Divine Plan Theory in regard to the issues of evil and human suffering. Because "we cannot comprehend the purposes that God may have for things. Mr. Beasley had sent his book, *A Vindication of the Argument, A Priori in the Proof of the Being and Attributes of God*

---

60   Virginia Declaration of Rights Article 16. [1776.]
61   James Madison to Frederick Beasley. November 20, 1825
62   Ibid

From the Objections of Dr. Waterland, which was published by Mr. Shoemaker in Philadelphia in 1825, the same year as James Madison's response to Mr. Beasley.[63] Mr. Beasley (1777–1845) was the fifth provost of the College of Philadelphia and wrote many theological essays and books including the one we have mentioned here,[64]

The book by Mr. Beasley mentioned above, as well as in James Madison response back to Beasley after receiving the volume, show lots of traits that both men believed in the Argument From Design, or Teleological Argument for God's Existence, as well as the First Cause or Cosmological Argument for the Existence of a Deity. Both of these philosophical arguments were employed by philosophers on both sides of the philosophical debate during the Enlightenment, for example by Madison's College mentor John Witherspoon, and most likely by Donald Robertson and the Rev. Thomas Martin, as well.

Mr. Hamilton's letter back to Mr. Beasley on November 20, 1825 also shows signs that the American statesman was an advocate of the "Divine Plan" Response to the Problem of Evil or Theodicy in the Christian tradition. This view essentially says that human beings are too limited in their knowledge to know much about God. Mr. Madison began the third paragraph in his return letter to Mr. Beasley by saying, "The finiteness of Human Understanding betrays itself on all Subjects but more especially when it involves Infinity."[65]

The 1825 correspondence to Mr. Beasley, James Madison also observed that at some point, "All philosophical reasoning on these Subjects must, perhaps, terminate. But I might not go farther beyond my depth and without the resources which bear you up in fathoming efforts."[66] Mr. Madison closes his letter to his Philadelphia friend. Mr. Beasley this way: I hasten to thank you for the favor which has made me your debtor and to assure you of my esteem & my respectful regards.[67]

---

63 Ibid
64 Ibid
65 Ibid
66 Ibid
67 Ibid

Of all of the *Collected Letters* of James Madison, this November 25, 1825 missive to Frederick Beasley displays more of the philosophical acumen of the fourth President of the United States than any other. It shows signs of his views on the existence of God, the Problem of Evil, as well as the nature and extent of Moral Goodness.

In an Amendment to the Virginia Declaration of Rights from June, 1776. Mr. Madison again asserts his belief in, "The duty of every man to render to the Creator such homage and such only as he believes to be acceptable to him."[68] The statesman goes on explicitly to relate: The duty is precedent, both in order of time and in degree of obligation to the claims of Civil Society.[69]

Mr. Madison makes the general claim here that our obligations to our Creator are far more fundamental than any duties we may be given by the government. The fourth President made this claim in a variety of ways in his life in which he indicated that God is more fundamental than any Civil Society or any human construction of a Government.

In that regard, Mr. Madison also frequently made the claim, as he did in a proposed amendment to the Constitution in a speech to the House of Representatives in 1789, and again in his "Essay on Property,'" published on March 29, 1792, that "Conscience comes from God and Conscience is the most sacred of all property."[70] Indeed, the statesman, Mr. Madison often voiced sentiments like this one in a letter to William Bradford, the future Attorney General of the United States, "So I leave you to pity me and to pray for liberty and Conscience to revive among us."[71]

James Madison also made some very general comments about God when discussing a clause on religious liberty, penned by fellow Virginian, George Mason, in which the fourth President made a suggestive substitute verbiage of the 'full and free exercise of religion according to Conscience,' a coded phrase that meant one's inherent understanding of the Moral Good that Mr. Madison had learned from

---

68   Virginia Declaration of Rights [June, 1776.]
69   Ibid
70   James Madison. "Essay on Property." [March 29, 1792]
71   James Madison to William Bradford. January 24, 1774

John Witherspoon when the former was a graduate student of the latter in 1771 and 1772.[72]

In fact, one of the assigned topics in James Madison's senior year of college was to defend the proposition, "Every religious profession which does not by it principles disturb the public peace, ought to be tolerated in a wise state."[73] This assignment, and the statement was devised by President John Witherspoon of the College of New Jersey And in Mr. Madison's Senior Thesis,' he went on to defend the proposition and to develop what would later be called by philosopher John Stuart Mill the "Principle of Harm."[74]

In his 1859 work, *On Liberty*, English philosopher, John Stuart Mill, suggested that people have a right to exercise their freedom only if it does not cause "harm' to others.[75] In his Senior Thesis at the College of New Jersey, James Madison essentially made the same argument.[76] He argued that the views of any 'religious professional' ought to be tolerated in a 'wise state' as long as it does not 'cause harm,' to third parties.[77]

In 1825, when asked to explain his own views of the being and attributes of God, James Madison answered the query by saying, "I have ceased thinking about those subjects for fifty years now."[78] In addition to these very general comments about God, James Madison—like many of the other Founding Fathers like Washington and Jefferson, for examples—avoided the actual employment of the word 'God,' in

---

72 After Mr. Madison completion of his BA, as we have indicated, he stayed an extra year to study Hebrew and Moral Philosophy with John Witherspoon

73 Quoted in Ketcham

74 'Mill's Moral and Political Philosophy," *Stanford Encyclopedia of Philosophy*. [2018.] J. S. Mill (1806–1873), was an English Utilitarian philosopher, political economist, and member of the British {Parliament. He was a member of the Liberal Party and was an early advocate for feminist issues, particularly in his book, *The Subjection of Women*

75 John Stuart Mill. *On Liberty*. (New York: Dover Editions, 2002.)

76 Quoted in Ketcham

77 Ibid

78 James Madison to Frederick Beasley. November 20, 1825

favor of substitutes or synonyms for that term. This is the subject of the Second Section of Chapter Two of this Study on James Madison's Religion to which we turn next.

Madison's Substitutes for the word God

In the period of the Founding Fathers of America, particularly in the latter half of the 18th Century, we see a pronounced and common practice of the avoiding of the use of the word "God" among the Founders. This practice can be seen in the works of George Washington who used nearly a hundred different substitutes for the word God[79] and Thomas Jefferson who only employed about two dozen synonyms for the Divine.[80] In this Second Section of Chapter Two, we will see that James Madison was no different than his contemporaries in this regard.

Of the 120 mentions of the Divine we have found in the *Collected Works of James Madison*, which do not use the word "God," ninety of those used the following terms:

- Governor of the Universe.
- Universal Sovereign.
- Supreme Law-Giver.
- Annals of Heaven.
- Nature's God.
- Supreme Law-Giver of the Universe.
- The Patronage of the Author.
- Creator.
- The Almighty.
- The Almighty God.
- Sovereign of the Universe.

---

79 See note 1. Of this Chapter
80 Ibid

- God.
- God All Powerful, Wise, and Good.
- Holy Name.
- Finger of the Almighty Hand.
- Holy and Omniscient Being.
- The Almighty Power.

Of the 120 references to the Divine in the corpus of the published works of Jams Madison, only thirty of those have employed "God" or the "Almighty God." In this Section of Chapter Two, we will analyze and discuss the other fifteen terms listed above in the works of James Madison.

James Madison used the "Annals of Heaven" to describe God in a letter dated November 9, 1773 to his friend William Bradford."[81] He called God "Creator," in another missive to Bradford on April 1, 1774.[82] In that letter the fourth President refers to the "duty that we owe our Creator."[83] In an Amendment to the Declaration of Rights, from June of 1776, Mr. Madison again referred to God as "Creator."[84]

In a letter to Frederick Beasley, dated November 20, 1825, the fourth President speaks of a 'God All Powerful, Wise, and Good."[85] In the fight to pass the Virginia Bill for Religious liberty, James Madison referred to the "reverence for the Holy Name."[86]

In his essay, *Memorial and Remonstrance Against Religious Assessments*, from 1785 James Madison referred to God as the "Governor of the Universe," in Sections one and fifteen of that work. And he affirmed that "Almighty God hath created the mind free in the same work."[87] Mr. Madison also employed 'Creator' and 'Creator of the Universe,' in the opening Section of the *Memorial and*

---

81 James Madison to William Bradford. November 9, 1773
82 James Madison to William Bradford. April 1, 1774
83 Ibid
84 Amendment to Virginia Declaration of Rights. [June, 1776]
85 James Madison to Frederick Beasley. November 20, 1825
86 Virginia Bill for Religious Liberty [1779]
87 James Madison. *Memorial and Remonstrance*. [1775.] Section 1

Remonstrance, as well.⁸⁸ In Section nine of the same work, James Madison related:

> Before any man may be considered as a member of Civil Society, he must be considered as a subject of the Governor of the Universe... Religion... must be considered as the basis of the Government.⁸⁹

James Madison, in a letter to his friend, Edward Livingston from July 10, 1822, also referred to God as the "Supreme Law Giver."⁹⁰ And in a Spring, 1832 letter to Rev. Jasper Adams, the statesman called God the "Patronage of the Author of the World."⁹¹ In an essay entitled the "Interest of Man," the fourth President referred to the deity as the "Universal Sovereign."⁹²

James Madison also employed the Enlightenment "Nature's God,' on a number of occasions such as in *Federalist Papers* Number 43 where he referred to "The transcendent law of nature and Nature's God."⁹³ Madison added, "The safety and happiness of society are the objects at which all political institutions aim, and to which all such institutions must be sacrificed."⁹⁴

The opening line of the Declaration of Independence from the Continental Congress with which James Madison had a hand, invoked

---

88 Ibid

89 Ibid., section nine

90 James Madison to Edward Livingston. July 10, 1822. Livingston (1764–1836) was an American statesman and Jurist. He represented New York and Louisiana in the U.S. Congress. He also served as the U.S. Secretary of State from 1831 until 1833

91 James Madison to Rev. Jasper Adams. May18, 1832. Adams (1793–1841) was an American clergyman, professor and College President He received his MDiv. degree from Yale Divinity School in 1819 and his S.T. D. from Columbia University in 1827

92 James Madison. "Interest of Man." See: *Federalist Papers*. number fifty-one

93 Ibid., number forty-three

94 Ibid

the "Laws of Nature and Nature's God" to claim title for the United States to an independent sovereign existence "among the powers of the earth."[95]

In *Federalist Papers* number 22, James Hamilton makes a familiar claim when he wrote, "The streams of national power ought to flow immediately from that pure, original fountain of all legitimate authority."[96] And in *Federalist* 49, Madison added, "The people are the only legitimate fountain of power,"[97] but the ultimate power Mr. Hamilton had in mind, of course, was God.

In Section 15 of *Memorial and Remonstrance*, the fourth President also employed the name "Supreme Law-Giver of the Universe," and the statesman speaks of the earnest praying and being duty bound to that Law-Giver.

In *Federalist Papers* number 37, James Madison related:

> It is impossible for the man of pious reflection not to perceive in the Constitutional Convention a finger of that Almighty Hand, which has been so frequently and signally extended to our relief in the critical stage of the Revolution.[98]

In another part of essay 37 of the *Federalist Papers*, James Madison again refers to God as the "Almighty," whom "when he Himself transcends to address mankind in their own language, his meaning, luminous as it may be, is rendered dim and doubtful in the cloudy medium by which it is communicated."[99] This suggests that Mr. Madison had what is called a 'Divine Plan" Theory explanation for the origin and meaning of Evil and suffering with respect to the Problem of Evil or Theodicy in the Christian Tradition. That is, that the purposes of evil and suffering are "beyond the understanding of mere humans."[100]

---

95 Declaration of Independence. First paragraph. [1776]
96 *Federalist Papers* number twenty-two
97 Ibid., number forty-nine
98 Ibid., number thirty-seven
99 Ibid
100 Ibid

The ideas of the "Hand," or "Finger' of the Almighty was ubiquitous among the Founding Fathers, Charles Pinckney said about the Constitution, "When the great work was done and published, I was struck with amazement. Nothing less than the superintending hand or Providence that so miraculously carried us through the War."[101]

On June 30, 1788, after the Ratification of the Constitution, George Washington wrote to Benjamin Latrobe to tell him that "The Great Governor of the universe had led us too long and too far, to forsake us in the midst of it. And the Hand of God is always in this place."[102] Washington wrote of "traces of the finger of Providence through the dark times now can be visible."[103]

In a May 28, 1788 correspondence to the Marquis de Lafayette, the General again speaks of the "finger of Providence' as an explanation of "any event in the course of human affairs." So it is not completely unprecedented when President James Madison employed similar language to indicate the Deity.

In August of 1814, Jams Madison had to flee from the British attack on Washington. The White House was burned. On November 16, he issued a Proclamation of a "Day of Public Humiliation, Fasting, and of Prayer to "the Almighty God."[104] On July 23, 1813, the year before. Mr. Madison also issued a "Proclamation for a Day of Thanksgiving," on which he called the Deity, the "Almighty Power," and the "Holy and Omniscient Being."[105]

In his First Inaugural Address, on March 4, 1809, the fourth President asked for, "The guidance of that Almighty Being Whose power regulates the destiny of nations and Whose blessings have been so conspicuously dispensed to this rising Republic, and to Whom we

---

101   For more on the Divine Plan Theory, see Stephen Vicchio. *The Voice From the Whirlwind: The Problem of Evil in the Modern World*. (Westminster: Christian Classics, 1989.), pp. 129–133

102   Charles Pinckney. Quoted at Constitutional Convention. [Summer, 1787]

103   James Madison to Benjamin Latrobe. June 30, 1788

104   James Madison. 'Day of Public Prayer." [August 10, 1814]

105   James Madison. "Proclamation for a Day of Prayer and Thanksgiving." [July 23, 1813]

are bound to address our devout gratitude for the past, as well as our fervent supplications and best hopes for the future."[106]

What is left unanswered, however, is why so many of the Founding Fathers chose the same kind of language when describing what they saw as the "miracle" of the United States of America. Ultimately, of course, this language about the hand or finger of God or the Lord goes back to the vocabularies of the Old and New Testaments in passages such as Psalm 23: 1 to 6; Psalm 63: 8; and Psalm 138: 7; as well as First Peter 5: 6; the Gospel of John 10: 29; and Paul's letter to the Romans 8: 34.[107]

Some scholars suggest that the Natural Theology invoked by the Declaration of Independence is a subtle and intentional way of being subversive in regard to traditional Biblical ideas of the Deity. "Nature's God: is instead tied to the modern natural rights philosophies of Hobbes, Spinoza, John Locke as part of a larger project in which the new wine of the Enlightenment is poured into the old wine casks of the traditional Religious view in Europe.

Finally, in his first Inaugural Address from March 4, 1809, Mr. Madison also refers to God as 'that Almighty Being whose power regulates the destiny of nations whose blessings have been so conspicuously dispended to this rising Republic and to whom we are bound to address our devout gratitude for the past as well as our fervent supplications and best hopes for the Future."[108] At any rate, this brings us to the Third Section of Chapter Two in which we will explore the complicated relationship that James Madison appears to have had with the Christian faith, the next Subject-matter in this Second Chapter.

James Madison on Christianity

Among the many works in his published material, James Madison made over a hundred references to the Christian Religion. Most of these are very general. In this Third Section of Chapter Two we will give

---

106 James Madison. First Inaugural Address. March 4, 1809

107 These "hand of God" and "hand of the Lord" passages are throughout both the Old and New Testaments

108 James Madison. First Inaugural Address

several examples of the fourth President's comments on Christianity and afterwards we will make some general conclusions about what Mr. Madison thought about the Christian Faith.

This Third Section will be followed by a Fourth, and Final Section of the Chapter in which we will show more about what James Madison believed and wrote about the person of Jesus Christ, but first we discuss his understanding of the Religion of Christianity. In a letter to the Rev. Jasper Adams, Mr. Madison tells the minister his general view of the Christian Religion. He related in the letter:

> The people of the United States have retained the Christian Religion as a foundation of their Civil, Legal, and Political institutions, while they have refused to continue a Legal preference to any one of its forms over the other.[109]

This comment in the letter to the Rev. Adams is an ambivalent one. On the one hand, Mr. Madison is encouraged that the U.S. has retained the Christian Religion, while at the same time he is happy that none of Christianity's Sects has become the national Faith.[110] Another general comment about the Christian Religion made by James Madison can be seen in a letter to William Bradford from September 25, 1773, after the former had returned to the Montpelier estate after his time at the College of New Jersey. In the letter, Madison expresses his belief in a Heaven that men must strive to enter, and he also calls for political leaders to be 'fervent advocates of Christianity."[111] One might say, as many critics have about Mr. Madison, that these cannot be the words of a Deist. Such a pronouncement could only have come from one who genuinely believed that the Religion of Jesus Christ was superior to all others.

In another general comment about the Christian Religion—a comment we have employed as an epigram for this Chapter—in his comments on the 1776 Virginia Bill of Rights, Mr. Madison related,

---

109 James Madison to Jasper Adams. May 18, 1832

110 The bitterness between Christian Sects was an annoyance about which President Madison was particularly concerned

111 James Madison to William Bradford. September 25, 1773

'It is the mutual duty of all to practice Christian forbearance, love, and charity toward each other."[112] This is an interesting comment because it may imply that the fourth President believed that Christianity was the established Faith in America, or that he is merely pointing to the importance of virtues like forbearance, love, and charity among the citizens of the United States.[113] This latter view appears to be Mr. Madison's meaning.

In another letter to his friend William Bradford from January of 1774, in the context of the question of an Established Church in America, the future, fourth President of the United States asks his Philadelphia friend:

> Who does not see that the same authority which can establish Christianity, in exclusion of all other religions, may establish with the same ease and particular Sect of Christians, in exclusion of all of the other Sects?[114]

Lying just below the surface of this comment is what appears to be the total lack of the realization of the existence of Judaism, Islam, and other Faiths in Mr. Madison's view of America. This is peculiar given the fact that the statesman learned classical Hebrew from his College mentor, President John Witherspoon. In the same letter he does point out, however, that in Europe a "diabolical hell- conceived principle of persecution rages among some and to their eternal infamy, the clergy can furnish their quota of impasse for such business."[115] Mr. Madison was clearly against the idea of seeing Religious Wars in America as they have existed in Europe since the 16thCentury.[116]

Madison scholar, Garrett Sheldon, in his *Political Philosophy of James Hamilton* makes the argument that Madison's education, writings, and speeches all reveal 'a Christian worldview in the

---

112 Virginia Bill of Rights. [1776]
113 Ibid
114 James Madison to William Bradford. January 9, 1774
115 Ibid
116 Ibid

statesman."[117] In another essay for a volume entitled *Religion in the American Presidency,* published by Columbia University Press in 2009, Dr. Sheldon again maintained that Mr. Madison's intellectual life and long public service to his nation were directed "by his firm Christian Faith and principles."[118]

From these several comments about Christianity from American statesman, James Madison, we may make the following conclusions. First, that Mr. Madison was confident in the fact that Christianity, with its many Sects, was widespread in America. Second, that Madison did not believe that any Sect of Christianity should be the Established Religion. Third, that James Madison believed that Christianity was the 'foundation' for 'Civil, Legal, and Political institutions in America.

Fourth, Madison was fearful that America not experience Religious Wars like those in Europe in the 16th and 17th Centuries. Fifth, the fourth President thought that Christian Charity and Love should be extended among all Americans, Sixth, the American statesman, Mr. Madison was convinced that Christianity was the greatest Faith in the World. And finally, Mr. Madison appears to have little or no understanding that America would one day be a land of Religious Diversity.

This brings us to the Fourth and Final Section of Chapter Two in which we will identify and discuss several comments and written passages where James Madison specifically speaks about, or simply mentions, the person of Jesus Christ of Nazareth.

James Madison on Jesus of Nazareth

Before we move to Madison's views on Jesus Christ, we first must point to a trend among several of the American Founding Fathers that saw the teachings of Jesus to be the purest expression of a moral sense in the history of mankind and, as Thomas Jefferson put the matter, "The teachings of Jesus need no priestly interpretation or subtle

---

117 Garrett Sheldon. *Political Philosophy of James Madison.* (Baltimore: Johns Hopkins Press, 2004.) pp. 97–99

118 Garrett Sheldon [Ed.] *Religion in the American Presidency.* (New York: Columbia University Press, 2009.) pp. 43–59

commentary."[119] Mr. Jefferson wrote in 1821, "Had there never been a commentator, there never would have been an infidel."[120]

Mr. Jefferson, as well as other Founders like Madison, believed, as Jefferson put the matter that the followers of Plato and his philosophy injected into Christianity clouds of "whimsies, puerilities, and unintelligible jargon."[121] Jefferson added, "Calvin introduced new absurdities into the Christian Religion… Our Savior did not come into the world to save metaphysicians only."[122]

Mr. Jefferson, Mr. Madison and others wished to cleanse Christianity of seventeen centuries of corruption and to scrape off the barnacles and appeal again to the unvarnished "general precepts of Jesus himself." As Mr. Jefferson related in 1803, "I am a real Christian… sincerely attached to his doctrines, in preference to all others."[123]

When examining James Madison's observations about Jesus over the years, it is important to keep in mind this overall view of the man from Nazareth. In a fight to pass the Virginia Bill for Religious Liberty, Mr. Madison attempted to shame Christian Conservatives who tried to insert the words "Jesus Christ" in an amended preamble with the words, "The better proof of reverence for that holy name would not be to profane it by making it a topic for legislative discussion."[124]

Nevertheless, in a letter to Benjamin Rush in 1803, Mr. Madison assented to Mr. Jefferson's view about the teaching of Jesus being the best moral system devised by humans. "It is the most sublime,

---

119 Thomas Jefferson. The Philosophy of Jesus of Nazareth. [1804]

120 Thomas Jefferson to Mrs. Samuel H. Smith. August 8, 1816

121 Ibid

122 Ibid

123 Thomas Jefferson to Benjamin Rush. April 21, 1803. Benjamin Rush (1746–1813) was a signer of the Declaration of Independence, a physician politician, and social reformer in Philadelphia. He was also one of the founders of Dickinson College. Rush was also a delegate of the Continental Congress in h Summer of 1787

124 James Madison. Comments on Preamble to Constitution

and perfect, which is merely an estimate of the intrinsic merit of his doctrines."[125]

In 1795, during a Congressional debate over naturalization, James Madison bluntly repelled Anti-Catholic prejudices when he said, "In their religion there was nothing inconsistent with the purest Republicanism."[126] At the age of 65, in his retirement at Montpelier. Mr. Madison praised the separation of Church and State because by it, "the number, the industry, and the morality of the Priesthood & the devotion of the people have been manifestly increased."[127]

In his *Memorial and Remonstrance* James Madison chided the various Sects of Christianity for claiming that his particular Sect is the "true and only" one. He points out that each Sect 'has the same authority, the person of Jesus Christ.[128] Mr. Madison referred to "Jesus Christ, your Savior and Redeemer and to every other needful business of life," in a letter to George Washington.[129] It seems unlikely that these are the words of an 18th Century Deist, as some biographers of James Madison have claimed.[130]

In Section Seven of the *Memorial*, Mr. Madison spoke specifically of the "Primitive" Christianity when the statesman wrote:

> Because experience witnesses the ecclesiastical establishments, instead of maintaining the purity and efficacy of Religion, have had a contrary operation. During almost fifteen centuries has the legal establishment of Christianity been on trial. What has been its fruits? More or less in all places, pride and indolence in the Clergy, ignorance and servility in the laity, and in both superstition, bigotry and persecution.[131]

---

125 Thomas Jefferson to Benjamin Rush. April 21, 1803
126 James Madison on Senate floor. April 18, 1795
127 Ibid
128 James Madison. *Memorial and Remonstrance*. Section seven
129 James Madison to George Washington. November 4, 1796
130 See, for example, the biography of William C. Rives. *History of the Life and Times of James Madison*
131 James Madison. *Memorial and Remonstrance*. Section seven

James Madison referred to this primitive form of Christianity as well in another letter to the Rev. Jasper Adams when he wrote, "Cursed be all that learning that is contrary to the Cross of Christ," an obvious dig at the "Ecclesiastical Establishments."[132]

In the same section of the *Memorial and Remonstrance* mentioned above. Mr. Madison again referred to the primitive form of Christianity when he wrote: Enquire of the Teachers of Christianity for the ages in which it appeared in its grandest luster, those of every Sect, point to the ages prior to its incorporation with Civil policy; propose a restoration of this primitive state in which its Teachers depended on voluntary rewards of their flocks, many of them predicting its downfall on which side ought their testimony to have the greatest weight.[133] Here, Mr. Madison pointed out that every new version of Christianity says everything before it was wrong; that it is important to get back to the original, primitive form; and the end of the world will soon be at hand. And Mr. Madison is skeptical of the first and third of these pronouncements, while advocating, as Jefferson did, to the second of them.

In the same Section of the *Memorial and Remembrance*, the fourth President asks, "What influences, in fact, have ecclesiastical establishment had on society? His answer was that all the effects for society are negative ones—to erect spiritual tyranny on the ruins of Civil authority; upholding the thrones of political tyrants; or those who wish to subvert the public liberty. And, 'a Just Government instituted to secure and perpetuate it, needs them not."[134]

One final aspect of James Madison's views on Jesus Christ is an essay written by the American statesman entitled *A Syllabus of an Estimate of the Merits of the Doctrines Compared with those of Others*, completed in April of 1803.[135] In this work, James Madison compared the views of ancient philosophers with those of Jesus. This analysis

---

132 James Madison to Jasper Adams. April 23, 1833

133 *Memorial and Remonstrance.* Section seven

134 Ibid

135 James Madison. *A Syllabus of an Estimate of the Merits of the Doctrines of Jesus Christ Comparted to Others.* [April, 1803

included five "disadvantages" of the doctrines of Jesus, as well as four "advantages."[136]

Among the 'disadvantages' to the life and teachings of Jesus, Mr. Madison listed five. These were:

1. Like Socrates and Epicurus, he wrote nothing himself.
2. He got others to write about him like Xenophon.
3. He fell an early victim to jealousy and a combination of altar and throne.
4. The doctrines he preached were defective as a whole and seem disjointed when misstated.
5. They had been disfigured and corrupted.[137]

Mr. Madison also listed four "Advantages" to the life and teachings of Jesus. These included:

1. He corrected the Deism of the Jews.
2. His moral teachings were superb.
3. His teachings were more about actions than thought or words.
4. He taught the doctrine of the Afterlife.[138]

The most important advantage, at least for James Madison, are his "Moral Doctrines" which are "pure and more perfect than those of the philosophers." Mr. Madison concluded the essay by observing, "A development of this head will evince the peculiar superiority of the system of Jesus over all the others."

From these comments of James Madison on the person of Jesus of Nazareth, we may make the following conclusions.

1. Madison thought that Jesus was the greatest of all moral teachers and that Christianity is the greatest Faith in

---

136 Ibid
137 Ibid
138 Ibid

human history.

2. That the most Primitive Form of Christianity had been corrupted.

3. If it was not for the followers of Platonism there would have been no Christian Infidels.

4. That the history of the Roman Church and Calvinism had been responsible for the corruption.

5. That Jesus Christ is the "Savior" and "Redeemer" of Humanity.

6. That too many Sects of Christianity believe that they are the only authorized Sect.

7. That Madison was against the idea of adding the words "Jesus Christ" to the amended preamble of the Constitution against the wishes of some Conservative legislators.

8. That all these Christian Sects have the same Authority, that of Jesus Christ.

9. That many Christian beliefs in his day should be Cursed because they run counter to "the Cross of Christ."

10. That there is no contradiction between Republicanism and the genuine teachings of Jesus Christ.

This brings us to the major Conclusions of this Second Chapter of this Study on James Madison's Religion, followed by the notes of the same. The main focus of Chapter Three of this Study shall be what the fourth President of the United States, James Madison believed, said, and wrote about the Holy Scriptures, or the Bible.

Conclusions to Chapter Two:

In the Introduction to this Second Chapter, we have indicated that the Chapter will have four distinct parts. These were the following:

1. James Madison's General Comments About God.
2. James Madison's Substitute Words for God.
3. James Madison on the Christian Faith.
4. James Madison on Jesus of Nazareth.

In the First of these Sections of Chapter Two, we have introduced and discussed several observations that James Madison made about God, including comments from the Virginia Declaration of Rights from 1776, from letters to Frederick Beasley, a comment from Madison's Essay on Property, and in a letter to William Bradford, among other material. We also have shown in the First Section of Chapter Two that James Madison held a view in his college Senior thesis much like that of John Stuart Mill and the Englishman's 1859 *On Liberty*, on religious toleration.

In the Second Section of Chapter Two we began by introducing a tendency among many of the American Founding Fathers to minimize the employment of the word "God" in their discourses while also using many synonyms for the Deity. In fact, of the 120 uses of these synonyms, we have found seventeen separate names for God in the works of James Madison. Indeed of the 156 references to the Divine in the works of James Madison, only thirty of them employed "God" or "Almighty God," while in ninety others, the statesman used: Governor of the Universe, Universal Sovereign, Supreme Law-Giver, the Annals of Heaven, Nature's God, Creator, the Patronage of the Author, and many other substitutes for the Deity.

At the end of the Second Section of Chapter Two we also raised the question of why Mr. Madison, as well as many other of the American Founding Fathers, engaged in this process of circumlocution, but with no definitive answer to that question. Most scholars, however, point to the propensity among many of the Founding Fathers to avoid the use of the word "God" in deference to the new "Enlightened" ideas of the 17th and 18th Centuries that had begun to occupy the minds of many European philosophical thinkers. In this view, the Americans were simply following suit, while avoiding and traditional Biblical language in their documents.

In the Enlightened mind, "Nature's God" is tied to the modern natural rights philosophy developed by Hobbes, Spinoza, Locke, and others as part of a larger project to supplant the traditional Biblical understanding of God and his relation to humankind. Nature's God, for those of the Enlightenment that may have included some of the American Founding Fathers was tantamount to a rational, organized principle of the universe and is thus radically different from the Providential, moralistic Creator, or Father, of the universe.

At any rate, in the Third Section of Chapter Two, we have explored the phenomenon of what the fourth President of the United States, James Madison, had to say and wrote about the Christian Faith. Through the use of Madison's letters, his comments on the Virginia Bill of Rights, and other materials we then made seven conclusions in regard to President James Madison's views on Christianity. These may be summarized this way:

1. That Madison was confident that Christianity spread in America.

2. That Madison was against the idea of an Established Church.

3. That Madison believed that Christianity was the foundation for Civil, legal, and Political institutions in American life.

4. Mr. Madison feared that Religious Wars would come to America as in Europe.

5. That Christian Charity and Love should be extended among Americans.

6. Madison thought that Christianity was the greatest Religion in the history of the world.

7. Madison said little about the potential for Religious Diversity in the United States.

In the Fourth and Final Section of Chapter Two, we have dedicated the Section to what the fourth President of the United States,

James Madison, believed, said, and wrote about the person of Jesus of Nazareth.

We began the Fourth Section of Chapter Two by pointing out another tendency among the American Founding Fathers that the teachings of Jesus, the most Primitive of his teachings, have been corrupted by the history of the Church, particularly by Roman Catholicism and Calvinism.

Indeed, we have suggested in Section Four of Chapter Two that both Thomas Jefferson and James Madison held this view. In the remainder of Chapter Two, we have catalogued a series of remarks that James Madison has made about the person of Jesus Christ. In that analysis, we have quoted from the fourth President's remarks on the Virginia Bill of Religious liberty, a 1795 comment on Anti-Catholicism, a number of remarks from the American statesman's *Memorial and Remonstrance*, and some observations in a letter to the Rev. Jasper Adams in which Mr. Madison spoke of cursing all that is contrary to the Cross of Christ.

We also have introduced in the Final Section of Chapter two a work of James Madison entitled *A Syllabus of the Merits on the Doctrines of Jesus Christ Compared with Those of Others,* in which the fourth President compares and contrasts the beliefs of the doctrines of Jesus with those of prominent Greco-Roman philosophers. We also have shown that in the opinion of Mr. Madison, the Ethics of Jesus are far superior to Socrates, Plato, and Aristotle.

At the very end of this Second Chapter of this Study on James Madison's Religion, we have provided a summary of ten propositions that the American statesman held about the person of Jesus Christ. These ten propositions were summarized this way:

1. Jesus was the greatest of all moral teachers and Christianity was the greatest human Religion.

2. The most Primitive form of Christianity has been corrupted.

3. If not for the follower of Platonism, there would have been no Christian Infidels.

4. The history of Roman Catholicism and Calvinism have been responsible for the corruption of Christ's teachings.

5. That Jesus Christ is Savior and Redeemer of human beings.

6. That too many Sects of Christianity believe that they are the only true Faith.

7. That Madison was against adding the words "Jesus Christ" to the amended preamble to the Constitution.

8. That the competing Christian Sects all have the same Authority—Jesus Christ.

9. That many Christian beliefs in his day should be cursed because they run counter to the "Cross of Christ."

10. That there is no contradiction between Republican Government and the genuine, Primitive, teachings of Jesus Christ.

This brings us to the Notes of this Second Chapter, followed by Chapter Three. The central focus of Chapter Three of this Study on James Madison's Religion is what the fourth President of the United States, James Madison, believed, said, and wrote about the Holy Scriptures or the Bible.

Chapter Three:
James Madison on the Bible

Mr. Madison left the impression on my mind that his creed was not strictly regulated by the Bible.

—Bishop William Meade. "On James Madison."

During his study Madison came to understand the power of parallelism in Hebrew and the Old Testament, a literary device designed to explain difficult concepts with clarity and grace.

—Rodney K. Smith. *The Old Testament and Hebrew Influence on James Madison*.

Jesus is a Hebrew name and signifies a Savior. Christ is a Greek name and signifies Anointed.

—James Madison. *Notes on Commentary on the Bible*.

Introduction

The central purpose of this Third Chapter of this Study on James Madison's Religion is to give a thorough account of what the fourth President of the United States believed, said, and wrote about the Bible. In his lifetime. We will begin Chapter Three by speaking about the principal sources for James Madison's perspectives on Holy Scripture. In the Second Section of Chapter Three our central focus will be on Mr. Madison and the Hebrew Bible or Old Testament, including a discussion of what has come to be known as the "Ten Commandment Hoax."

Mr. Madison's views on the New Testament will be the major focus of the Third Section of this Chapter Three. The Third Section will be the Final Section of the Chapter followed by the Conclusion and the Notes of Chapter Three.

Sources of Madison's Views on the Bible

In the course of this Third Chapter, we will speak of seven major sources in helping to understand the view of James Madison's on the Bible. We will list these seven sources here and then discuss them one at a time in this First Section of Chapter Three. These seven sources are the following:

1. Madison's knowledge of Classical Hebrew.
2. Madison's knowledge of Classical Greek.
3. Madison's knowledge of Medieval Latin.
4. Donald Robertson.
5. Madison's Notebooks and Reading List Before College.
6. The Reverend Thomas Martin.
7. President John Witherspoon.

James Madison learned his Classical Hebrew in the Post-Graduate year he spent studying with President John Witherspoon. Two repercussions from that study were first, it allowed the future statesman to read the Old Testament in its original language. And secondly, Mr. Madison learned a number of forms of Classical Hebrew poetry such as the Antithesis form, the Hebrew Parallelism Form, and the Synthetic Form.[139] In the Parallel Form, also known as the Synonymous Form, two lines of Scripture say precisely the same thing. Two examples in the poetry of the Old Testament can be seen as Psalm 2: 4 and 2: 9. The first of these tells us:

> He who sits in the Heavens laughs.
> The Lord scoffs at them.[140]

---

139 For more on these Hebrew poetic forms, see: Wilfred Owen. Classical Hebrew Poetry. (Sheffield: Sheffield Academics, 2009.)

140 Psalm 2: 4. [New International Version.]

Psalm 2: 9 relates:

> You shall break them with a rod of iron
> And dash them to pieces like a potter's vessel.[141]

Psalms 1: 6 and 4: 4 provide examples of the Antithetical form of Hebrew poetry. The former tells us:

> 'For the Lord watches over the way of the righteous/ but the way of the wicked
> will perish."[142]

Psalm 4: 4 relates:

> When you are disturbed do not sin,
> Ponder it on your bed and be silent.[143]

In the Antithetical form line B gives the opposite of line A. In the Synthetic form of classical Hebrew poetry line B appears to be unrelated to line A. Thus, Psalm 55: 6 and 92:9 are illustrative of this form. The former of these tells us:

> Oh that I had wings like a dove
> I would fly away and be at rest.[144]

While, the latter, the passage from Psalm 92: 9 informs us,

> "For your enemies, Oh
> Lord/for your enemies shall perish."[145]

In this Classical Hebrew poetic form line A appears to have nothing to do with line B.

While Mr. Madison was studying classical Hebrew with Mr. Witherspoon, he came to understand the power, clarity, and grace of

---

141 Psalm 2: 9. [NIV.]
142 Psalm 1: 6. [NIV.]
143 Psalm 4: 4. [NIV.]
144 Psalm 55: 6. [NIV.]
145 Psalm 92: 9. [NIV.]

these forms. In fact, this can be seen in one of the fourth President's favorite verses of the Old Testament, Isaiah 4: 10 that relates an Antithesis: "For ten acres of vineyard shall yield but one bath, and a homer of seed shall yield a mere ephah."[146] A homer is a large quantity, while an ephah is a small one.[147]

One contemporary scholar, Emmi Priddis Yildrim has suggested that if both phrases of the first Amendment are understood to be participle phrases, then the First Amendment is a fine example of an Antithetical expression in Classical Hebrew poetry. And where did this wording come from? James Madison.[148]

The second and third sources for aiding us in understanding James Madison's fluency with the Scriptures is the many years of study in which with Mr. Robertson and the Rev. Martin, he studied Greek and Latin with them. The former allowed Mr. Madison to read the New Testament in the original language, while the latter facilitated the young scholar in his ability in reading Latin poetry and Roman History, again in the original language.

Already we have spoken in this Chapter of Mr. Robertson's first year of teaching of James Madison concentrated in the fluency of the student in the English language. Madison learned English grammar thoroughly. But it is likely that the Rev. Martin, who was a graduate of the College of New Jersey, may very well have learned the three forms of ancient Hebrew poetry and taught them to his charge, the young James Madison.

Mr. Madison Notebooks from his years with Robertson and Martin gives us ample evidence of other sources for his early intellectual life. These adolescent Notebooks contain entries on Cicero, Horace, Justinian, Tacitus, and Vigil, as well as more modern Enlightenment thinkers such as John Milton, John Locke, Michel Montaigne, the Baron Montesquieu, and Joseph Addison's *Spectator*.[149]

---

146 Isaiah 4: 10. [NIV.]

147 Ibid

148 Emmi Priddis Yildrim. Quoted in Jean Jones' 'Hebrew Poetry,' @jean-jones.-net/2020/10/value-hebrew-poetry/

149 Joseph Addison. The Spectator. (New York: Palala Press, 2018.)

Earlier in this Study, we have suggested that Mr. Madison's reading of President Witherspoon's text, the *Lectures on Moral Philosophy*, may have been the greatest gift that President Witherspoon had given to the young Mr. Madison. One of the main reasons this is true is the moral sense that the work implies. Witherspoon tied the idea of the moral sense to his notion of moral responsibility. This become obvious in examples like this passage from the *Lectures*:

> The moral sense implies also a sense of obligation, that such and such things are right and others are wrong, that we are bound in duty to do the one, and that our conduct is hateful, blamable, and deserving of punishment is we do the contrary. And there is also in the moral sense or Conscience an apprehension or belief that reward and punishment will follow according as we shall act in the one way or the other.[150]

For President Witherspoon, the moral sense was what the Scriptures and the ordinary common language is called Conscience. This is the law written by our Maker, Dr. Witherspoon believed, into the hearts of all human beings. It is Conscience that also reenforces duty, which is more fundamental than human reasoning. Mr. Witherspoon also taught that Justice requires a person to live in accordance with his or her Conscience and to understand the moral obligations that we have toward others as well. For Witherspoon, morality, justice, and Conscience are all connected to each other and Mr. Madison learned that lesson well.

Roger Schultz, in his article, 'A Christian American: John Witherspoon and the Presbyterian Roots on American Independence," points to seven reasons that John Witherspoon was the best influence in James Madison's religious education. They may be summarized this way:

1. Witherspoon was a genuine Christian.
2. He was an advocate of Orthodox Christianity.

---

150 John Witherspoon. Lectures on Moral Philosophy. (New York: Wentworth Press, 2016.), p. 129

3. He had an unparalleled record as an educator.

4. He was a great patriot and statesman.

5. He had a leading role in forming the Presbyterian Church in America.

6. He was a staunch advocate of the free market system.

7. He was a vigorous Christian apologist.[151]

Of all the Biblical influences of the religious views of James Madison, President John Witherspoon, and his knowledge of classical Hebrew and of traditional Christian doctrine, is the most important of those sources, without doubt.

Mr. Witherspoon, while Mr. Madison was in college, often gave sermons at the required chapel service every morning. These morning devotionals often contributed to Mr. Madison's own capacity later in life in analyze Biblical verses or phrases in meticulous detail much like President Witherspoon who believed that religious understanding must come from diligent study, not a mere reading of chapter and verse.

President Witherspoon's method in parsing Scripture also helped to shape James Madison's careful choices of English words to clarify complex and complicated concepts in the rest of his life. Such early training at the hands of two master teachers—Robertson and Witherspoon—helped to make Mr. Madison a worthy words smith and a superb drafter of important documents. It would be difficult to declare that James Madison's exposure to these two great teachers could have been a matter of simple coincidence.

One final way that James Madison's views on the Bible may be seen is in the context of how he and other of the Founding Fathers made Biblical and Classical allusions in his works. In a recent study of the "Frequency of Historical Allusions by the Patriots and the Tories," conducted by Lumen Learning, Jams Madison had 1.5 Biblical allusions per page, while John Adams had 1 per every seven pages and Thomas

---

151 Roger Schultz. "A Christian American: John Witherspoon and the Presbyterian Roots on American Independence." In Christianity and the American University. In Liberty Journal. [February 26, 2019.]

Jefferson no Biblical allusions per page.[152] On the other hand, when it came to Classical allusions, we find far more per page in Mr. Jefferson and John Adams than the published works of the fourth President of the United States, James Madison.[153]

Scholar Daniel Dreisbach. In an article entitled "To Better Understand the Constitution," he makes the point of how persuasive the Bible was among the Founding Fathers. As he put the matter:

> Yet the Bible remained the most accessible and authoritative text in 18th Century America, and no worked was references more frequently than the Bible in the political deliberations that led to independence and produced new national and state governments.[154]

Professor Dreisbach adds, "If we miss or dismiss the Bible's contribution to the American Constitutional tradition, we distort our understanding of the nation's bold experiment in republican self-government and liberty under the law."[155] At the close of the same article, professor Dreisbach also points out that too many "New Historians," as he calls them, do not consider the importance of the Bible as a source for the Constitution and the writings of the Founding Fathers. Daniel Dreisbach tells us:

> New historians are discovering that the Bible, perhaps even more than the Constitution. Is our founding document... In an increasing secular age the Bible's role in the nation's founding is much contested. The evidence suggests, however, that the Bible is among the sources that informed the American constitutional experiment.[156]

---

152 Anonymous. "Frequency of Historical Allusions by the Patriots and Tories." Lumen learning Center. [February, 2017.]

153 Ibid

154 Daniel Dreisbach. "To Better Understand the Constitution." Philadelphia Inquirer. September 17, 2018

155 Ibid

156 Ibid

Thus, Professor Dreisbach seems to suggest that these "New Historians" have not given the Bible its due with respect to the role it played in the formation of the United States of America. Perhaps this has to do with an increasing secular age in Contemporary America, but it may well have to do with shared Biblical values that Americans have held since its founding.

This brings us to the Second Section of Chapter Three in which we will examine what we know of James Madison's relationship with, and uses of, that he had of the Old Testament. We also will discuss in Section Two what has come to be called the "Ten Commandment Hoax" in regard to James Madison.

James Madison and the Old Testament

Before we move to what Mr. Madison said and believed about the Old Testament, we must first identify two primary sources for understanding his views The first of these is the Madison Family Bible which was a copy of William Burkitt's *Expository Notes of the Bible.*[157]

William Burkiitt (1650–1703) was a vicar and lecturer in Dedham, England. His *Expository Notes* only treats the New Testament. He said his purpose was to write "with practical observations on the new Testament of our Lord and Savior, Jesus Christ, wherein the Sacred Text is at Large recited, the Sense explained and the instructive Example of the Blessed Jesus, and his Holy Apostles to our Imitation Recommended."[158]

Much of what James Madison had to say about the New Testament, as we shall see in the Third Section of Chapter Three, comes directly from the observations of Mr. Burkitt. The first edition of the *Expository Notes* was published in England in 1700, and this is the edition owned by James Madison.[159]

The other source in examining James Madison's views on the Bible is that of his College mentor and signer of the Declaration of

---

157 William Burkitt. Expository Notes of the Bible. (Jerusalem: Ulan Press, 2016

158 Ibid

159 Ibid

Independence and ratifier of the U.S. Constitution, President John Witherspoon (1723–1794.), Scottish-American Presbyterian minister. Mr. Witherspoon wrote extensively on the Bible and, as we have indicated earlier in this Study, tutored the young James Madison in Classical Hebrew, the Old Testament, and the forms of ancient Hebrew poetry.

Among the *Collected Sermons* of John Witherspoon, there are thirty separate homilies from Exodus; Deuteronomy; Samuel; Psalms; Proverbs; Isaiah; the Book of Daniel; Hosea; and the Book of Job.[160] There are also twenty-five sermons from the New Testament that will be discussed in Section Three of this Chapter.

In regards to the Old Testament, we shall examine what Dr. Witherspoon observed about Job 42: 5 and 6, Psalm 1: 1 to 6, Isaiah 50: 10 and 11, and Daniel 5: 24 to 28. Presumably, may of the observations that President Witherspoon made about these passages were passed on to the future American statesman, James Madison.

The text from the Book of Job mentioned above, in English translation looks something like this:

> Before I have heard of You by the hearing of the ear, but now my eyes see You. Therefore, I despise myself and repent in dust and ashes.[161]

Dr. Witherspoon began his sermon on this text by saying that at times Job has exhibited impatience as well as being "disrespectful to the conduct of his Lord and Maker."[162] President Witherspoon points to the fact that there are really two Jobs to be found in the text, a patient Job, and an Impatient Job, a morally good Job and an angry, or iconoclastic Job.

In his sermon on job 42: 5–6, Dr. Witherspoon also alludes to two theories about the origins and meaning of evil and suffering. In this first of these, the scholar related, "Glory humbles the soul." By this, the

---

160 Ibid

161 Job 42: 5–6. [Author's translation.]

162 John Witherspoon. Collected Sermons. (London: Kessinger, 2010.), pp. 429–430

Scot meant that sometimes God uses evil and suffering to make souls more humble than they otherwise might be.[163]

A few paragraphs later, in the same sermon on the Book of Job, President Witherspoon related, "Nothing makes any quality appear so sensibly as a comparison with its opposite."[164] This is a theological application of a theory known as the Contrast View that essentially says in order to know or understand an idea, you must understand or know its opposite. Thus, in order to know or to understand the Good, one must first know or understand Evil, or *Ra* in Hebrew.[165] Witherspoon goes on in the same sermon to suggest that before Chapter 42, Job was in a state of "ignorance," but now in 42: 5 and 6 there is an indication that the patriarch now understands the power and the glory of God. What was anger from the personality of Job now becomes a realization that God is Just and Good.

The text about which Mr. Witherspoon comments is, "Blessed is the man that walks not in the counsel of the ungodly, nor stands in the way of sinners."[166] The Scottish scholar indicated that this passage from Psalm 1: 1 to 6 is principally about sin and the sinner. He made observations about the text like 'We are prone to sin,' an indication perhaps in the belief in Original Sin; 'that the young are ignorant and unsuspicious,' and that 'vice is usually baited with pleasure,' another nod in the direction of the Contrast View of Evil and Suffering.[167]

In his sermon on Isaiah 50: 10 and 11, a good English translations of the couplet looks like this:

> Who among you fears the Lord and obeys the voices of His
> servants who walks in darkness and has no light,
> yet trusts in the name of the Lord and relies upon his God.
> But all of you are kindlers of fire, lighters of firebrands.
> Walk in the flame of your fire

---

163 Ibid

164 Ibid., p. 430

165 There are many words for "Evil" is the Hebrew Bible. Ra is the most often used term

166 Witherspoon. Sermons. Pp/ 451–452

167 Ibid., p. 452

And among the brands you have kindled.
This is what you shall have from my hand,
You shall lie down in torment."[168]

President Witherspoon mainly preached that this text is about the fear of God and those who "walketh in darkness and hath no light,' and the 'duty to trust in God and the foundation of it.' In fact, Witherspoon said the text relates to three different kinds of promises—to God, to other person, and to ourselves.'[169]

Dr. John Witherspoon's sermon on Daniel 5: 24 to 28, is entitled, "The Handwriting on the Wall." The Scottish scholar primarily saw this text as an apocryphal, future-time narrative about the "End of probation, the door of disinheritance, and the sentence of condemnation."[170] Ultimately, Witherspoon saw the text as about a "Repentance long deferred, which may come too late."[171]

Many of these same theological reflections—or ones similar to them—can be seen in James Madison's observations about the Old Testament. Judging by notations he made in the margins of his own copy of William Burkitt's *Expository Notes*, we have some ideas of which Old Testament passages and books were his favorites.

Among these favorites were passages like Job 4: 12 to 18, where Madison found a series of parallelisms in a form of Hebrew poetry he had learned from Dr. Witherspoon. Or consider two other favorites of the fourth president, Psalm 4: 10 and Isaiah 2: 4. Both of these exhibit another Hebrew form, that of Antithesis, which Mr. Madison again learned from Dr. Witherspoon.[172]

In the notes of his personal Bible, James Madison showed a fondness for the Book of Daniel 3: 8 to 12, primarily because it shows a proper view about how to handle political authority. Daniel disobeys Persian law by refusing to bow down to Nebuchadnezzar.[173] The fourth

---

168 Ibid., pp. 390–392
169 See Isaiah 50: 190 and 11. [Author's translation.]
170 Witherspoon. Sermons. 517–518
171 Ibid., p. 518
172 See: note 1 of this Chapter
173 Daniel 3: 8–12. [Author's translation.]

President had a similar affinity to Exodus 1: 15–17, where the Hebrew midwives refuse to kill Jewish babies.[174]

The most in-depth treatment of an Old Testament texts by James Madison comes in his analysis of the Book of Proverbs on which he gives an extensive commentary. About Proverbs 9: 7 and 8, Madison tells us:

> **He that reproveth a scorner getteth to himself shame. Reprove not a Scorner, lest he hate thee.**[175]

This, of course, is an example of parallelism, and he says about Proverbs 10: 26, 'As vinegar is to the teeth, and smoke to the eyes, so is the sluggard to them that sent him." At first, this appears to be a version of Parallelism, but v. 26c shows that the passage is a synthetic one for it has nothing to do with verses a and b.[176]

Mr. Madison speaks of his belief in the Omniscience of God when he said of Proverbs 15: 3, 'The eyes of the Lord are in every place, beholding the Evil and the Good.[177] And Mr. Madison finds great advice from proverbs 18: 13, "He that answers a matter before he hears it, it is folly and shame unto him."[178]

In his commentary on the Book of Proverbs, James Madison also endorses a number of theological beliefs that he finds in the text, such as the Omniscience of God. In fact, the American statesman alludes to another answer as to why evil exists when the fourth president related, 'God's foreknowledge does not compel, but permits it to be done."[179] This theological view is sometimes called the "Permission Theory." It says that God does not cause evil and suffering, he merely permits or allows it.[180]

---

174 Exodus 1: 15–17. [NIV.]
175 James Madison. "Notes on the Bible."
176 Proverbs 10: 26. [NIV.]
177 Proverbs 15: 3. [NIV.] (Author's translation.)
178 Proverbs 18: 13. In Madison's "Noes on the Bible."
179 Ibid
180 For more on the "Permission Theory" see: Stephen Vicchio. Theodicy in the Christian Tradition. (Pittsburgh: Rose Dog Books, 2020.), pp. 22–23

In his remarks and notes on the Book of Proverbs, Mr. Madison also show assent to resurrection of the body and to immortality of the soul, though there is much more on these ideas to be found in Mr. Madison's remarks on the New Testament, which is the subject-matter of the Next Section of Chapter Three. Before we get to that Section, however, we must address one final issue in the Old Testament. What has come to be called the 'Ten Commandments Hoax' among James Madison scholars.

In his 1882 book, on p. 120, David Barton in the *Myth of Separation*, quotes James Madison as saying the following:

> We have staked out the whole future of American civilization not upon the power of government, far from it. We have staked the future of all of our political institutions upon the capacity of mankind for self-government, upon the capacity of each other and all of us to govern ourselves, to control ourselves, to sustain ourselves according to the Ten Commandments.[181]

As a footnote to this passage, Mr. Barton cites Harold K. Lane's *Liberty, Cry Liberty*, pp. 32–33 and Fedrick Nyneyer's *First Principles in Morality and Economics*, p.31.[182] Robert Alley, an historian at the University of Richmond made an attempt to follow up on these citations and their origins, and he reporter his findings in his essay, "Public Education and the Public Good," in the *William and Mary Bill of Rights Journal*. [Summer of 1995, pp. 316–318.[183]

The upshot of Robert Alley's piece is that he could not find the quote in any of James Madison's works. Next, the editors of the *Papers of James Madison* received a letter inquiring about the authenticity of the Madison quote on November 23, 1993. Mr. David Mattern, one of the editors responded to the letter this way:

---

181 David Barton. The myth of Separation. (Washington: Wallbuilder Press, 1992.) p. 63

182 Ibid

183 David Barton. "Public Education and the Public Good," William and Mary Bill of Rights Journal. [Summer, 1995.], pp. 316–318

> We did not find anything in our files remotely like the sentiment expressed in the extract you sent us. In addition, the idea is inconsistent with everything we know about Madison's views on religion and government, views that he expressed time and time again, in public and in private.[184]

Even with the expert opinion from the editors of the *James Madison Papers*, a number of American writers have continued to give the what appears to be the phony quotation. In 1964, for example, Clarence Manion repeats the Ten Commandments quote [on p. 259.] and he suggested that the source is the *Federalist Papers*.[185] With a careful perusal of the essays of the *Federalist Papers* written by James Madison, however, reveals that the Ten Commandments, nor any reference to them, appear in the *Papers*.[186]

The bottom-line conclusion about this issue should now be clear. The supposed quotation of the fourth President of the United States, James Madison, that the foundations of American political institutions is the Ten Commandments is nothing more than a Hoax, and perhaps a contrived Hoax. This brings us to James Madison and the New Testament.

James Madison and the New Testament

When it comes to the sources of James Madison's views on the New Testament two principal ones can be pointed to. The Greek language that the statesman learned in his years before College with Mr. Robertson and the Rev. Martin, so that he could read the Koine Greek of the New Testament in the original language.

The other source for James Madison's perspectives on the New Testament was the twenty-five New Testament homilies of President John Witherspoon, on the New Testament in the latter's *Collected Sermons*. Witherspoon used these sermons in a course he taught on the

---

184 David Mattern, quoted in Robert Alley's James Madison on Religious Liberty. (New York: Prometheus Books, 1985.) pp. 111–112

185 Clarence Manion to David Mattem. November 23, 1993.)

186 Ibid

New Testament.[187] Of these 25 sermons there are:

- 3 on the Gospel of Matthew.
- 2 on the Gospel of Mark.
- 3 on the Gospel of Luke.
- 2. on the Gospel of John.
- 5 on Acts of the Apostles.
- 6 on the Letters of Paul.
- 2 from First Peter.
- 2 from the Book of Revelation.[188]

Mr. Witherspoon, in describing his class on the New Testament employed five descriptions he got from New Testament passages. These were:

1. Christ Jesus—the promise of the old made unto the fathers and the hope of Israel. [Acts 28: 20.
2. The light of the World. [John 8: 12.]
3. The end of the law for righteousness to everyone that believes. [Romans 10: 4.]
4. He is the only Savior in opposition to false religions. [John 14: 6.]
5. There is no salvation in any other way. [Acts 4: 12.][189]

In his *Notes on the Commentary on the Bible*, of the twenty-seven books of the New Testament, James Madison comment extensively on five of them. These are the four Gospels and the Acts of the Apostles. Of these comments, the most thorough reading of these books is what the fourth President said about Acts. Our analysis will begin there and then move to Matthew, Mark, Luke, and John.

---

187 Witherspoon. Sermons
188 Ibid. p. 211
189 Ibid. p. 219

About Acts 18, Mr. Hamilton relates that, "Paul went to the Feast at Jerusalem, not to observe the Ceremony but to preach to a large multitude he knew would be there. [verse 21.]"[190] Mr. Madison also mentions the Baptism of John the Baptist in regard to verse 24, and the 'learned men' among those assembled but no priests to teach in the Synagogues.[191]

In regard to Acts 19, Mr. Madison comments upon the 'Holy Ghost' in verse 2, that the Apostles did greater miracles than Christ in verse 11, and he speaks of Evil Spirits and some possessed by them in verse 13.[192]

In Chapter twenty of Acts, the fourth President comments on keeping the Sabbat [verse 7.]; those who sleep under God's word in verse 9; the nature and extent of humility in verse 19; grace as a free gift of God [verse 32.]; and that the Giver is more blessed than the Receiver in verse 35.[193]

in Mr. Madison's commentary on Chapter twenty-one of Acts, he sees connections to Isaiah in verse 11, Ezekiel in v. 11 To the Jews in v. 20 To Turkey& Spain in verse 37. And he tells us about St. Paul in regard to verse 39 that, "St. Paul was a Jew by birth & a Roman by immunity & privilege."[194]

In regard to Chapter twenty-two of Acts, Mr. Madison only comments on verses 16 and 19. The former about Baptism and the latter about "Carnal Reason, when against the command of God, should be laid by.[195]

Mr. Hamilton believed that Chapter twenty-three of the Acts of the Apostles is a central one because of its emphasis on Conscience in the first verse and that it should be 'informed as well as followed." In verse 4 of Chapter 23, 'Madison relates that "Magistrates are not to be treated with 'ill words.' That the Sadducees deny the Resurrection and

---

190 James Madison. "Notes on the Bible."
191 Ibid. p. 19
192 Ibid. pp. 21–22
193 Ibid., p. 24–25
194 Ibid. p. 29
195 Ibid

the existence of Angels in verse 8; and that Magistrates ought not to perform their duties blindly or blind-folded at verse 35.[196]

The fourth President only remarks on five verses in Chapter Twenty-four of Acts [1, 2, 5, 10, and 14, and two more in Chapter twenty-five, verses 9 and 19. He speak of "persecuting spirits' in 24: 1; flattery in 24: 2; judgment and plague in v. 5; sedition in v. 10; and the Church of Rome in v. 14.[197] Mr. Hamilton also comments on Politicians, Right and Wrong, at 25:9 of Acts and "Dung-Hill Cocks in 25: 19.[198]

Finally, in his analysis of the Acts of the Apostles. Mr. Hamilton goes on to comment upon only two verses in Chapter twenty-six of Acts; one verse in twenty-seven; and five verses in Chapter twenty-eight. [2, 3, 4, 8, and 14.][199]

In regard to the four Gospels, James Madison provides commentary for only verse from Chapters one to eight of Mark, nine, ten, eleven twelve, thirteen, and twenty-one of Matthew, and only Chapter two of Luke. In the latter, Mr. Madison explains at 2: 8 that the "Idle are fit for nothing but Temptation. The fourth President also remarks about Islam in Luke 2: 29. He relates that:

> After some Turks have seen Muhamad's tomb, they put out their eyes that They may never defile them after they have seen so glorious an object.[200]

Presumably, Mr. Madison means here the cube shaped tomb the Ka'ba in the city of Mecca in Saudi Arabia.

There are also many theological theories and beliefs to be found among Mr. Madison commentaries on the Gospels. Among these, are the following comments about the Gospel of Mark:

1. That the Virgin Mary had no other children but the Savior. [Mark 1: 25.]

---

196 Ibid., pp. 32–33
197 Ibid., p. 33
198 Ibid
199 Ibid., pp. 36–39
200 Ibid., p. 40

2. That Bethlehem signifies 'the House of Bread." [Mark 2; 4.]

3. That Mark 3: 3 is about 'Papists and Confession. [Mark 3; 3.]

4. Adoption and "Satan's grand design is first to tempt the children of God to doubt. [Mark 4: 3.]

5. That Forgiveness is an indispensable Duty. [Mark 6: 14.]

6. That gifts are to be distinguished from grace. [Mark 7: 21.]

7. That marriage should not be censures not condemned among ministers. [Mark 8: 14.][201]

About the Gospel of Matthew, James Madison provided the following commentary:

1. That souls depart under the conduct of Angels and accompany them to their places of Bliss or Misery. [Matthew 9: 24.]

2. That the Apostles were Disciples before they were Apostles. [Matthew 10: 1.]

3. That the Soul does not die with the body. [Matthew 10: 28.]

4. That in Christ's coming we should distinguish between his intentions and the accidental event of it. [Matthew 10: 34.]

5. That Christ's teaching is for the conversion of sinners. [Matthew 10: 34 and 41.]

6. That there are degrees of punishment among the damned. [Matthew 11: 24.]

7. That unbelief obstructs Christ's works in Heaven. [Matthew 13; 58.]

8. That all reformation of manners must begin at the House of God. [Matthew 21: 13.][202]

---

[201] Ibid., pp. 19–40
[202] Ibid

In commenting on the Gospel of Luke, James Madison related:

1. That the idle are fit for nothing but Temptation. [Luke 2: 8.]
2. That women who have been blessed with the safety of deliverance should make their first visit to the Temple to offer up praise and thanksgiving. [Luke 2: 22.]
3. That parts and abilities for the ministerial function are not sufficient to warrant our undertaking of it without a regular Call from God. [Luke 2: 15.][203]

These *Notes on a Commentary on the Bible* in the Madison Papers are dated from 1770 to 1773, so the entries were written when the fourth President was nineteen to twenty-two years of age. They are also very sketchy and incomplete. There is nothing in the notes of the first seventeen Chapters of the Acts of the Apostles, nor any remarks on Mark one to for or anything after Chapter eight. [204]

No comments in the *Notes* appear regarding the first eight Chapters of Matthew's Gospel, nor anything after Chapter twenty-one. The notes in the *Notes* on the Gospel of Luke are incomplete for they only contain remarks about five verses in Chapter two of that Gospel. The only commentary on the Gospel of John in the *Notes* is a remark about John 20: 28 that refers to the Divinity of Jesus Christ.

Mr. Madison entitled his commentary on the Book of Proverbs, "Some Proverbs of Solomon," but more modern scholarship doubts the veracity that the book was written by the Jewish King. There is nothing in the *Notes*, however, before Chapter nine, and they then extend from Chapter nine only to Chapter twenty, so the text contains no remarks about Proverbs Chapters twenty-one to thirty-one, the final chapter of the book.

The Madison Family Bible MSS. 6: 4 M265: 1 was given to the Virginia Historical Society on March 25, 1954 by the Sarah Madison Macon Family. The 1759 London Bible printed by Thomas Baskett

---

203 Ibid
204 Ibid

may have been one of four Bibles purchased over the years by James Madison Sr., the father of the President.[205] This family Bible records the birth and death dates of various Madison family members. Some doubtful entries, whether illegible or missing, have been supplied by the staff of the Virginia Historical Society in Richmond. Most of these come from Irving Brant's biography of James Madison. The Madison family Bible also contains obituary notices clipped from newspapers with dates and ages supplied by hand.[206]

This brings us to the major Conclusions we have made in this Third Chapter on James Madison and the Bible of this Study of James Madison's Religion, followed by the Notes of the same.

One final point about James Madison's views on the Bible. In several of his essays in the *Federalist Papers*, he suggested that the real foundation for political power in America was the Bible. In *Federalist* 22, for example, he related, "The streams of national power ought to flow immediately from the pure, original fountain of all legitimate authority."[207] By this, of course, he meant God and the Bible.

In *Federalist* essay forty-nine, Mr. Madison again referred to the "only legitimate fountain of power."[208] In *Federalist* essay fifty-one, the fourth President of the United States spoke of "the same fountain of authority," meaning the Divine and his Holy Scriptures. Ultimately, then, the "fountain of legitimate authority, whether Ecclesiastical or Political, was seen by James Madison to be God and the Bible. As we shall see in Chapter Four, that is true of Mr. Madison's views on the foundation of Ethics, as well, as we shall see in Chapter Four.

The main topic of Chapter Four of this Study shall be the fourth President of the United States, James Madison's perspectives in Ethics and Morality. It is to Ethics and Conscience, then, to which we turn next.

---

205 Ms. 6.4 M265.1 Virginia Historical Society, Richmond, Virginia
206 Ibid
207 James Madison. Federalist Papers. Essay number 22
208 Ibid., number forty-nine

Conclusions to Chapter Three:

In the Introduction to Chapter Three of this Study on James Madison's Religion we have indicated that the Chapter would explore the phenomenon of the fourth President's views on Holy Scripture. We have fulfilled that central task of Chapter Three by dividing the Chapter into three parts or sections.

In the first of those, we gave an account of the main Sources of Madison's views on the Bible. Among these we have identified and discussed eight of these sources. These included: Mr. Madison's knowledge of Ancient Hebrew, Classical Greek, and Medieval Latin. Additionally, we have indicated that Donald Robertson, the Rev. Thomas Martin, and President John Witherspoon of the College of New Jersey, all were also influential sources for the development of James Madison's perspectives on Holy Scripture. At the end of the First Section of Chapter Three we also have indicated that Mr. Madison's uses of Biblical allusions in his works should be considered in the context of those of other American Founding Fathers such as John Adams and Thomas Jefferson.

The Second Section of Chapter Three of this Study on James Madison's Religion has concentrated on the many places where the fourth President has said something about the Old Testament. In that Section, we pointed out that the Madison family Bible was a copy of William Burkitt's *Expository Notes on the Bible* and that many of Mr. Madison's observations on the Old Testament were consistent with the views of the Anglican Vicar, Mr. Burkitt.

We also have indicated that another source for understanding Mr. Madison's views on the Old Testament was his mentor, president John Witherspoon (1723–1794), noted teacher, scholar, and signer of the Declaration of Independence.

Indeed, in the Second Section of Chapter Three, we have examined Mr. Witherspoon's treatment of five Old Testament texts in his *Collected Sermons* and the possible influences there may have been on the fourth President of the United States.

To that end, we have discussed many of the personal notes that Mr. Hamilton had made in his copy of the family Bible. Among these notes, we have discussed passages from the Book of Job, Psalms, the Prophet Isaiah, and the Book of Daniel, among other Old Testament texts.

We also have shown that among the books of the Old Testament of which Mr. Madison has made commentaries, he completed a more extensive treatment of the Book of Proverbs than any other Old Testament texts. In fact, we have shown that the fourth President's remarks on Proverbs contain assents to many of Mr. Madison's central theological tenets such as the Divinity of Jesus Christ, the existence of Angels and Devils, as well as beliefs in Immortality of the Soul and the Resurrection of the Body.

The focus of the Third Section of Chapter Three on Madison and the Bible, we have explored what the fourth President had to say and write about the New Testament. Again, we have indicated that the two primary sources for these perspectives of Mr. Madison on the new Testament were William Burkitt's *Expository Notes* and the notes that Mr. Hamilton took in John Witherspoon's course on the New Testament while in College and graduate school.

In the remainder of the Third Section of Chapter Three, we have examined and discussed many of the notes on the New Testament that Mr. Hamilton called his "Notes on the Commentary on the Bible," which, as we have indicated were completed from 1770 to 1773 when the fourth President was in College and Graduate School.

We also have indicated that in these New Testament notes, Mr. Madison gave a much more thorough account on the Acts of the Apostles than he did on the other books of the New Testament. Indeed, we have shown that many of the American statesman's key theological ideas can be seen in these remarks from Acts.

Among these theological ideas we have indicated the fourth President's emphasis on Conscience, his views on the Soul and survival after death, and his understanding that God does not cause Evil but He does "Permit" it. We also have indicated in the Third Section of Chapter Three that Mr. Madison only made very cursory remarks about the four Gospels and he made far more about the Synoptics Gospels [Matthew, Mark, and Luke, than he made about the Fourth Gospel, the Gospel of John.

Along the way in our analysis of James Madison's views on the New Testament, we also have indicated many central theological ideas that the fourth President of the United States appears to have assented to or endorsed in some way. Among these theological ideas were observations about:

1. The Virgin Mary.
2. The meaning of the word Bethlehem.
3. His views on Papists and Confession.
4. His understanding of Adoption.
5. His view of Forgiveness.
6. The difference between Gift and Grace.
7. And his understanding of Marriage for Ministers of the Faith.

We also have indicated, however, that Mr. Madison's *Notes on the Commentary on the Bible* were written at a youthful time i his life, and that these are many gaps in the document where the American statesman made no comment. There is nothing, for example, about the first eight chapters of the Gospel of Matthew, nor anything after Chapter twenty-one of that text; the only commentary on the Gospel of John in those *Notes* comes from Chapter twenty of the Fourth Gospel.

In regard to the Gospel of Mark, as we have indicated in the Third Section of Chapter Three, Mr. Madison only supplied commentary on chapters one to eight of that Gospel and only Chapter two of the Gospel of Luke. Indeed, as we have indicated, Mr. Madison appears to have made a reference to the K*a'ba*, the sacred shrine in Mecca in Saudi Arabia.

In short, as we have indicated, Mr. Madison's treatment of the new testament falls short of a thorough analysis of the twenty-seven books of the new Testament. Indeed, of those books, the fourth President only makes remarks on five of them—the four Gospels and the Acts of the Apostles.

At the very end of Chapter Three we also have related that the ultimate "Fountain" of all authority for Mr. Madison was God and His

Holy Writ, and the fourth President made this claim several times in his essays of the *Federalist Papers*.

This brings us to the Notes of this Third Chapter of this Study on James Madison's

Religion, followed by Chapter Four of this Study. The central focus of Chapter Four, as we shall see, is what the fourth President of the United States, James Madison believed and wrote about the Moral Good and Ethical Theory. Thus, we moved next to Ethics, Conscience, and the Good.

Chapter Four:
James Madison on Ethics and Conscience

There is not a single instance in history in which civil liberty was lost and religious liberty was preserved entire. If therefore we yield up our temporal property we at the same time deliver the Conscience into bondage.

—John Witherspoon, 'The Dominion of Providence."

Our perceptions reveal the world pretty much the way it is and are not merely "ideas" impressed upon our minds and Ethical Common Sense.

—Mark A. Noll, "Common Sense Tradition and American Evangelical Thought."

The civil rights of none shall be abridged on account of religious belief or worship, nor shall any national religion be established, nor shall the full and equal rights of Conscience be in any manner, or on any pretext, infringed."

—James Madison, "Essay on Property."

Introduction

The main focus of this Chapter Four of this Study of James Madison's Religion shall be what the fourth President of the United States has had to say and written about the ideas of the Moral Good and Religious Conscience. We will fulfill that aim by dividing Chapter Four into three Sections.

In the first of these, we will identify and discuss the major sources and influences on James Madison's perspectives on the Good and on Religious Conscience. In the Second Section of Chapter Four, we will provide a catalogue of the role that the phenomenon of Conscience played in the early development of political and religious ideas in the United States of America. In a Third Section of Chapter Four, we will identify and then discuss many of the places in the fourth President's *Collected Works*, where he said or wrote about Ethics and Conscience or indicated what he believed about these phenomena. This brings us to the Sources of the fourth President's views on Ethics and Conscience.

The Sources of James Madison's Views on Ethics and Conscience

Among the sources for ascertaining the views of James Madison on Ethics and Conscience, several come to mind including many Classical thinkers on the idea of Virtue, including Aristotle, Seneca, and Cicero. The School of Philosophy known as the Scottish Common Sense School represented by Thomas Reid. The views on Ethics and Conscience in Madison's mentor, president John Witherspoon, particularly in his *Sermons* and his book entitled. *Lectures in Moral Philosophy* [1774.], that James Madison and his fellow classmates used as a text book in their senior year of College's Moral Philosophy class.[209]

While working on his Doctor of Divinity degree at the University of Edinburgh, Mr. Witherspoon became familiar with the school of Thought known as the "Scottish Common Sense" of Philosophy, a movement devised by Scottish philosopher, Thomas Reid (1710–1796), noted Scottish philosopher and central figure in the Scottish Enlightenment.[210] In 1783, Reid was one of the joint founders of the Royal Society of Edinburgh, he was a contemporary of Scottish philosopher, David Hume and he was also one of Hume's earliest and fiercest critics.[211]

---

209 John Witherspoon. Lectures on Moral Philosophy. (New York: Wentworth Press, 2016.)

210 Thomas Reid. On the Intellectual Powers of Man. (New York: Wentworth Press, 2016.)

211 Ibid., pp. ix to xiii

Mr. Reid's theory was called the "Common Sense" View because it began with the understanding that his view took a common sense view to knowledge over and against the schools of European Philosophy known as the Rationalist [Descartes and Leibniz], as well as the Empiricists [Locke and Hume.][212] The Latin expression *Sensus Comminis*, or "Common Sense" is the expression Mr. Reid employed to speak of the nature and uses of knowledge in his Philosophy.[213]

In his view of Ethics and Conscience, Thomas Reid believed that all human beings are endowed by God with an innate understanding of the Moral Good. For Reid, this sense is both innate and universal. Reid started out, then, with a common sense of the Good, as well as the additional common sense beliefs that 'the physical world exists," and "that other minds exists" constitute other beliefs of Reid's Common Sense Approach in opposition to both Rationalism and Empiricism.

Thomas Reid's starting point, then, for his views on Ethics is that moral concepts, like Good and Evil, are related to certain feelings of approbation and disapproval that we feel when we make judgments like "That action is wrong," or "That action is morally good." And these are nothing more than simply saying, "I approve," or "I disapprove of an action."[214]

What Thomas Reid and his School believed is inadequate of both Rationalism and Empiricism is that they both are incompatible with Common Sense when it came to issues like personal identity, the existence of other minds, Ethics and Conscience and the existence of the material world.

In addition to Thomas Reid, the other members of the Scottish Common Sense School included Adam Ferguson, Henry Home, George Campbell, Dugald Stewart, and Sir William Hamilton. Each of these men employed the idea of Common Sense as a rebuttal to both Rationalism and Empiricism. Philosophically, Scottish Realism

---

212 Rationalism believed that all knowledge came from the use of the mind, while the British Empiricists suggested all knowledge came from the use of the senses

213 Reid, p. 17–18

214 Ibid., pp. 22–23

contradicted Rationalism and Empiricism, while at the same time adhering to the influential scientific teachings of Sir Isaac Newton and Francis Bacon.[215] The central concern of the Common Sense School, then, was to employ the idea of Common sense against philosophical paradox, Skepticism, and confusion.

Another source of James Madison's views on Ethics and Conscience was the various views on the concept of Virtue from Classical Greco-Roman Literature that the fourth President first learned at the feet of Donald Robertson and the Rev. Thomas Martin, in his adolescent years. In that time, Mr. Madison read and enjoyed the works in particular of Aristotle, Seneca, and Cicero on the notion of Virtue which we will now review.

The oldest of Greco-Roman accounts of Virtue comes from Aristotle's book, the *Nicomachean Ethics*.[216] In this book, the ancient Greek philosopher tells us that a Virtue is a mean between two vices, one being a deficiency of the vice and the other an abundance of the vice. Thus "Justice' for Aristotle is "getting what one is due," while injustice is "not getting wat one is do," and "over-justice" is getting "more than what one is due."[217]

Aristotle believed that moral Virtues are character traits that one acquires over time. Thus, over time one may become known as a liar in his view, because a man has a habit of not telling the truth. On the other hand, the man may come to be known as a truthful man because he had acquired the habit of veracity.[218]

Another of the Greco-Roman writers that wrote about Virtue, and that James Madison studied with Mr. Robertson, was the Roman, Stoic philosopher and poet, Seneca, the Younger.[219] Seneca discusses the idea

---

215 Isaac Newton (1642–1727) and Francis Bacon (1561–1626), of course, were the two greatest British scientists of the 17th Century

216 Aristotle. Nicomachean Ethics. (Chicago: University of Chicago Press, 2012.)

217 Ibid

218 Ibid

219 Senaca. Ad Lucilium Epistulae Morales. (Cambridge: Cambridge University Press, 2017.)

of Virtue in his work, *Ad Lucilium Epistulae Morales*, published by Cambridge Press in 2017.[220]

In his close reading of Seneca with Mr. Robertson, he must have learned that Seneca believed that there are two fundamental questions to be asked and answered about Virtue, what is its ontological status, and how is it to be defined?[221] Seneca also tells us that any Virtue is to be understood through three means. He calls these "analogy," "observation," and "deduction."[222]

For Seneca, the nature of virtue is reflected in human behavior. A virtuous man for Seneca is compassionate with friends, restrained with enemies, and able to endure hardship. The virtuous man strives to pay all his debts and "acts as a soldier and citizen of the universe."[223] Seneca observed that, "This kind of man is always the same kind of man and is never anyone else."[224] "By him," he says, 'we have understood in him that perfect virtue may exists."[225]

A third Greco-Roman figure that James Madison studied with Mr. Robertson was the poet/philosopher, Cicero. In his work, *De Officiis*, Cicero sketches out his account of Virtue, including what he saw as the "Cardinal Virtues." For Cicero, these were: Wisdom, Justice, Courage, and Temperance.[226]

Wisdom, or *Sophia/sapiential*, for Cicero, "is the ability to discern the appropriate course of action to be taken in a given situation." Justice is nothing more than Fairness. It also has the meaning of "righteousness." Courage, or *Virtus*, in Latin also called "fortitude" by the Romans, is forbearance, strength, and endurance, and the ability to face fear and intimidation. Temperance, for Cicero, is another name for restraint, or the practice of "self-control."[227] Aristotle's teacher, Plato,

---

220 Ibid
221 Ibid., p. 42
222 Ibid., pp. 44–45
223 Ibid., p. 47
224 Ibid
225 Cicero. On Duty. (London: Stonewell Press, 2016.)
226 Ibid. pp. 29–33
227 Virtus, of course, is the origin of the English word "Virtue."

considered *Sophrosyne*, or "Temperance" in classical Greek, to be the most important of the virtues.[228] Again, we know that James Madison read Cicero and his account of Virtue with Donald

Robertson, and what is important about all of these Greco-Roman sources on Virtue is that the fourth President read them all in their original languages, either Greek or Latin. It is also likely that the American statesman continued these studies when he was tutored in his home by the Reverend Thomas Martin in the late 1760s.[229]

We already have said a great deal about the influence that President John Witherspoon has had on the intellectual development of James Madison. This is also true when it came to Madison's sense of Ethics and Conscience because in his post-graduate year in which he studied Hebrew and the Moral Philosophy, the Scottish Calvinist was also a source of the American statesman's later pronouncements and writings that mentioned Ethics and Conscience.

John Witherspoon, when he studied for his Doctor of Divinity degree at the University of Edinburgh became familiar with the teachings of the Scottish Common Sense School and thinkers like David Hume and Thomas Reid. And it is likely that he passed some of this knowledge on to his student, the future fourth President of the United States, particularly Reid's understanding of Conscience and its innate and universal nature in the Scottish Common Sense View.

This brings us to the Second Section of Chapter Four on Ethics and Conscience of this Study on James Madison's Religion. In this Section, we will show the ubiquitous character that the idea of Conscience had among the other Founding Fathers in America in the late 18th Century.

Conscience in Many of the Other Founding Fathers

The idea of Conscience was one that was discussed by at least twelve other American Founding Fathers in addition to American statesman, James Madison. We will list these other twelve Founding Fathers here in this Second Section of Chapter Four and then discuss them one at a time.

---

228 The word Sophrosyne can be found in Thucydides, Plato, Aristotle, the tragic poet Euripides, and in many other classical Greek writers

229 Mr. Madison was tutored by the Rev. Martin in 1767 to 1869

1. Roger Williams
2. George Washington.
3. John Adams.
4. Thomas Jefferson.
5. John Jay.
6. John Witherspoon.
7. Benjamin Rush.
8. Patrick Henry.
9. Samul Adams.
10. William Livingston.
11. Charles Grandison Finney.
12. John Quincy Adams.

In the year 1664, Roger Williams of Rhode Island, in a work he entitled, "The Bloody Tenant of Persecution for Cause of Conscience," was the first of the Founding Fathers to write and discuss the idea of the liberty of Conscience. He did this in the tenth and eleventh propositions of that document. In the former proposition, Mr. Williams related:

> An enforced uniformity of religion throughout a nation or civil state confounds the civil and religious, denies the principles of Christianity and civility, and that Jesus Christ is come in the flesh.[230]

In the eleventh proposition of the same work, Roger Williams wrote:

> The permission of the other Consciences and worships than a state professeth, only can, according to God procure a pure and lasting peace, (good assurance being taken) according to the wisdom of the civil state for uniformity of civil obedience from all sorts.[231]

---

[230] Roger Williams. The Bloody Tenants of Persecutions. (London: Kessinger Books, 2010.) Proposition ten

[231] Ibid., proposition eleven

Mr. Williams speaks of what he calls the 'other Consciences and worships,' a reference to religious views other than the Established Church such as the Congregationalist Church from which he came in the Massachusetts Bay Colony, and he goes on to argue vehemently for Religious Tolerance of these other views.

Each of the other Founding Fathers listed above have also made extensive comments on the ideas of Conscience in the early history of the United States. George Washington, in a letter to the United Baptist Chamber of Virginia, in May of 1789, told the Chamber's members:

> Every man, conducting himself as a good citizen, and being accountable to God alone for his religious opinions, ought to be protected in worshipping the Deity according to the dictates of his own conscience.[232]

In a letter written a year later to the Touro Synagogue in Newport, Rhode Island. Mr. Washington wrote to the Jewish community at the Touro Synagogue:

> The Citizens of the United States of America have a right to applaud themselves for having given to mankind examples of an enlarged and liberal policy; a policy worthy of imitation. All possess alike liberty of Conscience and immunities of citizens.[233]

In another letter, while he was President, George Washington fiercely defended the right of Conscience, when he wrote:

> The conscientious scruples of all men should be treated with great delicacy and tenderness; and it is my wish and desire, that the laws may always be extensively accommodated to them.[234]

On another occasion, George Washington again remarked about the relation of religious sentiments and Conscience. He wrote,

---

232 George Washington to United Baptist Chamber of Virginia. May 14, 1789

233 George Washington to Touro Synagogue in Newport. [August 18, 1790.]

234 George Washington to Benedict Arnold. September 14, 1775

"I have often expressed my sentiments that every man conducting himself as a good citizen and being accountable to God alone for his religious opinions, ought to be protected in worshipping the Deity [the Lord], according to the dictates of his own Conscience."[235]

In the letter to the Touro Synagogue mentioned above, President Washington also related," It is now no more that toleration is spoken of as if it were the indulgence of one class of people that another enjoyed the exercise of their inherent natural rights."[236] For George Washington, one of those natural rights is the "liberty of Conscience." President John Adams expressed a similar point of view in a letter from 1814 to John Taylor. He wrote, 'Being men, they all have what Dr. Rush calls a moral faculty, Dr. Hutcheson a moral sense and the Bible and the generality of the world, a Conscience."[237] Here President Adams referred to Benjamin Rush, as well as one of the members of the Scottish School of Common Sense, Francis Hutcheson (1694–1746.)[238]

The "Dr. Rush" to whom President Adams referred in Dr. Benjamin Rush who in his *Enquiry into the Influence of Physical Causes Upon the Moral Faculty*, a 1786 address to the American Philosophical Society, affirmed his belief in an innate moral faculty and observed, 'Saint Paul and Cicero give us the most perfect account of it that is to be found in modern or ancient authors."[239]

Dr. Rush goes on to explain this moral sense:

The faculty has received different names from different authors. It is the moral sense of Dr. Hutcheson—the 'sympathy' of Dr. Adam Smith—the 'moral instinct' of Rousseau—and the 'light that lighteth every man that cometh into the world' of Saint John. I have adopted the

---

235 George Washington to United Baptists
236 George Washington to Touro Synagogue
237 John Adams to John Taylor. April 15, 1814
238 Ibid
239 Benjamin Rush. Enquiry into the Influence of physical Causes Upon the Moral Faculty. (New York: Gale Sabin Americana, 2012.)

term of 'moral faculty' from Dr. Beattie because I conceive it convey with the most perspicuity. The idea of a power in the mind of choosing good and evil.[240]

The "Dr. Beattie" to whom Dr. Rush referred was James Beattie (1735–1803), Scottish poet. Moralist and philosopher. Beattie was also a member of the Scottish Common Sense School, and as Dr Rush indicated, Beattie's name for the Conscience was the "Moral Faculty." Thomas Jefferson on several occasions also made observations like this one: 'I have ever thought Religion a concern surely between our God and our Consciences, for which we are accountable to Him, and not to the priests."[241]

In a letter to Jared Sparks from November 4, 1828, Mr. Jefferson wrote:

But our rulers can have authority over such natural rights only as we have submitted to them. The rights of Conscience we never submitted, we could not submit. We are answerable for them to our God.[242]

In another instance, the third President of the United States, Thomas Jefferson wrote, "No provision in our constitution ought to be dearer to man than that which protects the rights of conscience against the enterprises of the civil authority."[243]

John Jay, original Chief Justice of the U. S. Supreme Court, in one of the *Federalist Papers* he authored observed,

"Adequate security under our Constitution is also given to the rights of Conscience and private Judgment. They are by nature subject to no control but to the Deity, and in that free situation they are now left. Every man is permitted to consider, to adore, and to worship, his Creator in the manner most agreeable to his Conscience.'[244]

---

240 Ibid., pp. 14–15
241 Thomas Jefferson to Mrs. Samuel H. Smith. August 6, 1816
242 Thomas Jefferson to Jared Sparks. November 4, 1828
243 Thomas Jefferson to Richard Douglas. February 4, 1809
244 John Jay. Federalist Papers. essay number four

William Livingston (1723–1790), one of the signers of the U.S. Constitution, remarked about that,

> "The Consciences of men are not the objects of human legislation. For what business, in the name of Common Sense has the magistrates (distinctly and singly appointed for our political and temporal happiness) with our religion, which is to secure our happiness spiritual and eternal? The state has no concern in the matter. For what manner does it affect Society in what outward form we think it best to pay our adoration to God?[245]

Mr. Livingston referred to the idea of Common Sense and its relation to the Consciences of men, as well as suggesting that the 'Consciences of men" should not be the object of human legislation.[246] Many of the general comments from the Founding Fathers about the idea of Conscience frequently point out the relationship of Conscience with Freedom, such as this comment from Patrick Henry (1736–1799), American Attorney, planter, and politician:

> A vitiated, impure state of morals, a corrupted public Conscience is incompatible with the idea of Freedom.[247]

President John Adams made a similar remark in a letter to Mercy Otis Warren from April 16, 1776, when he wrote: 'Public Virtue cannot exist in a Nation without private Virtue, and public virtue is the only foundation of a Republic."[248] Benjamin Franklin agreed. He related, 'Only a virtuous people are capable of freedom."[249]

In a speech from August 1, 1776, Samuel Adams (1722–1803), American statesman and political philosopher, spoke about America

---

245 William Livingston quoted in Myron Magnet. "Concerned in Liberty." City Journal. [Summer, 2012.]

246 Ibid

247 Patrick Henry. Speech to Virginia Legislature. [June 1, 1788.]

248 John Adams to Mercy Otis Warren. April 16, 1776

249 Benjamin Franklin. Autobiography. (New York: Create Space, 2019.), p. 228

being a 'last refuge for the Conscience' when he said:

> Driven from every other corner of the earth, freedom of thought and the right of private judgment in matters of Conscience directs their course to this happy country as their last asylum.[250]

Charles Finney (1792–1875), American Presbyterian Minister, though not technically among the generation of the Founding Fathers, nevertheless, remarked about the idea of Conscience in his essay, "The Decay of Conscience," published in the *New York Independent*, on December 4, 1873:

> If there is a decay of conscience, the pulpit is responsible for it. If the public press lacks moral discrimination, the pulpit is responsible for it. If the Church is degenerate and worldly, the pulpit is responsible for it. If the world loses interest in religion, the pulpit is responsible for it.[251]

It is not clear in this quotation, nor in the remainder of his essay, what Reverend Finny meant by the "Pulpit." Did he mean the Clergy or was he simply referring to the corruption of human nature in his Calvinistic, Presbyterian view, or the Doctrine of Original Sin. Nevertheless, the Rev. Finney makes a number of other observations about the nature and extent of Conscience and how the idea had changed in his lifetime.[252]

President John Quincy Adams, in a work of his entitled, *A Discourse on Education at Braintree*, which was delivered on October 24, 1839, affirmed, "The transcendent and overruling principle of the first settlers of New England that was Conscience."[253]

Of all the Founding Fathers we have listed and discussed here,

---

250 Samuel Adams. Speech Before the Continental Congress. August 1, 1776

251 Charles Finney. 'The Decay of Conscience." New York Independent. December 4, 1873

252 Ibid

253 John Quincy Adams. 'A Discourse on Education at Braintree," [October 24, 1839.]

President John Witherspoon of the College of New Jersey was the most influential on the morality and views on Conscience of James Madison. Witherspoon's perspectives on these matters were mostly developed in his sermon, "The Dominion of Providence Over the Passions of Men," from May of 1776, from his 'Sermon Delivered at Public Thanksgiving After Peace,' Sermon XlVI of the third volume of his *Collected Sermons*.[254] And, of course, Witherspoon's *Lectures on Moral Philosophy*.[255]

From these three works, it becomes clear that Dr. Witherspoon was greatly indebted to the Common Sense Moral Theory of Francis Hutcheson and Thomas Reid. From them, he adopted the idea of what Witherspoon called the "Moral Sense," which was nothing more than the belief that God had implanted into the hearts of all men a common and universal sense of the Good. It is an ethical compass instilled by God in all human beings and developed through religious education [according to Reid], or civic sociability [according to Hutcheson.][256]

Dr. Witherspoon believed that Virtue may be developed through the use of the moral sense, which he believed had two elements, a spiritual component and a temporal component. Civil Government, for Witherspoon, was more related to the temporal element, Biblical accounts of the Good more related to the spiritual component.[257] Dr. Witherspoon's lectures on "Moral Philosophy," was a required course and reading for all third and fourth year students at the College of New Jersey, including for James Madison when he was Witherspoon's student in 1769 to 1671.[258]

We have to point out, however, that President Witherspoon is reported to have said about the fourth President, "During the whole time that Madison was under my tuition, I never knew him to do, or to

---

254 John Witherspoon. "The Dominion of Providence Over the passions of Men," Collected Sermons. Volume III, number CXIVI

255 Witherspoon. Lectures on Moral Philosophy. Pp. 100–127

256 Francis Hutcheson. A System of Morals. (New York: Palala Press, 2015.)

257 Witherspoon. "Dominion."

258 See note 1 of this Chapter, pp. 29–38

say, an improper thing."[259] Reportedly, Mr. Witherspoon said this to Mr. Jefferson who apparently brought it up on every occasion he could to Mr. Madison.[260] It is not clear, however, whether Madison's academic mentor was saying something positive or negative about his former charge.

Later, President Witherspoon was responsible for conferring an honorary Doctorate on James Madison, in his remarks about the President on that occasion. Witherspoon only said laudatory things about his former student, including, "All concerned in the College were not barely willing but proud to honor one of their own sons who has done so much honor to his public service."[261]

Finally, there was language about the protection of Conscience in many of the early state Constitutions and other official documents, including the 1649 Maryland Toleration Act, the 1663 Charter for Rhode Island; the 1664 Charter for New Jersey; the 1665 Charter for North Carolina; the 1669 Constitution of South Carolina; the 1701 Charter for Delaware; the 1682 frame of government for Pennsylvania, as well as many others.[262]

These teachings regarding the natural right of Conscience, our most 'sacred property and right,' deeply influenced the life of James Madison and it found its way into the fourth President's work on Religious Liberty, as we shall see in Chapter Five of this Study. Mr. Madison was inclined to accept these moral teachings of Mr. Witherspoon, which also echoed what he had learned from Mr. Robertson.

This brings us to the Third and Final Section of Chapter Four in which we will explore what the fourth President of the United States, James Madison, believed and wrote about Ethics and the idea of Conscience

---

259 Ibid., p. 56

260 John Witherspoon to Thomas Jefferson. March 1, 1792. Mr. Jefferson responded on March 9, 1792

261 Ceremony of Honorary Doctorate for James Madison. Remarks by John Witherspoon. He received a Doctor of Laws at Commencement in 1787

262 The word "Conscience" appears in all of these state charters

James Madison on Ethics and Conscience

James Madison's study under John Witherspoon at the College of New Jersey exposed the student to John Locke's expanded definition of Property as not just a man's stuff and his possessions, but his being as well—his ability to produce and most importantly his Conscience. This being "a property of peculiar value in man's religious opinions and free use of his faculties, and free choice of the objects on which to employ them."[263]

In the same essay, Mr. Madison related, "Conscience is the most sacred of all property. Other property depending in part on positive law, the exercise of conscience being a natural and an inalienable right."[264] The infringement of one's religious Conscience, in the view of James Madison, is to take one's soul without providing any compensation, what the fourth President called "an act of tyranny of the worst kind."[265]

In essence, James Madison believed that Conscience was an important yet often unrecognized division of man's property and could be violated, confiscated, and destroyed, just as temporal property of man could be stolen or violated. In fact, in his 1792 essay, "On Property," the fourth President said far more about the notion of Conscience than he did in any of his other works.[266]

In fact, in that essay, Mr. Madison made the bold claim that, "Conscience is the most sacred of all property, other property depending in part on positive law but the exercise of that being a natural and unalienable right."[267] Mr. Madison asks us to consider the following analogy:

> To guard a man's house as his castle, to pay public and to enforce private debts with the most exact faith, can give no title to invade a man's Conscience, which is more sacred than his castle; or to withhold from it that debt of protection

---

263 James Madison. "Essay on Property." [1792.]
264 Ibid
265 Ibid
266 Ibid
267 Ibid

for which the public faith is pledged by the very nature and original nature of the social pace."[268]

In other words, for Mr. Madison, "Conscience is the most sacred of all property."[269] Liberty of Conscience, in his view, was a natural right, one endowed by the Creator into the hearts of all human beings. At times when James Madison spoke of the idea of Conscience he did so in the context of speaking, as some of the other Founding Fathers did, as we have shown, in the relation of Conscience to Freedom such as this comment:

> There is not a truth to be gathered from history more certain or more momentous than this: that civil liberty cannot long be separated from religious liberty without danger and ultimately without destruction to both. Wherever religious liberty exists it will first or last bring in and establish political liberty.[270]

Here Mr. Madison seems to be following the views of Thomas Reid and John Witherspoon that there are two kinds of moral sense, one political and one religious, and that the existence of one kind of liberty is inextricably related to the other kind of liberty, much like the perspectives of other Founding Fathers we have discussed earlier such as John Adams, Patrick Henry, and Samuel Adams, as we have shown earlier in this Chapter.

The fourth President also found the same connection between Conscience and political Freedom when he observed, "To suppose that any form of government will secure liberty or happiness without any virtue in the people, is a chimerical idea." At other times, Mr. Madison spoke of Conscience in the context of Religious Toleration such as in the following remark:

> Toleration is not the opposite of Intolerance, but it is the counterfeit of it. Both are Despotisms. The one assumes

---

268 Ibid
269 Ibid
270 Ibid

to itself the right of withholding liberty of Conscience, the other of granting it.[271]

In Mr. Madison's first draft of the First Amendment, the fourth President also included some language about Conscience. He said, "Congress should not establish a religion, and enforce the legal observation of it by law, nor compel men to worship God in any Manner contrary to their Conscience."[272]

Mr. Madison's second proposed amendment, which also dates from May 29 to June 12, 1776, "would have protected the free exercise of religion, according to the dictates of Conscience,"[273] but this formulation was rejected, as well. Mr. Madison also made many comments on Conscience on the context of the separation of Church and State. Madison was convinced that separating Church and State and protecting the right of all people to follow the dictates of Conscience was an arrangement in freedom that would endure for the ages.[274]

After enacting the Act for Establishing Religious Freedom in Virginia in 1786, Madison wrote to Thomas Jefferson who was in Paris at the time, as the Ambassador there. Madison wrote, "I flatter myself that with this statute we have in this country extinguished forever the ambitious hope of making laws for the human mind."[275]

James Madison was, to put it mildly, overly optimistic. The United States did not live up to the full promise of religious freedom in the 18th Century—and we have struggled to do so ever since, as Native Americans, Catholics, Jews, Mormons, Jehovah's Witnesses, and now members of the Islamic Faith can now attest.[276]

In general, however, most of the many observations that James Madison made about Ethics and Conscience are very general remarks

---

271 James Madison. Speech to Virginia Legislature. [June 12, 1776.]

272 James Madison. First draft of the First Amendment was in the Winter of 1775–1776

273 James Madison. Second draft of First Amendment. [June 12, 1776.]

274 James Madison. Final draft of First Amendment. [1786.]

275 James Madison to Thomas Jefferson. [January 16, 1786.]

276 Each of these traditions suffered through religious persecutions in the 18th and 19th centuries in America, and beyond

like this comment about a "Holy and Omniscient Being" and the idea of Conscience:

> If the public homage of a people can ever be worthy of the favorable regard of the Holy and Omniscient Being to Whom it is addressed, it mut be that in which those who join in it are guided only by their free choice—by the impulse of their hearts and by the dictates of their Consciences.[277]

At other times, Mr. Madison made comments about the idea of Conscience in the context of one's other religious rights:

> Because, finally, the equal rights of every citizen to the free exercise of his religion according to the dictates of Conscience is held by the same tenure with all other rights. If we recur to the origin, it is equally the gift of nature, if we weigh its importance, it cannot be less dear to us if we consider the "Declaration" of those rights which pertain to the good people of Virginia, as the basis and foundation of Government. It is enumerated with equal solemnity, or rather studied emphasis.[278]

The fourth President of the United States, James Madison sometimes remarked about Conscience in the context of Compacts or Covenants such as in this remark from the *Writings of James Madison*, from 1790 until 1802:

> As compacts, charters of government are superior in obligation to all others because they give effect to all others. As truths, none can be more sacred because they are bound on the Conscience by the religious sanctions of an oath. As mete and bounds of government, they transcend all other landmarks, because every public usurpation is an encroachment on the private right, not of one, but of all.[279]

---

277 James Madison. Prayer Proclamation. [June 23, 1813.]
278 James Madison. Memorial and Remonstrance. [1785.]
279 James Madison. The Writings of James Madison. Volume VI: 1790–1802,

This lofty judgment by Mr. Madison was made many times throughout many of the statesman's works such as his admission in his "Essay on Property," that "Conscience is the most sacred of all property."[280]

In several places of his *Memorial and Remonstrance*, the fourth President also spoke of the idea of Conscience such as this pronouncement:

> The Religion of every man must be left to the conviction and Conscience of every man to exercise it as these may dictate. This right is in its nature an inalienable right.[281]

In another Section of the same work, James Madison related, "The equal right of every citizen to the free exercise of his religion according to the dictates of Conscience is held by the same tenure with all our other rights."[282] In the same work, Mr. Madison continued:

> The Religion of every man must be left to the conviction and Conscience of every man: and it is the right of every man to exercise it as these may dictate.[283]

In the same work, Mr. Madison observed:

> The Civil Rights of none shall be abridged on account of religious belief or worship, Nor shall any national religion be established nor shall the full and equal rights of Conscience be in any manner or on any pretext infringed.[284]

Altogether, James Madison made fifteen separate arguments in the *Memorial*, all designed to counter the idea that the Government has the power to establish Christianity as the state religion. The fourth president also argued that the inequality resulting from an Established

---

pp. 161–162

280 James Madison. "Essay on Property,"
281 James Madison. Memorial and Remonstrance [1785.]
282 Ibid
283 Ibid
284 Ibid

Church would be a "signal for persecution," and America would no longer be a "beacon of Freedom to the persecuted and the oppressed."[285] Mr. Madison even went so far as to say that an Established Church differs from the inquisition "only in degree."[286]

The writing of the *Memorial* had been occasioned by the introduction of a bill by Patrick Henry in 1784 that provided for an annual tax to "support the Christian Religion or some Christian Church, denomination, or worship."[287] It was supported by many of the most powerful men in the Legislature and backed by Anglicans, Presbyterians, and Methodists.

By 1775, the year before the Declaration of Independence, nine of the Colonies had Established Churches, three Congregational [Conn. Mass. and N.H.], and six the Anglican Church. [Ga., Md., N.Y., N.C., S.C., and Va.] By 1819, all of these states had disestablished these Churches.[288]

James Madison even spoke of the ideas of Ethics and Conscience in some of his letters. One good example is a missive to the Rev. George Eve, a Baptist minister, on January 2, 1789, was told, "If elected to the First Congress, I would do my best for the most satisfactory provisions for all essential rights, particularly the rights of Conscience in the fullest latitude."[289]

Another good example is a letter told his friend William 'Billy" Bradford on January 24, 1774 which the fourth president ends by writing, 'So I leave you to pity me and to pray for the property of Conscience to revive among us."[290] This is most likely a reference from the lectures of John Witherspoon on Ethics at the College of New Jersey—which the two friends attended together—in which Mr. Witherspoon suggested that the "Conscience is the most valuable of all property."[291]

---

285 Ibid

286 Ibid

287 Ibid

288 This is a summary of Established Churches in the Colonies in 1775

289 James Madison to George Eve. January 2, 1789

290 James Madison to William Bradford. January 24, 1774

291 Both Bradford and Madison took Mr. Witherspoon's class in the Fall of 1770

Mr. Madison also made similar assurances to other Religious Congregations in letters he wrote over the years, including to other Baptist Congregations, as well as Jews and Roman Catholics.[292] Another example of these is a letter to Bishop James Madison of Philadelphia, a cousin of the President, from January 31, 1800 in which the President tells the AME Church Bishop that he "will work hard to preserve the rights of Conscience for you and your followers."[293]

James Madison also mentioned the phenomenon of Conscience in a letter written from Montpelier to Thomas Jefferson on October 17, 1788. In the letter Mr. Madison tells Mr. Jefferson that many critics of the proposed Constitution wish to add more "guards to public liberty and individual rights, including Conscience."[294] Mr. Jefferson answered the letter from Monticello on March 15, 1789 in which the third President endorses the views of these critics.[295]

On June 8, 1789, Madison gave a speech introducing the Bill of Rights to the First Congress. The future fourth President proposed an amendment to assuage the anxieties of those who feared that religious freedom would be endangered by the unamended Constitution. According to the *Congressional Register*, Mr. Madison on June 8th moved "That the civil rights of none shall be abridged or account of religious belief or worship, nor shall any national religion be established, nor shall the full and equal rights of Conscience be in any manner, or on any pretext, infringed.[296] This wording is exactly the same as Mr. Madison used in his *Memorial and Remonstrance* in 1785.

Other arguments made by Mr. Madison in the same work include paragraph eight that, "History further testifies that civil government do not need religion for their support," paragraph ten, "That good citizens will be driven from the state if required to pay a religious tax," and

---

292 James Madison. Virginia Act for Establishing Religious Freedom. [1786.]
293 James Madison to Bishop James Madison. [January 31, 1800.]
294 James Madison to Thomas Jefferson. [October 17, 1788.]
295 Thomas Jefferson to James Madison. March 15, 1789
296 James Madison. Speech to Congress. June 9, 1789

paragraph eleven, "That religious strife and violence will be encouraged by laws that meddle with religion."[297]

James Madison biographer, Irving Brant, calls the American statesman's 15-point document, "The most powerful defense of religious liberty ever written in America."[298] One reason is that Mr. Madison made freedom of Conscience the centerpiece of all Civil liberties.

In the article on Religion adopted at the Continental Convention in the Summer of 1787, Mr. Madison was the author of a resolution that contained the words, "according to the dictates of Conscience, and that it is in the mutual duty of all to practice Christian forbearance, love, and charity towards each other."[299]

Finally, we must keep in mind that when it comes to discussions of James Madison's views on Ethics and Conscience, we must rely on something he learned from John Witherspoon back at the College of New Jersey. That is, that human beings are first subject to God and are only secondarily members of a Civil Society. Therefore, every man must be free to serve God according to his own Conscience and conviction without interference from the Civil Society.

For both Witherspoon and James Madison the liberty of Conscience is a natural and inalienable right of every human being. And since this is the case, all political rights in a Civil Society are derived from the natural rights like the one related to Conscience.

The fourth President of the United States called religious belief a 'precedent both in order of time and in degree of obligation, to the claims of Civil Authority. By placing Freedom of Conscience prior to and superior to all other rights, James Madison gave it the strongest political foundation possible.

This brings us to the major Conclusions we have made in this Chapter Four, followed by the Notes of the same. The subject matters

---

297 James Madison. Memorial and Remonstrance. Paragraph 10

298 James Madison. Proposal at Continental Congress. [Summer, 1787.] Also see Memorial. paragraph 11

299 James Madison. "On property." Also John Witherspoon's Moral Philosophy class, Autumn, 1771, in which both Mr. Madison and William Bradford were students in that class

of Chapter Five of this Study in James Madison's Religion shall be the phenomena of Religious Freedom and Religious Toleration in the Work of President James Madison.

Conclusion to Chapter Four:

The two main goals of Chapter Four, as we have maintained in the Introduction of this Chapter is to give a thorough account of what James Madison believed and wrote about the phenomena of Ethics and Conscience. We attempted to meet those goals by dividing the Chapter into Three Sections.

In the First of these Sections, we put forth an account of the major sources that went into the development of the fourth President of the United States on the issues at hand. Among those intellectual sources, we have mentioned the following:

1. The Scottish Common Sense School of Philosophy. [Thomas Reid and others.]
2. John Witherspoon's Sermons and Lectures on Moral Philosophy.
3. Aristotle's Nicomachean Ethics.
4. Seneca's Letters on Virtue.
5. Cicero's Account of Virtue.

After discussing the contributions that each of these five sources may have made in the early intellectual life of James Madison, we moved to the Second Section of Chapter Four in which we identified and discussed the ideas of Morality and Conscience in thirteen of the other American Founding Fathers. Among these other early American men who commented on the idea of Conscience, we have introduced the comments and views on the matter of the following Founding Fathers:

- Roger Williams.
- George Washington.
- John Adams.

- Thomas Jefferson.
- John jay,
- John Witherspoon.
- Benjamin Rush.
- Patrick Henry.
- Samuel Adams.
- William Livingston.
- Charles Grandison Finney.
- John Quincy Adams.

After a discussion of these twelve Founding Fathers and what each of them said or wrote about the idea of Conscience, we turned our attention to the Third Section of Chapter Four, the views of James Madison on Conscience. One thing we may conclude, however, about the other twelve men is how many of them appears to be cognizant of, or positively assented to, the Common Sense view of morality, including John Adams, Thomas Jefferson, Benjamin Rush, and John Witherspoon.

The main focus of the Third Section of Chapter Four has been what James Madison said and wrote about the phenomena of Ethics and Conscience. We began the Third Section by pointing out that many of the important things that James Madison related about Conscience can be found in his work called "An Essay on Property," in which Mr. Madison maintained that "Conscience is the most sacred of all property."

In the remainder of Section Three of this Fourth Chapter, we have quoted Mr. Madison in a variety of his works where he said, or wrote, something about the phenomenon of Conscience. These quotations included selections from his letters, in his *Memorial and Remonstrance*, and in the various drafts of the First Amendment.

A number of conclusions may be made about what James Madison believed and wrote about the idea of Conscience. First, he thought Conscience was an innate and universal sense of the Good. Second, he believed it was a gift from God, or a grace, if you will. Third, Mr. Madison firmly believed that no man has the right to interfere with in any way, the Conscience of another. And finally, like the Common Sense School and his mentor, John Witherspoon, the fourth President thought that the right to Conscience is more fundamental than any of a person's Civil rights because the former came first in time, as well as in space.

Finally, at the end of Chapter Four on Madison and Ethics and Conscience, we have shown that in several places of his essays in the *Federalist Papers*, including numbers 22, 49, and 51, Mr. Madison made the claim that God and the Bible are the foundational "Fountain" of all Ecclesiastical and Political Power. For the fourth President, as we have seen in the Chapter Four, God and the Bible are the "Fountains of Power" for the ideas of Ethics and the Conscience, as well.

This brings us to the Notes of Chapter Four, followed by Chapter Five. The central issues at the heart of Chapter Five are two in number, the ideas of Religious Freedom, or Liberty, and the notion of Religious Toleration and what Mr. Madison believed and wrote about these two matters.

Chapter Five:
Madison on Religious Freedom and Religious Toleration

If we really believed that the pen is mightier than the sword, the nation's capital would be named not for the soldier who wielded the revolutionary sword, but to the thinker who was ablest with the pen. It would be Madison, D.C. Yet, until recently, there was not even a government building named after him. And what has now been named after him? A library, for Pete's sake. What a put-down in a city with the world's highest ratio of action to reflection."

—George Will, "Essay on Madison." [1981.]

As the rights of Conscience are in their nature peculiar delicacy and will little bear the gentlest touch of the government hand.

—Daniel Carroll, "Address to Congress." [August 15, 1789.]

The right of Religious Conscience is unalienable…because what is here a right toward men is a duty towards their Creator. It is a duty of every man to render to their Creator such homage and such only as he believes is acceptable to him. This duty is precedent, both in order of time and degree of obligation, to the claims of Civil Society.

—James Madison, *Memorial and Remonstrance*

Introduction

The purpose of this Chapter Five is to explore what the fourth president of the United States, James Madison believed and thought and wrote about the phenomena of Religious Freedom and Religious Toleration. To that end, we will divide the Chapter into three main Sections.

First, what Madison believed, said, and wrote about Religious Freedom, or Religious Liberty. In the Second Section, we will explore that the American statesman believed, said, and wrote about Religious Toleration. As we shall see, Mr. Madison had a very different view on this matter than many of the other American Founding Fathers. In the spirit of the Chapter, In the Third and Final Section of Chapter Five, we will examine what James Madison thought said and wrote about Religious faiths other than his own. Particularly, we mean what the fourth President thought and wrote about Judaism, Catholicism, Presbyterianism, and members of the Baptist Faith.

James Madison on Religious Freedom

A wide-eyed, twenty-five year old James Madison, travelling in Culpepper County, Virginia, came upon a Jail that housed six Baptist preachers who were held there simply for publishing their religious views. Mr. Madison bristled with indignation at the 'diabolical Hell conceived principle of persecution."[300] Writing to his college friend, William Bradford, he ended a letter with this lament, 'So I leave you to pity me and to pray for Liberty and Conscience to revive among us."[301]

This was one of the earliest signs of James Madison's dedication to the idea of Religious liberty. That dedication would continue for the remainder of the fourth President of the United States' life.

March 16, 2021, marked the 260th anniversary of the birth of James Madison. While his role as the major architect of the U.S. Constitution is clear, this passion for securing religious freedom is not. Indeed, biographer Ralph Ketcham tells us, "There is no principle in all of Madison's wide range of private opinions and long public

---

300 James Madison to William Bradford. January 24, 1774
301 Ibid

career to which he held greater vigor and tenacity than this one of religious liberty."[302]

Many historians—particularly American ones—fail to see the importance of Mr. Madison's early education. Rather than going to William & Mary, closer to home in Virginia, The fourth President chose instead to go to the College of New Jersey as we have indicated earlier in this Study. The College of New Jersey, later Princeton University, was an Evangelical Seminary known as both a citadel for republicanism and a haven for dissenting Presbyterians.[303]

The intellectual influences of the College's President, John Witherspoon—under whom James Madison studied directly—is difficult to overstate, as we have shown earlier in this work. In fact, one of the assigned topics in Madison's Senior year of College was to defend the proposition, "Every religious profession which does not by its principles disturb the public peace, ought to be tolerated by a wise state."[304]

Madison's early zeal for religious freedom can also be seen in May of 1776, when state lawmakers in Virginia wrote a new Constitution for the state and James Madison had a hand in the document that was originally penned by George Mason. This document contained a clause on religious liberty written by Mr. Mason that sad, "All men should enjoy the fullest toleration in the exercise of religion, according to the dictates of Conscience," as we have indicated in Chapter Four of this Study.[305]

Mr. Madison, however, chose to amend the wording of Mr. Mason and to substitute, "All men are entitled to the full and free exercise of religion."[306] We will say more about why Mr. Madison suggested this revision in Section Two of this Chapter Five, when we will speak of Religious Toleration in James Madison.

---

302 Ketcham, p. 229

303 The College of New Jersey became Princeton University in 1896. The College of New Jersey was founded in 1746

304 Ketcham, p. 300

305 James Madison's reformulation of Mr. Mason's proposal on religious toleration was made on May 15, 1776

306 Ibid

From 1776 until the late 1780s, Mr. Madison was involved in various religious liberty battles in the Virginia State Legislature, from repealing penalties against dissenters to suspending the paying of taxes to support the Anglican Clergy of the State. These struggles came to a head in 1784, when a group of religious conservatives wanted the General Assembly to pass a bill to collect tax money to support all "Christian Churches in the Protestant Episcopal [Anglican] Church.[307]

Prompted by Baptist leaders like John Leland (1754–1841) and others, James Madison now wrote his famous *Memorial and Remonstrance Against Religious Assessment* in July of 1785 that we have introduced in Chapter Four of this Study.[308] We have also indicate in that Chapter that Madison biographer, Irving Brant called the *Memorial*, 'The most powerful defense of religious liberty ever written in America.'"[309]

James Madison picked up the fight for Religious Liberty again during the drafting of the First Amendment. As Chairman of the House of Representative Conference Committee on the Bill of Rights, the fourth President's original draft was among the most ambitious. It declared, 'The Civil Rights of none shall be abridged on account of religious belief or worship…nor shall the full and equal rights of Conscience be in any manner, or on any pretext, infringed."[310]

This formulation was somewhat less expansive in its protection of rights than the final version adopted by the U. S. Congress:

> **Congress shall make no law respecting an Establishment of Religion or prohibiting the free exercise thereof.**[311]

This point cannot be overstated. Thanks largely to James Madison, the idea of free exercise has replaced the notion of Toleration as the national standard for protecting the religious liberties of Americans. This was a standard Mr. Madison first raised in the state legislature of

---

307 This event took place on May 29, 1784 at the Virginia State Legislature
308 James Madison. Memorial and Remonstrance. [July, 1785.]
309 Irving Brandt. James Madison. (New York: Bobbs-Merrill, 1953.), p. 131
310 First Amendment of U.S. Constitution
311 Ibid

Virginia and then sustained it throughout the rest of his career. Again, we will say more about this standard in the Second Section of this Chapter Five.

The fight for Religious liberty was continued by Mr. Madison in the struggle to pass the Virginia Bill for Religious Liberty. This was one of the most important documents in early U.S. religious history that marked the end of a ten- year period of a struggle for the Separation of Church and State, as we shall see in Chapter Six.

This Bill also became the template behind the religious clause of the First Amendment of the U.S. Constitution that was ratified in 1791. The Virginia Bill was originally drafted by Thomas Jefferson in 1776 and accepted by the General Assembly of Virginia in 1786. Mr. Jefferson explained the Virginia Bill this way, "It is an attempt to provide religious freedom to the Jew, the Gentile, the Christian, the Mahometan, the Hindoo, and the Infidel of every denomination."[312] In effect, this was the first attempt to remove the government from any influences on religious affairs.

Mr. Jefferson's Bill was first introduced during the legislative session of 1779. The Episcopal Church had recently declared its independence from the Church of England. In 1784, the fiery and headstrong Patrick Henry countered the Virginia Bill with one of his own that called for a general assessment tax to "support Teachers of the Christin Religion."[313]

Under Mr. Henry's Bill, taxpayers were allowed to choose what Church or Minister could receive his tax money. It was an attempt to replace the Established Church with "Multiple Establishments" of Religion, which created a tight Church-State network in Virginia that would allow taxpayer money to support all Christian Churches, not just the Episcopal Church.[314]

Mr. Jefferson in this period was serving as the Ambassador to France during the 1780s. Thus, the task of responding to Mr. Henry's

---

312 Thomas Jefferson Virginia Bill for Religious Toleration. [first draft, 1776; first proposed 1779

313 Patrick Henry. Proposed this bill in the Summer of 1775

314 Ibid

bill fell to James Madison. The fourth President's strategy in responding to Mr. Henry's bill had three separate aspects. First, Madison made an alliance with the Evangelicals that were opposed to the Assessment Bill. Secondly, he supported Patrick Henry's election to the governorship of Virginia in 1784, thereby removing Henry from the legislature.

And thirdly—and most importantly—the American statesman wrote his pamphlet, *Memorial and Remonstrance Against Religious Assessment*, as a response to Mr. Henry's proposal.[315] All of this was part of a plan in the mind of Mr. Madison to oppose Henry's Bill, support Jefferson's Bill, and calling for a Separation of Church and State, as we shall see in Chapter Six.

In the fifteen points of the *Memorial and Remonstrance*, Mr. Madison eloquently articulated the principles he believed were at stake. He asks, "Who does not see that the same authority which can establish Christianity, in exclusion of all other religions, may establish with the same ease any particular Sect of Christianity, in exclusion of all other Sects?"[316]

James Madison's pamphlet was an instant success. It was widely circulated in Virginia and it was signed by over two thousand Virginians, including many who were Presbyterians and Baptists who believed that Mr. Henry's Bill posed a danger to religious liberty in the state of Virginia.

In the fight to get Mr. Jefferson's Bill passed James Madison shamed Christian Conservatives who tried to insert the words "Jesus Christ" in an amended preamble to Mr. Henry's Bill with these words:

The better proof of reverence for that holy name would be not to profane it by making it topic of legislative discussion.[317]

In 1795, during a Congressional debate about naturalization, Mr. Madison bluntly responded to anti-Catholic prejudices about which we will say more in Section Three of this Chapter. In an article for the *National Gazette* called "Who Are the Best Keepers of the People's

---

315 James Madison. Memorial and Remonstrance. [1785.]
316 Ibid
317 Ibid., section VII

Liberties?" Mr. Madison compared the answer the Republicans would give against that of the Anti-Republicans. He suggests in that essay, the way of the Republicans is nothing more than the "Way of the Almighty, and not to the works of Man."[318]

Even at the end of his life, James Madison's commitment to Religious Liberty can still be seen. At the age of 65, while in his retirement at Montpelier, he praised the idea of the Separation of Church and State because by it:

> The number, the industry, and the morality of the Priesthood and the devotion of the people have been manifestly increased...[319]

In the twilight of his life, the fourth President of the Unite States wrote;

> A belief in a God, All Powerful, Wise, and Good, is so essential to the moral order of the World, and to the Happiness of Man, that arguments which enforce it cannot be drawn from too many sources.[320]

Even to the end, the fourth president of the United States, James Madison, continued to show his support of the religious liberties of all Americans, as well as the idea of the Separation of Church and State.

This brings us to the Second Section of Chapter Five in which we will make some general observations about American statesman, James Madison in regards to the idea of Religious Toleration in America.

James Madison on Religious Toleration

The idea of Religious Toleration was a part of existence in America from the very beginning. Many Colonists came to America to escape religious persecutions in Europe. But Colonies soon adopted laws that

---

318 James Madison. "Who are the Best keepers of liberty?" National Gazette. [August 10, 1795.]

319 James Madison. "Comments on Church-State Separation." [February 21, 1834.]

320 Ibid

limited religious freedom and, as we have shown in Chapter Four, forced citizens to pay taxes to support Churches they did not believe in nor attend. Dissenters started protesting to abolish those laws.

An important change came in 1786 when Virginia passed its statute for Religious Freedom, which was drafted by Thomas Jefferson, as we have shown in the First Section of this Chapter Five. The new law served as a model for the First Amendment, as well as other states, and Mr. Jefferson saw his law as one of his greatest accomplishments.[321]

Most of the earliest settlers in America came from England. Many who settled in the South—the Plantation Colonies—belonged to the Church of England or Anglican Church. In Virginia, Ministers were required to preach Christianity according to the "doctrines, rites, and religion" practiced by the Church of England. A law passed in 1611 required everyone to attend Church on the Sabbath. A subsequent law imposed a tax to pay for the Church's ministers, as well as to build new Church buildings. It also mandated that only Anglican ministers or priests could conduct marriages.[322] Similar laws were passed in Georgia, and in North and South Carolina.[323]

The Anglican Church was also the Established Church in Maryland, but because many Catholics lived there, the Colony passed the first Act of Toleration in 1649. This law promised religious toleration to all Christians, but it also decreed the death penalty for people like Atheists and Jews, who denied the Divinity of Jesus Christ.[324]

Meanwhile, in New England, Colonists also passed laws involving the government in religion. Most of the earliest settlers in Massachusetts, Connecticut, and New Hampshire were Puritans who belonged to the Congregational Church. For the first fifty years of the Bay Colony—which later became Massachusetts—no resident could vote unless he belonged to the Congregational Church.[325]

---

[321] Thomas Jefferson. Virginia Statute on Religious Freedom. [1786.]

[322] Virginia law on Religion. [1611.]

[323] These laws were passed in Georgia in 1634 and North Carolina and South Carolina in 1629

[324] Maryland Act on Toleration. [1649.]

[325] Mass. Bay Colony. "Act on Religion." [1636.]

Later laws required each town to maintain an "able, learned, and orthodox minister" paid for by the town's taxpayers. Because the Congregationalists were the majority in most towns, the law left others, like Anglicans, Baptists and Quakers, out in the cold. Similar laws existed in Connecticut, New Hampshire, New York City, and other parts of the New York Colony.[326]

By the second half of the 18th Century in America, two separate views of the protection of religious Conscience were competing in the new nation. One of these views was that the protection of Conscience was a matter of utilitarian tolerance—sound public policy, neighborliness, good will, and expedient policies. We will call this position the Toleration View.

If that view had prevailed, only a weak and unreliable set of Civil Rights would have developed. It makes a big difference whether respect for another's moral convictions is simply a matter of expediency and tolerance—to be suspended when outweighed by other considerations—or whether it is a positive and basic Civil Right that all can exercise.[327] This latter view is the one adopted by James Madison. He shifted the debate from Toleration to Human Nature.

Earlier, in Chapter Four, we spoke of the substitute language that Mr. Madison suggested as replacements for George Mason's restrained language, "That all men should enjoy the fullest Toleration in the exercise of Religion according to the dictates of Conscience."[328] The fourth President amended the line to read, "All men ae equally entitled to the full and free exercise of religion."[329]

Mr. Mason was suggesting the Toleration View, while Mr. Madison was pointing to a view much deeper than this. For Mr. Madison, the right to a free Conscience is a natural right, endowed by God and written into the hearts of human beings. For the American statesman, as he tells us in the *Memorial and Remonstrance*:

---

326 These acts were passed between 1649 and 1673
327 James Madison. Memorial and Remonstrance. [1785.]
328 George Mason's proposal on Religious Toleration. January 16, 1786
329 James Madison. Memorial and Remonstrance

> The right of Religious Conscience is unalienable...because what is here a right toward men is a duty towards the Creator. It is the duty of every man to render to the Creator such homage, and such only, as he believes to be acceptable to him. This duty is precedent, both in order of time and degree of obligation, to the claims of Civil Society.[330]

Mr. Madison has moved the understanding from the Tolerance View to a Natural Right View by observing that the right to Conscience is more fundamental than any other right, including any Civil Right. The fourth President wrote, "Before any man can be considered as a member of Civil Society, he must first be considered as a subject of the Governor of the Universe."[331]

While many political prognosticators in the late 18th Century harped about 'Toleration" in religious matters. Mr. Madison's view was far more radical. He flipped the idea of toleration on its head. He thought that the people's right to worship in their own unique way—or even their right to not worship, if that is what they choose—was first and foremost a "gift from God," and therefore, the government should keep out of it.

To James Madison, the idea of Religion went much deeper than how one does, or does not, practice it. As we have seen in Chapter Four, he believed that "Conscience" was "the most sacred of all property," and, like a good scholar of English philosopher, John Locke, Mr. Madison felt strongly that one's property was a natural, and God-given right.

For Mr. Madison, defining the proper relation between Religion and Civil Government meant drawing a jurisdictional line between two potentially competing authorities, one spiritual and one political. That line was drawn with the understanding that one's duty to God, as perceived within the individual Conscience, is superior to political, legal, or social obligations.

In this view, then. Mr. Madison believed that Religion posited an ultimate limit on the power of the state In this sense, the fourth

---

330 Ibid
331 Ibid

president wanted the First Amendment to function as a kind of religious "Supremacy Clause" which presumes that God exists and makes claims on human beings and that those claims are prior in both time and importance to any claims of the State.[332]

James Madison's support for Religious Liberty and Conscience over Toleration may have had something to do with the reservations about conventional religion, as well as his immersion in 17th and 18th Century Enlightenment thinkers when he was at the College of New Jersey, such as the influence on his work by John Locke's *A Letter Concerning Toleration*, which was originally published in 1689.[333]

In fact, Mr. Madison's *Memorial and Remonstrance* was highly influenced by Locke's *Letter*. Mr. Madison, for example, appears to have appropriated some of the language and phrases of the Englishman's *Letter*. One specific element that the American statesman surely must have concentrated upon was the English philosopher's claim that, "Religious Truth and the means of Salvation are beyond the concerns of the State."[334] As Locke put the matter. "The Magistrate ought not to forbid the holding or teaching of any speculative opinions in any church, because they have no bearing on the civil rights of his subjects."[335]

John Locke was also the source for the famous phrase, "life, liberty, and property' that was later modified in America by Mr. Madison to become, "Life, Liberty, and the Pursuit of Happiness," which was incorporated into the Declaration of Independence.'

In a recent article in the *Oxford Journal of Law and Religion* by Kevin Vance argues that, "Although Locke did not directly link the duty of human beings to worship God according to one Conscience to the right of religious liberty," he, nevertheless, argued that each part of James Madison's argument "is already present in Locke."[336]

---

332 The Supremacy Clause can be found in Article VI, paragraph 2 of the U.S. Constitution

333 John Locke. A Letter on Toleration. [London, 1689.]

334 Ibid

335 Ibid

336 Kevin Vance. "Golden Thread of Religious Liberty." Oxford Journal of Law and Religion. Vol. VI, no. 2. [2017.]

We concur with Mr. Vance's conclusion. Madison's *Memorial and Remonstrance* was heavily influenced by John Locke's *A Letter Concerning Toleration* and the American also admired and employed ideas in many of Locke's other philosophical works like the Englishman's arguments against an Established Church, for example. The two disagreed, however, about Catholics and their right to Conscience. Locke was against it in England, while Madison was in favor of it in America.[337] Interestingly enough, Pierre Bayle also denied Religious Toleration should be extended to Catholics, as well.[338]

As we shall see in Chapter Nine, this concern about what might be called "comparative religions" is the central concern we take up in that Chapter where we will make further comments on Mr. Madison's views on religions other than his own.

This brings us to the Third Section of Chapter Five on James Madison's Views on Religious Liberty and Religious Toleration in which we will explore what the fourth President of the United States thought, said, and wrote about varieties of Religious Faith other than his own.

James Madison on Religious Points of View Other Than His Own

Another way to see Mr. Madison's commitment to Religious Toleration and the safeguarding of Religious Conscience is what the fourth President of the United States believed, said, and wrote about religions other than his own. We specifically have in mind here the Roman Catholics, Judaism, the Presbyterians, and the Baptists in the second half of the 18th Century and the beginning of the 19th Century.

Already in this Study of James Madison's Religion we have indicated that when Mr. Madison was a young man in Orange County, Virginia he was outraged by the imprisonment of Baptist Preachers for the crime of 'publishing their religious Sentiments." He wrote to his friend, William Bradford in describing the jailing of the Baptists as being 'that diabolical Hell conceived principle of persecution," and he asked him to 'pray for Liberty and Conscience to revive among us."[339]

---

337 Ibid

338 Ibid

339 James Madison to William Bradford. January 24, 1774

Pastor James Ireland was one of the Baptist jailed in Culpepper, yet he continued to preach through a grate to his followers. Ruffians harassed Ireland, however, some even urinating on the preacher as he attempted to preach to his followers. His antagonists also burned brimstone and pepper to try to silence Rev. Ireland by suffocating him.[340]

Even earlier, in 1771, when James Madison was twenty years old and still in college, an Anglican priest disrupted a Baptist service by beating the preacher at the pulpit and dragging him outside where the Sheriff of Caroline County gave him twenty lashes with a bullwhip.[341] The quick growth of the Baptists in the South challenged the Anglican establishment and the Baptist refused to give up their desire to obtain licenses to preach.[342]

As we have indicated earlier in this Study, Mr. Madison was aware of these abuses of the Baptists in Virginia and was vehemently against them. In the January, 1774 letter to Mr. Bradford, the American statesman said this:

> There are at this time in the adjacent County not less than 5 or 6 well-meaning men in close Gaol [Jail] for publishing their religious Sentiments which in the main are very orthodox. I have neither patience to their talk nor think of anything relative to this matter, for I have squabbled and scolded, abused, and ridiculed so long about it, to so little purpose that I am without common patience.[343]

As one of Mr. Madison's biographers put the matter, "These jailed Preachers, all Baptists, had done nothing more than bring vital religion to the unchurched or to the indifferent Anglicans."[344] Perhaps the most important Baptist thinker in Virginia in James Madison's early career was Rev. John Leland (1754–1841), who preached in Massachusetts

---

340 James Ireland. (1745–1806) was Pastor of the Buckmarsh Baptist Church from 1786 until his death in 1806

341 This event took place in February of 1771

342 Ibid

343 James Madison to William Bradford. January 24, 1774

344 Ketcham. P. 72

and then Virginia. He also became a well-known Abolitionist. Leland was an important voice in the struggle for religious freedom for minority religions in both Massachusetts and Virginia.

At one point James Madison visited the Rev. Leland's farm and the two thrashed out the differences the two had on Religious Freedom and Toleration. After their meeting, on June 7, 1789, Mr. Madison submitted the first version of the First Amendment to the Bill of Rights, and hereby Religious Freedom and Religious Toleration, became enshrined, to the delight of the Reverend Leland and other Baptist Preachers.

We also have indicated earlier in this Study that Mr. Madison reacted negatively to a number of Anti-Catholic sentiments that were expressed in his time in the Virginia Legislature. David Kopel, in an article entitled "Opinion: The Second Amendment vs. Anti-Catholicism," published in the *Washington Post* on November 20, 2015, also points to another connection between James Madison and Anti-Catholicism.[345]

Mr. Kopel pointed out that the English Declaration of Rights, enacted by Parliament in 1689 had said, "The subjects which are Protestants may have arms for their defense suitable to their conditions as and allowed by law."[346] This pronouncement, of course, said nothing about Catholics. Mr. Madison, as Kopel pointed out, wanted to change that, so that when the Second Amendment was formulated it included Catholics when speaking of the right to bear arms for safety and protection.[347]

When James Madison proposed the first draft of the First Amendment, the Catholic, Daniel Carroll was the only Congressman to support the measure explicitly in a speech to Congress on August 15, 1789. Mr. Carroll maintained that the amendment merely articulated what was the general sentiment concerning the right to religious liberty. In the *Congressional Register*, Thomas Lloyd wrote an account of the Carroll speech, Mr. Lloyd quoted Mr. Carroll as saying:

---

345 David Kopel. 'The Second Amendment vs. Anti-Catholicism." The Washington Post. November 20, 2015

346 Ibid

347 Ibid

> As the rights of Conscience are in their nature of peculiar delicacy, and will little bear the gentlest touch of the government hand; and as many Sects have concurred in the opinion that they are not well secured under the present Constitution,, he said he was much in favor of adopting the words; he thought it would tend more toward conciliating the minds of the people to the government than almost any other amendment he had heard proposed. He would not contend with gentlemen about phraseology, for his object was to secure the substance in such a manner as to satisfy the wishes of the honest part of the community.[348]

It is not important, of course, if Mr. Lloyd had accurately gave an account of Mr. Carroll's remarks before Congress. What is important for our purposes is that Mr. Carroll, a staunch Catholic, was the only member of Congress to support the first draft of Mr. Madison's formulation of the First Amendment; and the statesman from Virginia certainly greatly appreciated that support.

Thus, we have seen so far in this Section of Chapter Five that one way to see Mr. Madison's support for Religious Toleration is also to see the support that the fourth President of the United States, early on, had given to the Baptists and to the Roman Catholics. There is also significant evidence that the American statesman, James Madison had an admiration for the religion of Judaism and the Jews, as well shall see next.

James Madison, as well as Thomas Jefferson, corresponded about the subject of Religious Freedom and Religious Toleration with two of America's leading Jews, Mordecai Manuel Noah (1785–1851) and Dr. Jacob De La Motta (1789–1845.) Each of these Rabbis had dedicated a Synagogue, Noah in New York in 1818, De La Motta in Savannah in 1820. Each also sent published copies of their remarks to Mr. Jefferson and Mr. Madison.[349]

Rabbi de La Motta's letter to the fourth President is now in the *Papers* of his Presidential Library. In Mr. Jefferson's case, his response

---

348 Thomas Lloyd, quoting Daniel Carroll. Congressional Register. August 15, 1789

349 These rabbis are discussed more thoroughly in Chapter Nine of this Study

was completed on his device called a "Polygraph," which the third President called a "portable Secretary."[350] It was a writing device that used two pens, in tandem, so that two identical letters were produced at the strokes of the pen.

Rabbi Mordecai Noah dedicated the Shearith Israel new Synagogue in Savannah on April 17, 1818. Noah was the best known Jew in America at the time. He had served as the U.S. Consul in Tunis and was now the editor of the *National Advocate*.[351]

The response that Rabbi Noah received from President Madison was full of evidence of the statesman's commitment to Judaism and the Jews. Among the words in that response were the following two paragraphs:

> A statement of surprising significance by philosopher Thomas Jefferson on the nature of democracy, the frailty of human character, the power of the free human spirit, and the faith in humankind.
> More remains to be done for although we are free by the law, we are not so In practice.[352]

Mr. Madison's reply to Rabbi de La Motta from August 7, 1820 observed that, "The history of the Jews must forever be interesting. The modern part of it is… so little generally known that every ray of light on the subject has its value."[353] Mr. Madison also related in his letter to Rabbi De la Motta these words:

> Among the features peculiar to the political system of the United States is the perfect equality of rights which it secures to every religious Sect.[354]

---

350 Mr. Jefferson's "Polygraph" discussed in Monticello's blog of research and education. "Eight Objects in Our Collection." [July 23, 2020.)

351 The National Advocate was a newspaper published in New York City between 1812 and 1829 and edited by Rabbi Noah

352 Rabbi Noah. "Dedication of a Synagogue." April 17, 1818

353 James Madison to Rabbi Noah. August 7, 1820

354 Ibid

Mr. Madison then goes on in the letter to speak of other provisions of the American system and finally concludes about them, "The account you give of the Jews of your Congregation brings them fully within the scope of these observations."[355]

From these two responses to Rabbis Noah and De la Motta it should be clear that James Madison, the fourth President of the United States, greatly admired Judaism and the Jews and thought its principles were perfectly consistent with those outlined in the new American, political system.

We also have said a great deal about the respect and admiration that Mr. Madison had for certain leaders of the American Presbyterian Church, such as his Scottish teacher, Donald Robertson and his College mentor, President John Witherspoon of the College of New Jersey, later Princeton University.

As early as 1784, Mr. Madison was also in the thick of a battle over religious freedom and Virginia's role in mediating the grievances of various Sects, chiefly the Presbyterians and the Episcopalians. In a letter to Thomas Jefferson from Mr. Madison in 1785, the statesman related, "I am far from being sorry for it as a coalition between them alone endanger our religious rights and a tendency to such an event had been suspected."[356]

In this letter to Mr. Jefferson, James Madison exhibits an understanding of the self-interest that motivates these sects, but also the good that can come when they are in a constant state of conflict with each other. Perhaps the fourth President of the United States had read the old adage of Voltaire that, "The more religions there are, the more guarantee that they will all live in peace."[357]

Another thing that James Madison worried about when the early American government was getting started was the fact that there were so many sects and factions competing for allegiance from the people, it seemed unlikely that any one of them could become dominant to the rest. This was particularly true, Madison believed after the removals of the Established Churches in the various states, including Virginia.

---

355 Ibid

356 James Madison to Thomas Jefferson. October 17, 1788

357 Ibid

Nevertheless, in essay fifty-one of the *Federalist Papers*, Mr. Madison wrote about these various Sects:

> The society itself will be broken into so many parts, interests, and classes of citizens, that the rights of the individuals, or of the minority, will be in little danger from interested combinations of the majority.[358]

At the time, Mr. Madison believed he was writing about the various religious sects that existed in America in his time. In the 21st Century, however, we now see that Americans are chiefly categorized by their color and gender, so that the population is divided into a countless number of 'kinds" of human beings in America, all competing for the acknowledgement and validation of their rights.

Today, America is mostly divided into White, Black, Asian, straight, Queer, Transgender, and so many other American "kinds," that there are now never any conversations about what each of these "Sects" have in common. Mr. Madison would have found this reality strange and perplexing indeed.

In the first Legislative effort in his career, James Madison, when he was 25 years old, wrote a guarantee of Freedom of Conscience into the state of Virginia Constitution of 1776, whence it soon spread to the charters of other states. In his second act for Civil Liberty, he wrote the notion of the Separation of Church and State into the Constitution of the United States. This will be the central concern of Chapter Six of this Study on the Religion of James Madison.

This brings us to the major Conclusions we have made in Chapter Five, followed by the Notes of the same. The principal concern of Chapter Six of this Study on James Madison's Religion, as we have indicated, will be an analysis of his views on the Separation of Church and State.

Conclusions to Chapter Five:

As we have indicated in the Introduction of Chapter Five, the two central issues to be discussed in the Chapter were James Madison's

---

358 James Madison. Federalist Papers. Essay number 51

views on Religious Freedom and the idea of Religious Toleration. To that end, we have divided the Chapter into three Sections. In the first of those, we have set forth what the fourth President of the United States had to say and write about the phenomenon of Religious Freedom, or what was generally called "Religious Liberty" at the time.

In the Second Section of Chapter Five, our main focus has been on what Mr. Madison believed and wrote about the idea of Religious Toleration; and in the Third and Final Section of Chapter Five, we have explored what the American statesman, James Madison thought and wrote about religious traditions other than his own, including Catholicism, Judaism, the Baptists, the Presbyterians, as well as other points of view.

We began the First Section of Chapter Five by pointing out Mr. Madison's reaction to the jailing of six Baptist Ministers in Culpepper, Virginia, who appear to have done nothing more than professing their religious views.

Next in Chapter Five, we wrote of James Madison's amending of George Mason's formulation of a clause on religious liberty that "All men should enjoy the fullest toleration in the full exercise of religion." As we have indicated in Chapter Five, Mr. Madison's reformulation of Mr. Mason's idea was a radical shift, as we will discuss in our summary of the Second Section of Chapter Five.

In the First Section of Chapter Five we also have explored the attempt by Patrick Henry before the Virginia State Legislators to replace the Established Church in Virginia with "Multiple Established Churches," all to be supported by Virginia taxpayers. James Madison's *Memorial and Remonstrance*, written in 1785, as we have shown, was principally a negative response to the bill of Mr. Henry. Indeed, in the *Memorial*, Mr. Madison ushered fifteen separate arguments against Patrick Henry's proposal.

In the Section on Religious Toleration, we began by pointing out that the idea had been part of the American Colonies since the very beginning. We also have indicated that with the passing of a statute for Religious Freedom, drafted by Thomas Jefferson, served as a model for the First Amendment of the U.S. Constitution, as well as other state charters.

After sketching out the different and varied views about Established Churches in the thirteen Colonies, we returned to the attempt on the part of James Madison to reformulate George Mason's suggestion that "All men should enjoy the fullest Toleration in the exercise of religion." As we have indicated, the Fourth President amended the line to say, "All men are equally entitled to the full and free exercise of religion."[359]

In the Second Section of Chapter Five, we also have indicated that Mr. Madison's change in this formulation was a radical shift from one view about religious freedom to another perspective. More specifically, as we have indicated, it was a shift from what we have called the "Toleration View," to a perspective that suggested that the right to Conscience is far more fundamental and prior to any Civil Rights.

In the Second Section of Chapter Five we also have indicated the indebtedness of James Madison to the philosophical views of English philosopher John Locke, particularly in regard to the Englishman's *Letter Concerning Toleration*, as well as how far rights of religion should extend. In fact, as we have indicated, Mr. Locke and Pierre Bayle disagreed with Mr. Madison on whether Catholics have a right to free religious expression. Locke and Bayle said no, while Mr. Madison said yes.

At the close of Section Two of Chapter Five, we have introduced the scholarly work of Kevin Vance who suggests that all that Mr. Madison put forth about Religious Freedom and Religious Toleration could first be found in the works of John Locke, and we heartily agreed with that conclusion.

The Third Section of Chapter Five, as we have indicated earlier, was taken up with what the Fourth President of the United States believed and wrote about other religions other than his own.

We began that Third Section by reiterating Mr. Madison's reaction to the jailing of six Baptist Ministers in Culpepper, Virginia when the statesman was a young man. We also have noted that Mr. Madison was fully aware of the treatment of Baptist by Episcopalian clergy in 1771, when the Baptist were complaining about the Established Church in Virginia, the Episcopal Church.

---

359 See note number six of this Chapter

Next in the Third Section of Chapter Five, we turned our attention to James Madison's understanding of Catholicism, using an article written for the *Washington Post* by David Kopel who argued that the English *Declaration of Rights* enacted by Parliament in 1689, only granted religious liberties to "Protestant subjects of the Crown." Mr. Kopel concluded that the Second Amendment of the U.S. Constitution was a by-product of the English statute that included the "right to bear arms" for Catholics.[360]

We also have indicated that when James Madison proposed the first draft of the First Amendment to the U.S. Constitution that Catholic, Daniel Carroll, was the only member of Congress to support that formulation of Mr. Madison. Indeed, we have supplied a summary of Mr. Carroll's remarks to Congress from August 15, 1789 supplied by Thomas Lloyd.

In addition to support of, and from Baptist and Catholics in Section Three of Chapter Five, we also went on in that Section to speak of the admiration that the Fourth President of the United States had for Jews and for Judaism. In fact, in that portion of Chapter Five we spoke of letters between Thomas Jefferson and James Madison, back and forth, to two prominent, 18th Century members of the American Jewish community, Rabbi Mordecai Manuel Noah and Dr. Jacob De la Motta.

We have shown that in Mr. Madison's two letters back to the two Rabbis, the American statesman had the opportunity to express his dedication and admiration for the Jewish Faith, as well as his commitment to the Religious Toleration that he thought should be extended to that Faith.

Next in Chapter Five, still in its Third Section, we went on to speak of the many relationships that James Madison had to the American Presbyterian Church, including his time with Donald Robertson and his College mentor, President John Witherspoon.

We also have indicated at the end of Chapter Five that in his *Federalist Papers* essay number fifty-one, James Madison voiced a displeasure at the growing number of religious Sects that were

---

360 See note 46 of this Chapter

proliferating in the U.S. in his day, and that he was concerned that this would turn America into "too many tribes" and factions, while giving up on what they have in common.

Indeed, we have argued in the close of Chapter Five that Mr. Madison's fear in *Federalist* 51 is precisely what is occurring in American political culture of the 21st Century. Too many factions, too many interests groups, Mr. Madison feared, destroys unity, and he was entirely correct about that. As Mr. Madison put the matter at the time:

> The Society would be broken into so many parts, interests, and classes of citizens that the rights of individuals, or of the minority, will be in little danger from interested combinations of the majority.[361]

Thomas Jefferson disagreed with Mr. Madison on this pronouncement and he encouraged his fellow Virginian to change his mind about the idea of the "Consent of the People." Madison, in turn, unwilling to let the Anti-Federalist undo the Constitution and eager to get himself elected to Congress, Madison ultimately supported the Amendment.[362]

James Madison's talent for negotiation also helped in the passage of the Bill of Rights that included the guarantee of Religious Liberty to be found in the First Amendment. And, ultimately, then, Mr. Jefferson and Mr. Madison were on the same page when it came to Religious Freedom, Religious Toleration, and the Separation of Church and State, as we shall see in Chapter Six of the Study on James Madison's Religion.

This brings of this the Notes of this Chapter Five, followed by Chapter Six. The main focus of Chapter Six to follow, as we have indicated, is what James Madison, the Fourth President of the United States believed, said, and wrote about the Separation of Church and State in the United States of America.

---

361 James Madison. Federalist Papers. Essay number 51

362 Thomas Jefferson to James Madison. July 21, 1788

Chapter Six:
James Madison on the Separation of Church and State

God has therefore ordained two regimens, the Spiritual which is of the Holy Spirit...and the Secular ways which retrains un-Christian and Evil Folk.

—Martin Luther. "Commentary on Genesis."

Those with different religious views are both equally fit for being employed in the service of our Country. It is imperative to build an impenetrable wall of Separation between things Sacred and things Civil.

—James Burgh. "Political Disquisitions."

I contemplate with sovereign reverence that act of the whole American people which declared that their Legislators should 'Make no law respecting an established religion or prohibiting the free exercise thereof. Thus building a wall of separation between Church and State.

—Thomas Jefferson 'Letter to Danbury Baptists.'

Introduction

The main purpose of this Sixth Chapter is to identify and discuss what the fourth president of the United States, James Madison thought, said, and wrote about the phenomenon of the Separation of Church and State. To that end, Chapter Six will be divided into Four Sections. In the first of these we shall explore the major sources for determining Early American views about the Separation of Church and State.

In the Second Section of Chapter Six, we shall give a short history of how the idea of the Separation of Church and State was commented upon from the time of Roger Williams in 17th Century Rhode Island to more 18th and 19th Century views on the matter including those of Thomas Jefferson and a number of other thinkers in that time, including, of course, James Madison.

In the Third, and most important, Section of Chapter Six, we will identify and discuss the major places in the works of President James Madison where he spoke or wrote directly about the phenomenon of the Separation of Church and State. Many of these direct references, as well shall see, come directly from the letters of James Madison, as well as other of his major works, such as the *Memorial and Remonstrance*, his contributions to the *Federalist Papers*, as well as his *Detached Memorandum*.[363]

Finally, the Fourth and Final Section of Chapter Six, we shall explore what President James Madison had to say about the Separation of Church and State after the time he was President. As we shall see the American statesman appears to have change his mind about some questions pertaining to Church and State Separation, particularly in his *Detached Memorandum*, where Mr. Madison pointed out some inconsistencies he saw between the government practice and the spirit of Church-State Separation embodied in the First Amendment of the US Constitution.

Sources For Views on Separation of Church and State

In terms of American Sources for understanding Views on the Separation of Church and State, the following items must be kept in mind:

1. The Religious Clause of the First Amendment.
2. Madison's original Proposal for the Bill of Rights.

---

363 James Madison. Detached Memorandum. There is some dispute about the date of this text. William Cabell Rives, in his Letters and Other Writings of James Madison says it "came after his retirement in 1817." [vol. III, p. 243.] Gaillard Hunt, in his essay, 'Aspects of Monopoly One Hundred Years Ago," [Harper's Magazine, March 1914.], p. 489 said "It is before 1832."

3. Justice Joseph Story's Comments on Church and State.
4. Everson v. Board of Education. [1947.]
5. Lemon v. Kurtzman. [1971.]

The first of these items refers to what is called the 'Establishment Clause" of the First Amendment, as well as the "Free Exercise Clause." The former prohibits the Government from "Establishing' a state Religion. There has been some disagreement over the years about what counts as an 'Establishment,' but historically, it has meant prohibiting state-sponsored Churches, such as the Church of England in Britain.[364] The wording of the Establishment Clause is this:

> Congress shall make no law respecting as establishment of religion or prohibiting the free exercise thereof; or abridging the freedom of speech, or of the press, or the right of the people peaceably to assemble, and to petition the Government for a redress of grievances.[365]

Today, what counts as an 'establishment of Religion" is often governed by a three-part test put forth in the Supreme Court decision called *Lemon v. Kurtzman* [1971.] Under the *Lemon* test, the government can assist religion only if (1.) the primary purpose of the assistance is secular. (2.) the assistance must neither promote nor inhibit religion. And (3.) There is no excessive entanglements between Church and State.[366]

The free exercise clause protects citizens' rights to practice their religion as they please, so long as the practice does not run afoul of a "public morals," or a "compelling" government interest. For example, in *Prince v Massachusetts*, the Supreme Court held that a state could force the inoculation of children whose parents would not allow such actions for religious reasons. The Court ruled that the state had an overriding interest in protecting the overall public health and safety.[367]

---

364 "Establishment Clause." First Amendment of U.S. Constitution
365 Ibid
366 Lemon v. Kurtzman. [1971.]
367 Prince v. Massachusetts. 321 U.S. 158. [1944.]

At times, the Establishment Clause and the Free Exercise Clause may come into conflict with each other. The Federal Courts help to resolve such conflicts, with the U.S. Supreme Court being the final arbiter of such disputes.

James Madison's original proposal for a Bill of Rights had a provision concerning that read, "The Civil Rights of none shall be abridged on account of religious belief or worship, nor shall any national religion be established, nor shall the full and equal rights of conscience be in any manner, or on any pretense, infringed."[368] This language was altered in the House of Representatives to read, 'Congress shall make no law establishing religion, or to prevent the free exercise thereof or infringe the right of conscience."[369] In the Senate, the body adopted, "Congress shall make no law establishing articles of faith, or a mode of worship, or prohibiting the exercise of religion."[370]

Justice Joseph Story did an explication of the religious clauses and their meaning in which he wrote, "The right of a society or government to interfere in matters of religion will hardly be attested by any person who believes that piety, religion and morality are intimately connected with the wellbeing of the state, and indispensable to the administration of civil justice."[371]

Judge Story also wrote:

> At the time of the adoption of the constitution and of the amendment to it, now under consideration, the general, if not the universal, sentiment in America was, that Christianity ought to receive encouragement from the state, so far as we are not incompatible with the private rights of Conscience and the freedom of religious worship. An attempt to level all religions, and to make it a matter of state policy to hold

---

368 James Madison. Original proposal for the Bill of Rights. June 8, 1789. This document had 39 separate proposals all related to possible Amendments of the U.S. Constitution

369 House of Representatives proposal on Bill of Rights. [June, 1789.]

370 Senate proposal on Bill of Rights. [June, 1789.]

371 Joseph Story. "On Religious Clause." In Comments on the Constitution. [1833.] Document 69

all as utter indifference, would have created universal disapprobation, if not universal indignation.[372]

Finally, the Supreme Court in the 1947 decision of *Everson v. Board of Education*, the Court saw a direct link between Thomas Jefferson's "wall of Separation" and the First Amendment's Establishment Clause.[373] Indeed, we move now to Section Two of Chapter Six in which we will examine the History of Views about the Separation of Church and State going all the way back to the very early 18th Century in America.

The History of Views on Church and State Separation in America.

In the history of the Christian Church, the first attempt at separating the Religious and Secular realms came in Saint Augustine's *City of God*, where he made a distinction between the 'City of God" and the "City of Men."[374] The Bishop of Hippo first introduced this distinction in Book IV, Chapter four of his work. Augustine's basic claim about the two cities is that they have little to do with each other.[375]

Saint Augustine believed that the City of God was created when God made the Heavens. The City of Man, on the other hand, came into being when Adam and Eve created and
committed the first human sin. The City of God symbolizes the Christian Community. The City of Men is characterized by Original Sin, rebelliousness, envy, and greed.[376]

The two cities also correspond, for Augustine, with two forms of Love. The first kind is Holy, the other kind is Foul. The first is Social, the second is selfish. The first kind of love worries about the General Welfare and Good, the second kind of Love cares little about one's fellow humans.

---

372 Ibid

373 Everson v. Board of Education. 330U.S. 1 [1947.]

374 Augustine of Hippo. City of God. (New York: Penguin Books, 2003.) Book IV, chapter 4

375 Ibid

376 Ibid

Eleven hundred years later, Martin Luther appropriated Augustine's view of two cities to put forward a doctrine of "Two Kingdoms," that says that God is the Ruler of the Whole World and that He rules in two separate ways, one Kingdom related to the Earth and the other to the Heavens.

Martin Luther's account of his Two Kingdoms are also called the "Kingdom of Grace," which is made up of "true Christians," and the "Kingdom of the Devil," that is made up of Secular Un-Christian and Evil folk. Luther tells us:

> God has therefore ordained two regimens, the Spiritual which is of the Holy Spirit and produces Christians and the pious folk under Christ and their Secular ways which restrains Un-Christian and evil folk, so that they are obliged to keep outward peace, albeit by no outward merit of their own.[377]

The people of the First Kingdom act from the Grace of God. Those in the Second Kingdom act from self-interest, the most far thing from the Grace of God. John Calvin significantly modified Martin Luther's original Two Kingdoms Theory, and certain Neo-Calvinists call their theory "transformationalism."[378] John Calvin wrote about the idea of the Two Kingdoms in his *Christian Institutes* [2.213], where he wrote:

> I call earthly things those which do not pertain to God or his Kingdom, to true Justice or to the blessedness of the future life, but which have their significance and relationship with regard to the present life and are, in a sense, confined within its bounds. I call 'Heavenly Things' the pure knowledge of God, the nature of true righteousness and the mysteries of the Heavenly Kingdom. The first class includes government,, household management, all mechanical skills, and the liberal arts. In the second are the knowledge of God and of His Will and rules by which we conform our lives to it.[379]

---

377 Martin Luther. "The Two Kingdoms." Discussed in Diarmaid MacCulloch. The Reformation: A History. (New York; penguin Books, 2003.) pp. 157–164 and 238

378 Ibid., p. 164

379 John Calvin. Institutes of the Christian Religion. (Peabody, Mass: Hen-

The first political pronouncement to comment on the idea of the Separation of Church and State in America was Baptist dissenter, Roger Williams. In a 1702 book, he wrote:

> When they [the Church] have opened a gap in the hedge or wall of separation between the garden of the church and the wilderness of the world, God has ever broke down the wall itself, removed the Candlestick, etc. and made His Garden a Wilderness, as it is this day.[380]

Mr. Williams had been among the earliest settlers to America, arriving in 1631. He was a Baptist and took pride in the idea of religious freedom in his Rhode Island Colony, while scoffing at the idea that New England was a "New Israel," as they called themselves. In 1644, Roger Williams wrote *The Bloody Tenent of Persecution*, in which we called for the separation of Church and State. He wrote, "Enforced uniformity confounds civil and religious liberty and denies the principles of Christianity and Civility."[381]

Roger Williams also insisted that no man should be required to worship or to maintain a worship against his will and that to do so was to force a guilt of hypocrisy. He thought government to be 'merely human and civil with no appropriate religious function, and he noted that good government exists in "nations, cities, and kingdoms…which never heard of the true God, nor His only Son."[382]

Williams believed that efforts by the state to involve itself in religion were likely to "corrupt both government and religion."[383] Therefore, in the same work he called for a "wall or hedge of separation between the wilderness of the world and the Garden of the Church."[384]

---

drickson Publishers, 2010.) Vol. II, p. 213

380 Roger Williams. The Bloody Tenant of Persecution. (London: Kessinger, 2010.)

381 Ibid., pp. 17–18

382 Ibid., pp. 21–22

383 Ibid., p. 22

384 Ibid

A century later, near the time of the American Revolution in 1767, a Scottish dissenting Minister named James Burgh—a man whose work was known by both Jefferson and Madison—published his *Political Disquisitions*, which went on to be called 'one of the key books of the Revolutionary generation.'[385] The Reverend Burgh at the time wrote:

> Those with different religious views are both equally fit for being employed in the service of our country. It is essential to build an impenetrable wall of Separation between things sacred and things Civil.[386]

Around the same time in a January 1, 1802 letter by Thomas Jefferson to the Danbury Baptist of Connecticut, and also published in a Massachusetts newspaper, the third President wrote:

> Believing with you that religion is a matter which lies solely between Man & his God, that he owes account to none other than his faith or his worship, that the legitimate powers of government…I contemplate with sovereign reverence that act of the whole American people which declared that their Legislature should "Make no law respecting an establishment of religion, or prohibiting the free exercise thereof, thus, building a wall of separation between Church & State.[387]

Scholars Jack Plano and Milton Greenberg, in their book, *The American Political Dictionary*, suggested that Mr. Jefferson's view of the Separation of Church and State may be summarized in four propositions. They related:

1. It is a basic principle of American government that Church and State not mingle.
2. The Supreme Court argued that the State must neither advance nor retard Religion.

---

385 James Burgh. Political Disquisitions. (New York: Palala Press, 2015.)
386 Ibid
387 Thomas Jefferson. "Letter to the Danbury Baptists. [January 1, 1802.]

3. The state must not use funds to favor one Church over others.
4. Public institutions should not be embroiled in Sectarian controversies.[388]

Proposition number one is related to the First Amendment. The second proposition is related to the balance of power among the three forms of Government. Proposition three is related to the Established Clause. And proposition four speaks of absolute separation. For some, the Treaty of Tripoli has sometimes been quoted as early support of the American separation of Church and State, particularly Article 11 of that document. Joel Barlow represented the United States in the treaty between the United States and the Bey and Subjects of Tripoli of the Barbary States in 1796. Its purpose was to secure commercial shipping rights, but it is also cited in discussions regarding the role of Religion in early America. Clause eleven of the Treaty says: The Government of the United States of America is not, in any sense, founded on the Christian Religion.[389]

The Treaty was subsequently broken by Tripoli and after the First Barbary War a superseding treaty of Peace and Amity was signed between the two nations on July 4, 1805.[390] Some also point to George Washington's 1790 letter to the Newport Rhode Island Jewish community in which the First President gave an unequivocal guarantee in his return letter to the Jews stating boldly that the new American Government "would give to bigotry no sanction, and to persecution no assistance."[391]

We also have already spoken in this Study of how Baptist Preacher John Leland is often overlooked when speaking of the issue

---

388 Jack Plano and Milton Greenberg. "Separation of Church and State." American Political Dictionary. (New York: Harcourt Books, 2001.)

389 The "treaty of Tripoli," between the United States and the Bey and Subjects of Tripoli, was signed in November 4, 1796

390 Treaty of peace and Amity. [July 4, 1805.]

391 George Washington to the Jewish Community of Newport. [August 21, 1790)

of the Separation of Church and State in America. Rev. Leland played an important role in the development of the Bill of Rights and was a persistent advocate of the Separation of Church and State. It is also true that nowhere else is there a more

commitment dedication to the idea of the Separation of Church and State in America, with the possible exception of Thomas Jefferson, than the views of the Fourth President of the United States, James Madison. Those views are the focus the Third Section of Chapter Six.

Finally, as another source for Mr. Madison's views on the Separation of Church and State we must add the great American statesman's College mentor and professor, President John Witherspoon. Mr. Witherspoon assented to the Lutheran and Calvinist idea of the "Two Kingdoms," on religious and one secular, in regard to the nature of power. But ultimately, the "Fountains" for both of those Kingdoms—for both Witherspoon and Mr. Madison—are God and the Bible.

Mr. Witherspoon advocated a "Republic" or "Free Government" that would balance national and state interests as well as legislative, executive, and judicial functions of the government, ultimately in a structure that would, as the Preamble of the Constitution proposes, "form a more perfect Union, establish Justice, ensure domestic Tranquility, and provide for the common Defense."[392]

We should not, therefore, dismiss John Witherspoon as a source for the fourth President of the United States, James Madison's formulation of his doctrine of the Separation of Church and State. Witherspoon's commitment to Calvin's idea of "Two Kingdoms," is clearly most relevant in that regard. This brings us to Mr. Madison's actual statements that he made about the Separation of Church and State over the years, the focus of the next Section of Chapter Six.

James Madison on the Separation of Church and State

There are countless reference in the works of James Madison that speak about the phenomenon of the Separation of Church and State in America. He speaks about the issue, for example, in several of his letters such as this missive from March 2, 1819, when Mr. Madison wrote:

---

392 Preamble to U.S. Constitution. September 17, 1787

> The Civil Government, though bereft of everything like an associated hierarchy, possesses the requisite stability and performs its functions with complete success, whilst the number, the industry, and the morality of the priesthood and the devotion of the people, have been manifestly increased by the total Separation of the Church from the State.[393]

Eight years earlier, in a June 3, 1811 letter to the Baptist Churches of North Carolina, Mr. Madison had also written quite explicitly about the matter at hand. The great, American statesman told the Baptists:

> I have received fellow citizens your address, approving of my objections to the Bill containing a grant of public land to the Baptist Church at Salem Meeting House, in the Mississippi Territory. Having always regarded the practical distinction between Religion and Civil Government as essential to the purity of both, and as guaranteed by the Constitution of the United States, I could not have otherwise discharged my duty on the occasion which presented itself.[394]

Perhaps the most important of James Madison's letters that speak of the Church-State issue is the Fourth President's missive to the Reverend Jasper Adams, from the Spring of 1832. Mr. Madison told Mr. Adams:

> I must admit, moreover, that it may not be easy, in every possible case, to trace the line of separation between the right of Religion and the Civil Authority with such distinctness as to avoid collisions and doubts of unessential points. The tendency on the one hand to a usurpation and on the other to a corrupting coalition or alliance between them will be best guarded against by entire abstinences of the Government from interference in any way whatever beyond the necessity of preserving public order and protecting each Sect against trespasses on its legal rights by others.[395]

---

393 James Madison to Edward Livingston. March 2, 1819
394 James Madison to the Baptist Churches of North Carolina. June 3, 1811
395 James Madison to the Rev. Jasper Adams. May 15, 1832

In the same letter to Preacher Jasper Adams (1793–1841), American clergyman, college professor and college President of the Geneva College in New York, Mr. Madison argued on behalf of letting Religion finding its own way and to survive on its own merit.

In a letter to his friend, Edward Livingston from July 10, 1822, James Madison wrote to Mr. Livingston:

> Every new and successful example, therefore, of a perfect separation between the Ecclesiastical and Civil matters is of importance.; and I have no doubt that every new example will succeed, as every past ones have done, in showing that Religion and Government will both exist in greater purity the less they are mixed together.[396]

In another of Madison's letters, this one to F.L. Schaeffer from December 3, 1821, Mr. Madison writes of "Without a legal incorporation of religious and civil polity, neither could be supported."[397] He added, "A mutual independence is found most friendly to practical Religion, to social harmony and to political prosperity."[398]

In this letter we see a repetitive theme about the issue of the Separation of Church and State in the writings of James Madison. That is, that is the two realms are indeed kept separate then both are stronger and more pure in the process. Mr. Madison makes the same kind of claims in a letter to Edward Everett on March 18, 1823, in which in the end of the missive Mr. Madison related, "This proves rather more that the law is not necessary to the support of Religion."[399]

In addition to these mentions of Church State Separation in his letters, Mr. Madison also speaks of the same phenomenon in some of his other works. Consider this portion of the statesman's *Detached Memorandum*, written sometime around 1820:

> Strongly guarded as is the Separation between Religion and Government in the Constitution of the United States, the

---

[396] James Madison to Edward Livingston. July 10, 1822
[397] James Madison to F.L. Schaeffer. December 3, 1821
[398] Ibid
[399] James Madison to Edward Everett. March 18, 1823

danger of encroachment by Ecclesiastical Bodies may be illustrated by precedents already furnished in their short history.[400]

In fact, a good deal of the *Detached Memorandum* is concerned with the issues of Religious Liberty. The work is also important because it gives Madison's views on a number of related issues like Congressional Chaplains and Days of Thanksgiving and Prayer, we shall see in Section Four of this Chapter Six.

In another place in the *Detached Memorandum*, the fourth President of the United States again hints at his desire to keep Church and State separated when he asked, "Why should the expense of a religious worship be allowed for the Legislature, be paid by the public, more than for the Executive or Judicial branches of Government?[401] Mr. Madison's answer was a clear one: None of them should be.

James Madison's views on the Separation of Church and State can also be seen in two vetoes he issued during his time as President. The first of these came on February 21, 1811, when he vetoed a bill that was entitled, "An Act Incorporating the Protestant, Episcopal Church in the Town of Alexander, in the District of Columbia." In his veto of the bill, Mr. Madison quotes the Establishment Clause and he indicates the bill may "infringe on the Separation of Church and State."[402]

The other relevant veto of Mr. Madison's was issued just three days before the first on February 18, 1811. The bill would have supplied "relief" for five Baptist Ministers and the Salem Meeting House in the Mississippi Territory.[403]

In his letter of Veto to the House of Representatives, the Fourth President made these objections to the bill in question:

> Because the bill in reserving a certain parcel of land of the United States for the use of said Baptist Church it comprises

---

400 James Madison. Detached Memorandum

401 Ibid

402 James Madison. 'An Act Incorporating the Protestants, Episcopal Church in the Town of Alexandria." February 21, 1811

403 James Madison. "Relief for Five Baptists Ministers." February 18, 1811

a principle and precedent for the appropriation of funds of the United States for the use and support of religious societies, contrary to the Article of the Constitution which declares that "The Congress shall make no law respecting a religious establishment.[404]

It is an interesting fact that in both of these vetoes, Mr. Madison actually misquotes the Establishment Clause. In neither case, however, did he quote from the Bill of Rights which would have helped to make his point.

Mr. Madison was proud of his two vetoes in 1811 including a bill to incorporate an Episcopal Church in Alexandria—the first veto mentioned earlier—by then the issue of incorporation of religious societies was percolating in Virginia. Most denominations and Sects considered it unfair that the Virginia Assembly resolutely refused to give them the benefit of incorporation, even if it issued charters to them, or for many other conceivable enterprises such as railroads, copper mines, and even mineral springs in the State.

What the leaders of these other denominations and Sects desired was a general incorporation law, similar to denominational equality with is sister confession. This would allow all churches to obtain charters and this more allow a more efficient administration of their affairs and it would permit them to serve the Virginia, religious community more robustly in their role as "religious charities."

James Madison also referred to the Separation of Church and State in several letters he wrote to College and University Presidents who wished to have their schools add theological professorships as an integral part of their curricula. To one College President, Mr. Madison wrote:

> I am not surprised at the dilemma produced at your University by making a
> theological professorships an integral part of your system. The anticipation of such a one led to the omission in ours; the visitor bring merely authorized to open a public hall for religious occasions, under impartial regulations, with

---

[404] Ibid

the opportunity to establish different Sects. The village of Charlottesville also, where different religions worship will be held is also so near, that resort may conveniently be had to them.[405]

In this same letter, Mr. Madison not only points out that there was no theology faculty at the original University of Virginia, but he also adds this note in the same letter to the University president above:

A University with Sectarian Professorships becomes, of course, a Sectarian monopoly, with Professorships of rival Sects. It would be an arena of Theological Gladiators. Without any such professorships, it may incur for a time, the least imputation of irreligious tendencies, if most designs. The last difficulty was thought more manageable than either of the others.[406]

The fourth President sums up his views about theological studies at public universities when he wrote, 'On this view of the subject, there seems to be no alternative but between a public university without a theological professorship, and Sectarian Seminaries without a University."[407]

Mr. Madison wrote about a similar situation at the College of William and Mary when local clergy complained of no theological professorships at the College and wished to use public funds to institute some. This letter was written to Edward Everett from Montpelier on March 18, 1823. Mr. Madison related to Mr. Everett that, "Some of the Clergy did no fail to arraign the peculiarity but it is not improbable that they had an eye to the chance of introducing their own creed into the Professor's chair."[408]

James Madison also complained about the same issue in a letter to Thomas Jefferson on December 31, 1824 in which he complained

---

405 James Madison "Letter to College Presidents." [May 13, 1815.]
406 Ibid
407 Ibid
408 James Madison to Edward Everett. March 18, 1823

about Presbyterian "Sectarian Seminaries," armed with charters of incorporation, disseminating obsolete religious doctrines by which he clearly meant the Determinism of Calvinism and many of its other doctrines.[409]

Before the year 1786 most of James Madison's comments about the Separation of Church and State had been about how the phenomenon could be secured in the statesman's home state of Virginia. After 1786, however, the fourth president's involvement with Church-State issues shifted to the national level. In fact, he was the principal architect on the federal Constitution, drawn in Philadelphia in the Summer of 1787.

The drafters of the Constitution were far from being irreverent, but some pious citizens still complained that they paid too little attention to religion. This was in addition to the criticisms of some of the other Sects and denominations other than the Episcopal Church. Robert L. Maddox, in his book, *Separation of Church and State: Guarantor of Religious Freedom*, quotes Mr. Madison as saying, "The people have been manifestly increased by the total Separation of Church and State."[410]

In another of his letters, written in 1803, Mr. Madison related what he saw as the "purpose" of the doctrine of the Separation of Church and State. He said:

> The purpose of Separation of Church and State is to keep forever from these shores the ceaseless strife that has soaked the soil of Europe in blood for centuries.[411]

Mr. Madison, of course, was speaking of the many religious wars in Europe from the 16th and 17th centuries. And early 18th century. These were a series of wars waged in Europe after the beginning of the Protestant Reformation in the early 16th Century, including the Thirty Years War (1618 to 1648), the Huguenot Rebellion in France (1621 to 1629), what is called the "Nine Years War (1688 to 1697), that included

---

409 James Madison to Thomas Jefferson. December 31, 1824

410 Robert L. Maddox. Separation of Church and State: Guarantor of Religious Freedom. (New York: Crossroads Books, 1987.) pp. 191–192

411 James Madison [1803 letter] quoted in William D. Graves. 'Separation of Church and State: Historical Fact or Myth?"

the Glorious Revolution of 1688 and 1689, and the War of Spanish Succession from 1701 until 1714.[412]

Mr. Madison was gravely concerned that these Religious Wars do not spill over in the United States, and luckily, they did not. In his mind, this was a very important reason for the development of the idea of the Separation of Church and State in America. After his Presidency, however, mostly in his Detached Memorandum and other works. Mr. Madison began to show some inconsistencies in his views about the Separation of Church and State. These are the focus of Section Four of this Chapter Six.

Madison and Separation After His Presidency

In his retirement at Montpelier, his estate in Orange County, Virginia, Mr. Madison spoke out against the disruptive states' rights influences that by the 1830s threatened to shatter the Federal Union, in the mind of James Madison. In a note opened after his death in 1836, the great American statesman had written, "The advice nearest to my heart and deepest in my convictions is that the Union of the States be cherished and perpetuated."[413]

James Madison enjoyed nearly twenty years of retirement. As he aged, he suffered increasingly from rheumatism; at time he could scarcely hold a pen to respond to his voluminous correspondence. His mind, however, remained sharp and as aware as ever, and he maintained an active interest in the progress of the nation and in his native state of Virginia. On this latter front, James Madison became an advocate of scientific agriculture in order to diversify the economies of both Montpelier and Virginia.

Nevertheless, as indicated above, Mr. Madison after his presidency began to exhibit some inconsistencies from his earlier views on the Separation of Church and State. For one thing, the statesman opposed having government money pay for Chaplains in the military, as well as in Congress, calling the practice "unconstitutional."

---

412 For more on these religious wars, See: Giordano Tarantino. Feeling Excluded. (London: Routledge, 2019.)

413 James Madison note was opened after his death. [1836.]

Mr. Madison also referred to attempts made by some delegates in Virginia to insert the words "Jesus Christ" after "Our Lord" in the preamble to Thomas Jefferson's *Statute for Religious Freedom*. The term "Lord" at this time primarily meant "God," though, as we have pointed out, many of the Founding Fathers tended to avoid using that word in favor of many substitutes.

After his Presidency, Mr. Madison, in his *Detached Memorandum*, criticized the issuing of religious proclamations by government entities, national, state, and local. He said about this phenomenon, "Although they may only be recommendations, they imply a religious agency… and seem to suggest and imply and certainly nourish the erroneous idea of a National Religion."[414]

A related problem that Mr. Madison saw after his Presidency was that the practice tends to 'narrow the recommendation to the standard of the predominant Sect.' And this, 'naturally terminates in a conformity to the creed of the majority.'[415] The fourth president finally concluded about this issue:

> Members of the Government can in no sense be regarded as possessing an advisory trust from the Constituents in their religious capacities. They cannot issue decrees or injunctions addressed to the faith or the Consciences of the people.[416]

Around the year 1832, James Madison penned another Memorandum in which he called upon states that still had formal ties with religious bodies to emulate Virginia's example of religious freedom through Thomas Jefferson's Church and State Separation. Mr. Madison wrote at the time, "Make the example of your Country as Pure & Complete in what relates to the freedom of the mind and its allegiances to its Maker, as in what belongs to the legitimate objects of political and civil institutions."[417] In other words, James Madison

---

414 James Madison. Detached Memorandum
415 Ibid
416 Ibid
417 Ibid

was asking for a pure and complete Separation of Religion from the Government.

Very late in his life, James Madison addressed "The great and interesting subject of tax support for Religion" to what he called "a decisive test." He meant by this that "No religious test should ever be requited for holding a public office."[418]

Finally, President James Madison had some qualms about the idea of Presidential Proclamations calling for Days of Prayer and Thanksgiving at the end of his life. Very late in his life, he said that the believed the two Days of Thanksgiving and Prayer that he proclaimed during his time as President were "ill-conceived" and he regretted having done so.[419]

From October 3, 1789, with President George Washington's first prayer proclamation until March 4, 1815, when Mr. Madison made his second and final Proclamation for a "Day of Thanksgiving and Prayer," each of the first four Presidents of the United States declared days of Prayer, Thanksgiving, and even of Fasting.

Thus, Presidents Washington, Adams, Jefferson, and Madison each proclaimed Days of Thanksgiving, Fasting, and Prayer. And in each of these the name of God was addressed by each of these American heads of state.[420]

Mr. Madison, while the fourth President of the United States, on November 16, 1814 and March 4, 1845, referred to both of his proclamations as "Thanksgiving Proclamations. Both were given in the city of Washington, D.C., and both proclamations refer to the Deity in their texts.

In his first Thanksgiving Proclamation, Mr. Madison referred to the Deity as the "Almighty God," as the "Great Sovereign of the Universe," and as a "Beneficent Parent of the Human Race" that "He would be graciously pleased to pardon all of their offenses against Him."[421] Mr.

---

418 James Madison to Thomas Jefferson. February 21, 1832

419 These were on November 16, 1814 and. March 4, 1815

420 Among the first four Presidents, George Washington [2.]; Adams. [1,]; Jefferson [1.]; Madison. [2.]

421 James Madison. Day of Prayer and Thanksgiving." November 16, 1814

Madison added, "To support and animate them in the discharge of their respective duties; And to continue to them the precious advantages flowing from political institutions so auspicious to their safety against dangers from abroad, to their tranquility at home, and to their liberties Civil and Religious."[422]

The following year, on March 4, 1815, the Fourth President again declared a 'Thanksgiving Proclamation." Mr. Madison referred to the Deity four times with four separate titles. These were "Almighty God," "the "Great Disposer of Events of the Destiny of Nations," as the 'Divine Author of Every Good and Perfect Gift," and finally, at the end of the Proclamation as the "Heavenly Benefactor."[423]

At the close of Mr. Madison's second Thanksgiving Proclamation, the great American statesman related:

> That now I recommend that the second Thursday in April next be set apart as a day on which the people of every religious denomination may, in their solemn assemblies, unite their hearts and their voices in a Free Will offering to their Heavenly Benefactor of their homage of thanksgiving and of their songs of praise.[424]

Although Mr. Madison, while President, offered two Thanksgiving Proclamations In 1814 and 1815, at the end of his life he regretted doing so, even though every President before him had done so, as well. The chief reason that the great American statesman had these regrets he revealed at the end of his life, was principally because these two, state-sponsored "Prayers of Thanksgiving," in his later view, were encroachments of his long-held dedication to the idea of the Separation of Church and State. He also observed that the Prayers may have been infringements of the Establishment Clause.[425] Thus, at the end of his life, James Madison regretted the use of public funds for religious institutions, as well as his two

---

422 Ibid
423 James Madison. "Day of Prayer and Thanksgiving." March 4, 1815
424 Ibid
425 Detached Memorandum

Thanksgiving Proclamations, in 1814 and 1815, that he made during his time as President.

This brings us to the Major Conclusions we have made in this Chapter Six, followed by the Notes of the same. This will be followed by Chapter Seven in which our main focus shall be what James Madison believed about the Soul and Survival After Death.

Major Conclusions to Chapter Six

As we have indicated in the Introduction to Chapter Six, the major focus of the Chapter was the idea of the Separation of Church and State and what Thomas Jefferson and James Madison believed and wrote about that phenomenon.

We began the First Section of Chapter Six by supplying a catalogue of sorts of the major Sources for Views on the Separation of Church and State. Among these sources that we then went on to explicate and discuss were the Religious Clause of the First Amendment, James Madison's original Proposal for the Bill of Rights, Joseph Story's remarks on Church and State Separation, and two U.S. Supreme Court cases, *Everson v. Board of Education* [1947.] and *Lemon v. Kurtzman.* [1971.][426]

The main focus of the Second Section of Chapter Six has been to give a short history of Western Views on Church and State. Among these views we have introduced and then discussed were Augustine of Hippo's idea of "Two Cities,"; Martin Luther's descriptions of 'Two Kingdoms,' which John Calvin also discussed in his *Institutes of the Christian Religion*; Roger Williams and his *The Bloody Tenant of Persecution*, in which he called for the Separation of Church and State; the Rev. James Burgh who also put forth a claim of Separation in his *Political Disquisitions*; and Thomas Jefferson and his letter to the Danbury Baptist in which he sketches out the idea of the Separation of Church and State most thoroughly in his works.

We also have indicated in the Second Section of Chapter Six that other early evidence for American views on the issue of Church and State may be found in Article 11 of the Treaty of Tripoli, Baptist

---

426 Ibid

Preacher, John Leland, and George Washington's 1790 letter to the Jewish Community of Newport.[427]

In the Third and Central Section of Chapter Six, we have sketched out the views of the fourth president of the United States on the phenomenon of the Separation of Church and State. Many of Mr. Madison's comments about the matter, can be found in his letters to Christian organizations, like the Baptist Churches of North Carolina, or to Madison's friends and acquaintances like the Rev. Jasper Adams, Edward Livingston, and to Edward Everett, among others.

We also have indicated in the Third Section of Chapter Six, that the Fourth President of the United States also endorsed the phenomenon of the Separation of Church and State in his *Detached Memorandum*, as well as two bills he vetoes about the matter when he was President, one in 1814 and the other in 1815.

In Section Four of Chapter Six we have turned our attention to some matters in President Madison's retirement where he appeared to have had some reservations about some issues related to Church and State Separation. Among these issues were the use of Government funds for religious institutions like the Baptist in the American West, for example, the making of Prayer and Thanksgiving Proclamations, of which Mr. Madison made two in his Presidency, and the idea of having Chaplains in both the military and the Houses of Congress.

About all these issues, as we have shown, Mr. Madison changed his mind in his retirement, for the later believed that each of these ideas was nothing more than infringing on his long-held dedication to the idea of the Separation of Church and State.

This brings us to the Notes to Chapter Six, followed by Chapter Seven of this Study on James Madison's Religion. The focus of Chapter Seven of this Study shall be what the Fourth President of the United States, James Madison believed and wrote about the Soul, Immortality and the idea of Resurrection of the Body.

---

427 Lemon v. Kurtzman. [1971.]

Chapter Seven:
James Madison on the Soul and Immortality

And the dead shall be raised, some to everlasting life and some to infernal perdition.

Book of Daniel 12: 1–3

Now to the King Eternal, Immortal, Invisible, the Only God, be honored and glorified forever and ever. Amen.

First Timothy 1:17

The Government is capable of embodying of what can only be called a National Spirit.

James Madison *Federalist Papers*

Introduction

The major focus in the Chapter Seven is on the phenomenon of Survival After Death and more specifically what the fourth President of the United States, James Madison appears to have believed and written about the idea. We will begin the Chapter by identifying and discussing the distinction between the Hebraic idea of Resurrection of the Body and the Greek notion, mostly Platonic, of Immortality of the Soul.

Next, we will open Chapter Seven by speaking of how the question of Survival After Death was dealt with in 18th Century Western Philosophy, using one figure, Immanuel Kant who believed in Immortality, and another philosopher, Scotsman, David Hume who was skeptical about the idea.

In the Second Section of Chapter Seven, we will speak more about background materials on Immortality and Resurrection that may also have influenced the beliefs of James Madison on these matters. More specifically, we will examine what Mr. Madison's college mentor, John Witherspoon thought about these issues and how they may have affected the views of the great American statesman.

Another source in the Second Section of Chapter is what has come to be called "Jefferson's Bible," an attempt to counter the four Gospels so they are consistent with the theological views of Thomas Jefferson, the third President of the United States.

In the Second Section of Chapter Seven we also will speak of what other Founding Fathers thought about Immortality, as well as some of the uses of the word "Soul' in the late 18th Century in America.

In the Third and central Section of Chapter Seven, we will introduce the few places in the works of James Madison's where he employs words such as 'Soul," "Immortality," "Survival," and "Resurrection." As we shall see, these references are few and far between in the works of the Fourth President, so it may be difficult to make a solid guess in terms of what he believed about these issues.

Finally, in the Fourth Section of Chapter Seven, we will add some other facts and items that may help us in deciding what Mr. Madison believed about Survival After Death, including his reading of the Greeks and Romans, as well as other miscellaneous facts that may assist us in discerning his views about these matters.

One point must be made before we move to 18th Century Views on Immortality and the Soul, and that is this—there is far less clear information about what the fourth President of the United States believed and professed about these issues than information on any other topic discussed in this Study. Mr. Madison said next to nothing about the Soul and Immortality, at least in his public life, save a few references in his essays of the *Federalist papers*.

Resurrection of the Body and Immortality of the Soul

In New Haven, Connecticut, there is an 18th and 19th Century Burial Ground known as the Grove Street Cemetery. Very near the front gate of the cemetery are the graves of a 19th Century, Presbyterian couple, the husband was Ralph and the wife's name was Edna. These graves are important for our purposes because of what they say on their tombstones. On Ralph's burial marker it says:

> Ralph
> Sleeping in the Dust
> But one day will meet his
> Maker.[428]

On the other hand, the tombstone of his mate, Edna boldly proclaims:

> Edna
> Gone to her Eternal
> Reward.[429]

Ralph and Edna were married. They live from the early 19th Century until the late 19th Century, and they were American Presbyterians. But the messages on their tombstones are very different because they call to mind two different senses of person identity, as well as two disparate views on Survival After Death.

Ralph's grave marker is associated with the Old Testament and a view of survival after death that is called Resurrection of the Body. What it means to be an individual self in the philosophical view behind Ralph's grave marker is a 'body that works.' After death, Ralph's body went into the grave and he is now "sleeping in the dust." At the end of time, however, his body will resurrect and be put back together again whereupon he will "meet his maker."[430]

Edna's tombstone on the other hand, suggests a different view of the Self, as well as a different view of survival after death than her husband's grave marker. The philosophical view that supports Edna's grave is that of the philosopher Plato. Like Ralph, when Edna dies, her body went into the earth; but who Edna is was no longer there for Edna is "gone" and where did she go? To attain her "eternal reward."[431]

---

428 Grove Street Cemetery. New Haven, Connecticut
429 Ibid
430 Ibid
431 Ibid

What it means to be a Self in Edna's view is a Soul that disconnects from the body at death. The form of survival after death that is implied in Edna's tombstone is Immortality of the Soul. Not only did Edna experience survival after death, she achieved it eternally.

These two views on survival after death, Resurrection of the Body and Immortality of the Soul have both developed in the Christian tradition, with various thinkers attempting to combine the two views. Among these Christian thinkers were Saint Paul, Augustine of Hippo, Thomas Aquinas, Martin Luther, John Calvin, and many others. Saint Paul, for example, suggested in the 15th chapter of First Corinthians that when one dies, he goes into the ground as a "physical body," but it will be raised as a *psychikos*, or a 'spiritual body." It is enough like a body that the noun is still "body," but enough like a spirit that the adjective is "spiritual." [See First Corinthians 15: 44.] Paul may be comparing the Hebrew idea of Resurrection of the Body to Immortality of the Soul, or he may have been attempting a compromise solution for bringing the two views together.

At any rate, Paul tells us at First Corinthians 15: 37 that one is "sown as a corruptible" body' but will be raised as an "incorruptible body."[432] First Corinthians 15: 35 to 49 describes how the resurrected bodies of believers will be different from our current bodies. Resurrected bodies will not be reanimated corpses or some lesser version of pre-death frame. The opposite is true. Our current bodies are like "seeds' that are sown to bring life. But this form is temporary and will change with the resurrected, 'spiritual body."

Thomas Aquinas proposed four places the soul might go upon the death of the body. These were Heaven, Hell, Purgatory, and Limbo, the latter a place where unbaptized babies and morally good people who did not know about Jesus Christ. Both Luther and Calvin rejected both the ideas of Purgatory and Limbo, as did most Protestant Churches during and after the Reformation. 5 And both reformers saw Resurrection of the Body as much more fundamental than Immortality of the Soul, in much the same way that Easter, a celebration of the resurrection of Jesus Christ, is the most important day on the Christian calendar.

---

432 First Corinthians 15: 37. [NIV.]

In more modern times, French philosopher Rene Descartes was one of the first Modern thinkers to propose philosophical arguments for the soul's survival of bodily death. He asks to begin a thought experiment. You wake up, go to the mirror but nothing is there. You feel for your face and only get air. Descartes asks, 'Who is the "I" feeling for the face?" His answer is it is the soul, the disembodies Spirit that does one's thinking. Thus, Descartes dictum: *Cogito ergo Sum*, or I think, therefore, I am.

A second argument that Rene Descartes makes in the same book his *Meditations on First Philosophy*, turns out to be a version of Plato's the Eternal Knows the Eternal argument discussed earlier in this Chapter Seven.[433]

The 18th Century Enlightenment became a time when many traditional Christian theological ideas were called into question, many of them because they did not pass the test of Reason.

By the birth of James Madison in 1751, in the context of the Enlightenment, two major views arose pertaining to the notion of Immortality of the Soul. One view assented to belief in the idea, while the other view did not.

We will explore these contrasting 18th Century understanding of Immortality in the Second Section of this Chapter Seven. We will employ the view of David Hume as a representative figure of the denial of immortality, while German philosopher, Immanuel Kant will be used as an example of those philosophers who assented to Immortality of the Soul in the late 18th Century.

Two Eighteenth Century Views on Immortality of the Soul

Scottish philosopher David Hume (1711–1776), in two of his major works examined the idea of Immortality of the Soul. These were *An Enquiry Concerning Human Understanding*, published in 1748, and *Dialogues Concerning Natural Religion*, which was written in 1750 but not published until after his death in 1776.[434]

---

433 Rene Descartes. *Meditations on First Philosophy*

434 David Hume. *Dialogues Concerning Natural Religion*. (New York: Hackett Books, 1998.)

The first enemy of David Hume in regard to Immortality are the Platonic Dualists off his day like Frenchman Rene Descartes.[435] Against Descartes view, Hume was skeptical that human beings are Substances at all, let alone "immaterial Substances." Hume reiterates his Skepticism about arguments which attempt to show that the fact that humans think or feel imply that they have immaterial and immortal souls.

Hume points out, "Animals undoubtedly feel, think, love, hate, will, and even reason, though in a more imperfect manner than man. Are their souls also immaterial and immortal? Hume goes on in the *Enquiry* to make two separate points about Immortality. First, that even if humans are immaterial substances, this should give no reason to believe in Immortality.[436] Secondly, Hume maintains that the "kind of Immortality which would have guaranteed us, if this argument succeeded, would not be worth wanting.[437]

Against the view that Dualism leads naturally to Immortality, Hume suggested that if we do accept the idea of the existence of an immaterial substance, then:

> We have reason to conclude from analogy, that nature uses it after the manner she does the other substance matter. She employs it as a king of paste or clay, modifies it into a variety of forms and existences, dissolves after a time each modification, and from its substance erects a new form.[438]

What David Hume seems to be relating here is that the incorruptibility of the Soul is what guarantees the Immortality of the Soul. Hume goes on to say, "What is incorruptible must also be ingenerable. The soul, therefore, if immortal, existed before our birth. And if the former in no way concerned us, then neither will the latter.[439]

---

435 *An Enquiry Concerning Human Understanding.* (New York: Hackett Books, 1993.); Rene Descartes. *Meditations on First Philosophy* (New York: Hackett Books, 1999.)

436 Hume, *Enquiry*, p. 52

437 Ibid., pp. 54–55

438 Ibid., p. 55

439 Ibid

Hume then goes on to consider arguments from the "Justice of God." These are arguments that take God's existence as a given and says that if God is truly Good, then He would provide us with life after death. Hume counters this argument by suggesting, "Then we do not know very much about what the Justice of God is like."[440] Hume wrote:

> It is very safe for us to affirm, that, whatever, we know the deity to have actually done, is best; but it is very dangerous to affirm, that He must always do what to us seems best. In how many instances would this reasoning fail with regard to the present world.[441]

David Hume then adds that we can hardly argue for the Justice of God to Immortality when our ideas about Justice are seemingly in conflict with Christian ideas of what the afterlife is like. More specifically, Hume tells us, "Punishment, according to our conception, should bear some proportion to the offense. Why then eternal punishment for temporary offenses of "so frail a creature as man?"[442]

This assumes, of course, that our notion of Justice is the same as God's. Perhaps it is not. And if that is the case, Hume reasoned, then how can we talk about God's Justice in any case if it is different from our own?

Hume believed there is good reason to believe that, given what we know of people, a Just God would not have designed humans as we are if there was the possibility of survival after death. He gives four arguments in which he argues that some feature of human life does not fit with the view that we are designed for a future life by a Just God.[443]

These four arguments are the following:

1. People for the most part are only concerned with this life.
2. Too many people die young for this life to be a preparation for another life.

---

440 Ibid., p. 56
441 Ibid
442 Ibid
443 Ibid., p. 57

3. This makes our fear of death inexplicable.
4. The powers of reason and resolution between the sexes out to have been equal.[444]

Over and against these arguments, is Hume's claim that all the empirical evidence available about the question is on the side of finitude. This empirical evidence, in Hume's view, cries out forcefully that "When you are dead, you stay that way and do not survive the ordeal.

The conclusion of German philosopher, Immanuel Kant (1724–1804) about Immortality of the Soul is exactly opposite of that of David Hume. Kant found a close connection between his Theism and the Afterlife in arguments for what he called the 'postulates of Practical Reason.'"[445] Kant gives very different reasons for postulating God and for Immortality of the Soul, and the ends served by these postulations are ostensibly different, as well.[446]

In actuality, however, it is highly plausible that the two postulates are inseparable. We ought to postulate God because only in this way is it possible that the end happiness should be enjoyed by every person. Given the conditions of the present life, it is clear that not all of us have achieved that happiness in this life. From this it follows, in Kant's view, that there must be a "second life" in which human happiness is to be achieved. Thus, for Kant enters the idea of Immortality of the Soul, as a postulate of Practical Reason.[447]

It is likely that James Madison, beginning at the age of twelve, in his studies with Donald Robertson, became aware of the views of both Hume and Kant on Immortality of the Soul. There were several other sources of what Mr. Madison's views of Survival After Death may have been, and this is the topic of the next Section of Chapter Seven.

---

444 Ibid., pp. 57–58

445 Immanuel Kant. *Critique of Practical Reason*. (New York: Hackett Books, 2002.)

446 Ibid., pp. 25–26

447 Ibid., p. 26

Sources For Madison on Survival After Death

To ascertain the views of James Madison on Survival After Death, we can point to the following Sources that may be of some help:

1. The philosophy of Plato.
2. The philosophy of Aristotle.
3. The Views of John Witherspoon on Resurrection and Immortality.
4. Thomas Jefferson's Bible and other Mentions of Soul and Immortality.
5. Comments From Other Founding Fathers About the Soul and Immortality.
6. Enlightenment Ideas Related to Immorality, including an emphasis on Reason.

In this Third Section of Chapter Seven, we will comment on each of these Sources that may have influences James Madison's perspectives on the Soul, its Immortality, Resurrection of the Body and other ideas about Survival After Death.

It is likely that Donald Robertson read the philosophy of Plato with his student James Madison. In Plato's *Republic*, as well as a number of his other dialogues, he wrote a great deal about his belief in the Immortality of the Soul. Plato believed that the soul has three parts. He calls these the Appetitive part, the Spirited Part, and the Rational Part of the Soul. The Appetitive part of the Soul for Plato are one's emotions, passions, feelings, and instincts. It is the most basic of the three parts of the Soul.

The Spirited element of the soul for Plato are the rules of Society and Religion, and the Rational element is Reason. Plato gives a metaphor about the nature of the soul when Socrates was asked about it. He said the Soul is like a chariot, a charioteer and two horses. One horse is full of passion and is very dark, while the other horse is very obedient to the Charioteer, who stands for Reason in the metaphor. The dark horse is the Appetitive element of the Soul and the lighter horse, of course, is the Spirited element.[448]

---

448 Plato. *The Republic*. (New York: Hackett Books, 1992.)

Plato also believed it was only the Rational part of the Soul, symbolized by the Charioteer in Plato's analogy, which survives death and he offered several arguments for how he was certain that the soul of a human survives in an immortal state.[449]

Aristotle's understanding of the Soul was radically different from his teacher, Plato. Rather than parts or elements of the Soul, Aristotle believed that the Soul has functions, and like Plato the number of functions is three. The first of these is the Nutritive function, the part of a person that eats, excretes and reproduces.[450] The Appetitive part of the Soul is the seat of various desires for food, drink, sexual gratification and other such pleasures, as well as other desires that should be limited such as eating a ten pound sirloin steak at every meal and other unlawful desires lie the desire to eat one's children.

Even though the Appetitive part of the Soul lusts after many things, Plato dubs it as "money loving, "since money is required for satisfying most of the desires in a just and fair human.[451] The Appetites should fully be controlled by Reason and Reason's accomplice, the Spirited element.

The second function of the Soul for Aristotle he calls the Sensitive function. This is the function of the Soul that controls one's senses, both internal [memory and instinct] and external [the five senses.]

The final function of the Soul for Aristotle is the Rational function, or Reason. For Aristotle, anything that is alive has a soul. The smallest things alive only possess the Nutritive function, larger animals have the Nutritive and Sensitive, but not Rational. Human beings have all three functions of the Soul; and since God is pure Reason, He only has the Rational function.[452]

The Spirited part of the Soul also controls one's beliefs, which constitutes the lowest part of cognitive abilities. The object of beliefs are in the physical realm, the realm of the uses of the senses. A man in a state of belief has no access to the highest form of knowledge, the

---

449 Aristotle. *On the Soul*. (Oxford: Oxford University Press, 2018.)

450 Ibid

451 Ibid

452 Adams met John Witherspoon on August 29, 1774

realm of the Eternal Forms, but instead the Spirited element takes the realm of the senses to be the most real.

The Eternal Forms, for Socrates and Plato is a spaceless, timeless realm of reality, the most real part of reality. For them, the Rational part of the Soul is capable of apprehending the Eternal Forms, or these ideal versions of physical objects and Virtues, like Justice, Courage, and the Good. Indeed, for Plato, the Good is the highest of the Forms and it is represented by the Sun, for it illuminates everything else in the sensible World.

Because the Rational part of the Soul is capable of knowing the Eternal Forms, it is also the element of the soul that survives death. In fact, Plato provides a series of arguments for establishing the Soul's Immortality, including an argument called the "Eternal Knows the Eternal and another called "Argument From Opposites.

If something of the Soul knows the Eternal Forms, then that thing must itself also be eternal. Thus, the Eternal Knows the Eternal." In the argument From Opposites, Plato points out that many things spring from their opposites. Thus, for example, we were not alive, then we were, so life sprang from death. At the end of our lives, we will be dead again, so death came from life. It follows then that some kind of life must come from death, and for Plato that is Immortality of the Soul.

Another big difference between Plato and Aristotle on the Soul is that the latter believed that the Soul did not survive death. He thought when you are dead, you stay that way forever, unlike his mentor, Plato, who was certain that the Rational element of the Soul survives death.

It is likely that these two points of view were taught to James Madison by his teacher Donald Robertson and may have been reaffirmed by the Reverend Thomas Martin. When the fourth President entered College at the College of New Jersey, it is likely that Madison learned the Enlightenment ideas about survival of Hume and Kant, as well as renewed his knowledge of Plato and Aristotle in that period as he had learned from Mr. Robertson.

Perhaps the most fundamental source for Survival after Death in the life of James Madison was his Presbyterian college mentor, John Witherspoon who wore three different hats: President of the College of New Jersey; Presbyterian Clergyman; and a member of the Continental Congress. After a distinguished career as a pastor in the Church of Scotland, he was called in 1768 to lead the struggling College of New Jersey in America. At that point he could not have known how he would get caught up in America's struggle for independence, but he observed from the start that there was a contagious air of freedom in the New World environment.

In 1774, John Adams passed through Princeton, New Jersey on his way to the Continental Congress which was meeting in Philadelphia, and he visited President Witherspoon and he marveled at the College President's demeanor and brilliance.[453]

Dr. Witherspoon's views on survival after death, which undoubtedly he taught to his students, can be seen in a number of his works, including many of his sermons, including on Job 42: 5 and 6 and the Gospel of Mark 10: 13 to 16. In the former, Mr. Witherspoon revealed about the patriarch Job, He was "Not only impatient, but also of disrespect to the conduct of the Lord his Maker."[454]

President Witherspoon also observed in the same sermon that "The Glory of God sometimes humbles the soul," an example of the Moral Qualities view that says God sometimes sends evil and suffering to make people more humble.[455] In the same sermon, Witherspoon also observed, "Nothing makes a quality appear so sensibly as a comparison with its opposite." This is an example of the Contrast View. In order to make sense of the Good, we must also have knowledge of Evil.[456]

In his sermon on Mark 10: 13 to 16, John Witherspoon spoke of Resurrection of the Body and Immortality of the Soul. About "Of such is the Kingdom of God," the College President related, "It is perhaps most commonly the case that the seeds of Resurrection were sewn in infancy."[457] In the same sermon, Witherspoon speaks of the "deep

---

453 John Witherspoon. *Collected Sermons*. (Philadelphia: Franklin Classics, 2018.) p. 131

454 Ibid

455 Ibid., p. 132

456 For more on the Contrast View, See: Stephen Vicchio *The Voice From the Whirlwind: The Problem of Evil in the Modern World*. (Westminster: Christian Classics, 1986.), pp. 126–129

457 Witherspoon. *Sermons*. P. 218

sleep" that humans will experience "until the last," and "as the saying goes, they die so they may live."[458] This should be seen as assenting to both Ralph and Edna's points of view described on the tombstones earlier in the Chapter.

In the same sermon on the Gospel of Mark, John Witherspoon wrote about the "graces of the spiritual life," an obvious reference to Immortality of the Soul; and a little further on, he spoke of good human beings who were "born for immortality."[459] At the close of the same sermon, President Witherspoon asked God "To give us a new heart and a new spirit to create in us anew in Christ Jesus unto our good works, which God has before preordained, that we should walk in His ways."[460]

In another of his works known as the "Dominion of Providence," John Witherspoon begins by observing:

> I would take this opportunity on this occasion, and from this subject, to press every hearer to a sincere concern for his own soul's salvation.[461]

Witherspoon goes on in the same work to cite passages from Saint Paul in Second Corinthians, from Chapter six and fifteen, that support the idea of Resurrection of the Body in those Pauline texts.[462]

In short, it is clear that John Witherspoon, the President of the College of New Jersey, was a firm believer, in both Resurrection of the Body and Immortality of the Soul. We only wonder how much of this commitment was adopted by his student, the fourth President of the United States, James Madison.

Another source for Mr. Madison's views on Survival After Death may well have been Thomas Jefferson, particularly a text of the third President that has come to be known as "Jefferson's Bible."[463] This was

---

458 Ibid

459 Ibid., p. 219

460 Ibid

461 John Witherspoon. *Dominion of Providence*. (London: Kessinger Books, 2010.), p. 53

462 Ibid

463 Thomas Jefferson. *Jefferson's Bible*. (London: A & D Books, 2009.)

an attempt on Jefferson's part to edit the four Gospels. He wrote way to a published in Philadelphia to get the four Gospels in the original Greek, in the Latin Vulgate, in French, and in English. Mr. Jefferson then placed the four versions side by side in four columns.

Next, using a razor, he cut out of the four columns what he did not believe in and then pasted together what he had left. This exercise is significant for our purposes because much of what he cut out was anything related to Jesus' miracles, as well as any references to Resurrection of the Body and Immortality of the Soul.[464] We know that James Madison had a copy of Jefferson's Bible and apparently read it thoroughly. But we cannot be sure how much the fourth President agreed with these views of the third President.

We do know, however, that in many other places of the writings of Thomas Jefferson he did refer to the Soul and to Immortality, such as in his "Syllabus of an Estimate of the Merit of the Doctrine of Jesus Comparted With Those of Others," written on April 21, 1803.[465] In that work, Mr. Jefferson explicitly told us about Jesus:

> "He taught, emphatically the doctrines of a future state, which was either doubted or disbelieved by the Jews, and wielded it with efficiency, as an important incentive supplementary to the other motives to moral conduct."[466]

Although Mr. Jefferson spoke of the teachings of Jesus about survival after death, he said nothing about whether the third President agreed with Jesus. In a letter to John Adams, however, from October 28, 1813, Mr. Jefferson did seem to deny survival when he spoke to the second President of the "Immortality of the Race being taken away."[467] It is not entirely clear, however, what Mr. Jefferson meant by that statement.

---

464 Ibid

465 Thomas Jefferson. Syllabus on the Estimate of the Merits of the Doctrines of Jesus Christ Comparted with Those of Others. (Philadelphia: Arkose Press, 2015.)

466 Ibid., p. 17

467 Thomas Jefferson to John Adams. October 28, 1813

Charles B. Sanford, in his book, *The Religious Life of Thomas Jefferson* suggests that two of the third President's letters to John Adams, om August 9, 1816 and December 8, 1818, maintains that "Jefferson was influenced by Adams' arguments about spirit to find room in belief in immortality among the wondrous attributes of certain forms of matter."[468]

At any rate, it is pretty clear that Thomas Jefferson did not ascribe to either Resurrection of the Body or Immortality of the Soul. What is not clear, however, is how much the two Virginia friends shared these negative beliefs about Survival After Death, if they shared them at all.

There is, however, sufficient evidence of other of the Founding Fathers about whether they did, or did not, believe in Resurrection and Immortality. Benjamin Franklin, for example, in an attempt to summarize his religious beliefs wrote, "...That the Soul of Man is Immortal and will be treated with Justice in another life, respecting its conduct in this life."[469]

Thomas Paine, in his *Common Sense*, wrote about the American Revolution, "These are the kinds of times that tests man's Souls," but it is unlikely that he meant the immaterial element of a human being.[470]

A number of scholars who study the life and beliefs of Daniel Webster also suggest that the New Hampshire native was a firm believer in Immortality of the Soul, including his famous last words, "I still live."[471]

Joseph Ellis, in an article on "The U.S. Founding Fathers: Their Religious Belief," tells us about many of the Founding Fathers in America, "The only afterlife that they considered certain was in the memory of subsequent generations, which is to say, in this sense, testimonials to a kind of everlasting life."[472] What Mr. Ellis has in

---

468 Thomas Jefferson to John Adams. August 9, 1816 and December 8, 1818

469 Benjamin Franklin. *Autobiography*. (New York; Norton, 2012.)

470 Thomas Paine. *Common Sense*. (New York: Independently Published, 2010.)

471 Daniel Webster, quoted by John F. Kennedy. *Profiles in Courage*. Kennedy says of Webster, "Webster was undoubtedly the most talented figure in our Congressional history."

472 Joseph Ellis. 'The Founding Fathers: Their Religious Beliefs." *Encyclopedia Britannica*. [February 23, 2007.]

mind here is a kind of "Social Immortality," in which the Founding Fathers have become immortal, if you will, by virtue of what they did in America in the second half of the 18th Century.[473]

This brings us to the few instances when James Madison did have something to say about the ideas of the Soul, Immortality, and Resurrection of the Body, the topic of the next Section of Chapter Seven to follow.

Madison on the Soul, Immortality, and Resurrection

The only place that James Madison discusses these issues at any length is in his essays of the *Federalist Papers*. In this Section of Chapter Seven we will explore what Mr. Madison said about the Soul. One way to see this is to return to the philosophy of Plato and his idea in Book V of his *Republic*, where he discussed the notion of an Ideal State or the *Kallipolis* in classical Greek.[474]

In the *Republic*, as we have suggested earlier, Socrates claims that the human soul is divided into three parts—Appetitive, Spirited, and Rational. The Appetitive is the origin of emotions and desires. The Appetitive provides the raw materials upon which the other parts of the soul can function.

The Rational part of the soul deliberates and organizes the Appetitive desires into a coherent order. It determines which of the Appetitive desires ought to be fulfilled. The Spirited element of the soul enforces and carries out the decisions of the Rational element.

Each of these three parts of the soul for Socrates/Plato represents three separate elements of Society. The Rational part is the leader who ought to rule by Wisdom. Plato calls this figure the "Philosopher-King." The Spirited element of the Soul is the army and the polices. They are known by their Courage. The Appetitive element of Society is the "Makers," 'Artisans," or 'manufacturers.' These are the aspect of Society that makes things that are necessary for the well-being of the ideal State, or *Kallipolis*. The virtue associated with the Makers is Temperance.

---

473 Ibid
474 See note # 20 of this Chapter

James Madison believed that the three branches of Government work in a similar way or at least ought to will Justice of the State is the final goal. For Madison, the Legislative branch in the Appetitive part of the Society. It is the origin of many competing proposals. It provides the raw material upon which the other branches may operate.[475] The Judicial system is the Rational element of the State or Republic. It deliberates upon the legislative proposals, determining which should be struck down and which should remain. Finally, the Executive branch is the Spirited part of the Republic. It enforces and carries out the desires that have been approved by the Judiciary.[476]

In the mind of James Madison, the *Federalist Papers* outlines the balances that ought to exist among the three branches. The ultimate goal is to create a balance in the State in the same way that there is a balance in the individual Soul. Plato, through Socrates explains that a Democracy allows desires, a lack of Reason and Moderation and ultimately individual freedoms to over-indulge the appetites.[477]

Mr. Madison, in his essays of the *Federalist Papers,* aimed to use the factions of free thought in order to restrict the appetites and to create moderation. The fourth President asserted that in order to have a stable Republic, you must account for the flaws of human nature. In fact, in *Federalist* number 18, human nature has been the cause of the deterioration of many past governments.[478] We will say more about Mr. Madison's views on human nature in Chapter Eight of this Study.

Mr. Madison's thinking about Democracy offered a timely antidote to what might be called populist Democracy. While he began from premises that the will of the people ought to govern us he insisted that political institutions and intermediary Civic institutions were essentially for cultivating the "cool and deliberate sense of the community." Madison also famously insisted that we should not design a government trusting that "Enlightened statesman will always be at

---

475   Ibid., p. 100
476   Ibid
477   James Madison. *Federalist Papers*. essay 10
478   Ibid. essay number 18

the helm. He did believe, however, that political leadership is essential to educating the public md, or what he called the "Societal Spirit."

To return to Plato, he also relates about the passions, "They never fail to wrestle the scepter from Reason. Mr. Madison tells us in *Federalist* 55, "Had every Athenian been like Socrates, every Athenian Assembly would still have been a mob."[479]

James Madison, in many of his essays of the *Federalist Papers*, through Publius, had a similar conception of the Soul as Socrates did. Like Socrates, Publius asserted that passions will always overcome reason at some point, the necessity of acknowledging passions into the system becomes clear. Mr. Madison explained that instead of attempting to cure factions, 'by giving every citizen the same opinion, the same passions, and the same interests," a government can control the effects of factions," or so Mr. Madison said in *Federalist* number ten.[480]

In *Federalist* number 10, Mr. Madison quoted David Hume on the idea of ruling solely by Reason. Hume observed:

> To balance a large state or society, whether a Monarchy or a Republic, on general laws, is a work of so great a difficulty that no human genius, however, comprehensible, is able by the mere dint of Reason and Reflection, to effect it. The judgment of many must united in the work; experience must guide their labor; time must bring it to perfection, and the feeling of inconvenience must correct the mistakes which they inevitably fall into in their first trials and experiments.[481]

In *Federalist* numbers 46 and 51, the fourth President told us that, "The Government is capable of embodying a national Spirit."[482] This Spirit is composed of local problems but at the same time detached from them as an aggregation of many opinions. States will 'fight for public liberty by national authority, according to *Federalist* 28.[483]

---

479 Ibid., essay 55
480 Ibid., essay number 10
481 Ibid
482 Ibid., essay number 46
483 Ibid., essay no. 51

Mr. Madison suggested that both the Judicial and the Legislative branches serve as Guardians for the State and for the People [*Federalist* 17.] In the *Republic*, the Guardians are most aligned with the Good, or the virtues of the Republic, and thus they are tasked with enforcing these virtues and values. The Judges and Representatives also are the voice of the Spirit of the State, one of which originates in the people and the other in the State.[484]

In short, James Madison appears to have taken the idea of Plato's *Republic* and its metaphors and connections between the State and the individual human Soul and modified the idea of the three branches of Republican Government in America to fit these Platonic ideas. Beyond these few references to "Soul" and "Spirit" in Mr. Madison's essays of the *Federalist Papers*, there are no other mentions of these terms in his *Collected Works*. There is also no evidence that the fourth president appropriated any of the ideas about Resurrection of the Body, nor Immortality of the Soul, that he was taught by Donald Robertson and President John Witherspoon.

There is no evidence in any part of James Madison's life from his adolescence until his death that Mr. Madison assented to either of these Biblical beliefs. He did, however, chose instead to use Plato's idea of the structure of the Soul and of the Society, to speak of the idea he called the "Spirit of Society." And along the way, he said a great deal about the ruling by Reason or by Passion alone, as well as what he saw as the "dangers of Democracy."

In the Introduction to Chapter Seven we indicated that there is nearly no evidence concerning what James Madison believed about Survival After Death. Other than these metaphorical uses of terms like "Soul" and "Spirit" in his essays of the *Federalist papers*, there is absolutely no evidence that the fourth President of the United States assented to beliefs that there is life beyond the grave.

Earlier in this Study, in the Chapter on Madison and the Bible, we have indicated that Jams Madison found immortality of the soul in Matthew 9: 24 and that he found both Resurrection of the Body and Immortality of the Soul in certain passages in the Book of Proverbs.

---

484 Ibid., essay no. 17

We also have shown in the same Chapter that in Mr. Madison's "Notes on the Bible," which he scribbled in the Madison family Bible, also suggested a belief on the part of Mr. Madison that Immortality of the Soul can be detected in the Acts of the Apostles, as well, at 2: 6–11; 2: 27; 7: 59; and 17: 32.

This brings us to the major Conclusions of Chapter Seven, followed by the Notes of the same. The central focus of Chapter Eight, as we will soon see, is what the fourth President of the United States, James Madison believed and wrote about the phenomena of Human Nature and Democracy.

Conclusions to Chapter Seven

We have begun this Chapter Seven on James Madison's views on Survival After Death by pointing out that the Chapter would unfold in four principal parts. In the first of those, we have sketched out the contrasting views of Resurrection of the Body and Immortality of the Soul in the history of the Judeo-Christian Tradition.

As we have shown, the former view is an Old Testament and thus Hebraic idea, while the latter idea has been gleaned from Greek philosophy or, more specifically from the works of Athenian philosopher, Plato.[485]

In order to explicate the differences between these two views, we have employed the grave markers of a 19th Century couple of Presbyterians, one of whom is "sleeping in the dust," while the other has "gone to her eternal reward."[486]

We also have indicated in the First Section of Chapter Seven that James Madison was fully aware of the arguments of Greek philosopher, Plato on survival after death, but we have no indication of what the fourth President of the United States thought about that series of arguments that established, at least in Plato's mind, that the human soul survives bodily death and is immortal. There is no evidence, however, that Mr. Madison employed these Platonic arguments in any way.

---

485 See, for example, the Book of Daniel 12: 1–3
486 Grove Street Cemetery. New Haven, Connecticut

In the Second Section of Chapter Seven, we have introduced the two major views on Survival After Death that existed in late 18th Century, European and American philosophical thought. One of these views, was that of David Hume who was skeptical about the matter, while the other view, held by German philosopher, Immanuel Kant, who proposed that Immortality of the Soul may be proven through a series of complicated philosophical arguments of what he called "Practical Reason."[487]

Among the 17th and 18th Century philosophers who thought Immortality can be proved were Rene Descartes and Bishop Joseph Butler in addition to Immanuel Kant. Among those who denied Immortality were the Baron D'Holbach and French philosopher Voltaire. **60** James Madison, as we have shown, would have been aware of this literature on Immortality of the Soul, going all the way back to Plato and his student, Aristotle.

In the Third Section of Chapter Seven we have explored what we have called the "Sources for James Madison's views on Survival After Death." In that Section, we pointed to six principal sources. These were: Plato, Aristotle, John Witherspoon, the Thomas Jefferson Bible, other American Founding Fathers, and Enlightenment ideas from people like Rene Descartes, David Hume, Immanuel Kant, Bishop Joseph Butler, the Barons Montesquieu and D'Holbach, and many other thinkers he learned of from Mr. Robertson and President Witherspoon.

Of these sources, as we have indicated, Thomas Jefferson's project to eliminate with a razor all the evidence of miracles and survival after death in the "Jefferson Bible," may have been the major force behind the lack of information about these matters to be found in the works of James Madison.

If the Jefferson Bible was not the major source behind the lack of information about survival after death in the works of James Madison, then it was many of the sermons of his College mentor, President John Witherspoon in which he indicated his assent to both Resurrection of the Body and to Immortality of the Soul.

The fourth President of the United States was also fully aware of the arguments of both David Hume and Immanuel Kant on Survival

---

487 See note no. 17 of this Chapter

After Death which he must have learned from Donald Robertson and, of course, from President John Witherspoon who often spoke of both Resurrection of the Body and Immortality of the Soul in his sermons and other published works In the 18th Century during the Enlightenment Period.

In the Fourth and Final Section of Chapter Seven, we have sketched out the few places in the *Collected Works*, where the fourth President of the United States said or wrote anything about Immortality and Resurrection. As we have indicated in Section Four of Chapter Seven these few references all came from James Madison's essays of the *Federalist Papers*.

Indeed, we have shown that the meager references to Survival After Death of Mr. Madison's may be found in essays 10, 17, 18, 46, 51, and 55. And in each of these he used the words 'spirit' and or 'Soul,' but most often not in a metaphysical or theological context. The overall pieces of evidence, however, in regard to James Madison's views on Survival After Death, are few and far between, and there is little evidence to assert that James Madison was an active believer in either Resurrection of the Body or Immortality of the Soul.

This brings us to the Notes of this Chapter Seven, followed by Chapter Eight in which we will discuss two separate but related issues in the views of James Madison. The first of these is the issue of human nature, and the second is what the fourth President of the United States really thought about the notion of Democracy.

Chapter Eight:
James Madison on Human Nature and Democracy.

> He who refuses to rule is liable to be ruled by one who is worse than himself.
>
> —Plato. "The Republic."

> The heart is more deceitful than all else and is desperately sick.
>
> —Jeremiah 17: 9. [Author's translation.]

> The latent cause of human nature, therefore, is sown in the nature of man.
>
> —James Madison. Federalist Papers.

Introduction

The purpose of this Chapter Eight is to ascertain what the views of the fourth President of the United States, James Madison were in regard to two issues, human nature and Democracy.

The Chapter will begin by looking at 17th and 18th Century views about human nature prior to the time of James Madison.

In the Second Section of Chapter Eight, we will explore what Mr. Madison himself thought and wrote about human nature. As we shall see, his views on the matter can principally be found in four of his *Federalist Papers* essays, numbers 10, 34, 37, and 51.

The views of James Madison on the ideas of Democracy versus Republicanism will be the focus of the Third and Final Section of Chapter Eight. As we shall see, he is quite negative about the former and positive about the latter in his speeches and published works.

Human Nature in the 17th and 18th Centuries

The idea of human nature certainly must be the beginning of any discussion of the nature of the State, for states are nothing more than an aggregate of humans. Some political theorists like Plato believed that the ideal state could be achieved by all the parts of the State to work in harmony and to be ruled by Justice.

In the mind of Plato, human beings were basically good and is true whether a person was a slave or a Philosopher-King.[488] On the other hand, Bishop Augustine of Hippo and Italian philosopher, Thomas Aquinas, held the view that humans are born basically Evil because of their doctrine of Original Sin.[489]

In the Modern Era of History, in the 17th and 18th Centuries, the debate about basic human nature was again a central concern of Philosophy and the Enlightenment. On the one hand, Thomas Hobbes, in his 1651 book, *Leviathan*, agreed with the Augustine/Aquinas view.

In the state of nature, Hobbes related about human beings:

> In such condition there is no place for industry, because the fruit thereof is uncertain, and consequently no culture of the earth; no navigation, nor use of the commodities that may be imported by sea; no commodious building; no instruments of moving and removing such things as require much force; no knowledge of the face of the earth; no account of time; no arts; no letters; no society; and what is worse of all, continual fear and danger of a violent death, and the life of man is solitary, poor, nasty, brutish, and short.[490]

This description is one of the most famous in all of Western Political Philosophy. This description is what Thomas Hobbes suggested life would be like without a strong central government to protect human beings from themselves. Furthermore, Hobbes suggested that the Sovereign, or Leader of the Government, had the authority to control all aspects of his Subjects.

---

488 Plato. The Republic. (New York: Hackett Books, 1992.)

489 Thomas Aquinas. Summa Theologica. (New York: penguin Books, 1993.) Part One, Question 82.1–4

490 Thomas Hobbes. Leviathan. (New York: Digireads. 2017.), p. 35

Thomas Hobbes did not believe in the idea of the Separation of the Powers of Government. But he did believe, like Augustine an Aquinas, that human beings are basically Flawed, or as Thomas Hobbes said, "The life of man is solitary, poor, nasty, brutish and short.⁴⁹¹

On the other hand, French philosopher, Jean Jacques Rousseau (1712–1778), in his work the *Social Contract*, related that in the state of nature human beings are innocent and at their best.⁴⁹² Rousseau also suggested that the nature of humans became corrupted with the introduction of society.⁴⁹³ Rousseau also believed in the state of nature people tended to be isolated, there was no war, and human desires were limited and circumscribed, mostly consistent with their survival needs. In Rousseau's view, people did not have the constant desire to acquire things, for in the state of nature egoism was absent.

Rousseau proclaimed the idea, then, that human beings are basically good and that any one man's nature is as good as any other man. Rousseau also believed a man could be just without virtue and be good without much effort, principally because of his nature. The French philosopher believed that in the state of nature humans were free, wise, and good and the laws by which they lived were benevolent.⁴⁹⁴

For Jean-Jacques Rousseau, evil did not arise from human nature but instead in human social institutions. He believed that Society corrupts the innocent nature of human beings, they become evil by having contact with social arrangements. Rousseau wrote, "The first person to mark off a plot of land and then call it his own, that is the beginning of the origin of hum Inequality."⁴⁹⁵

Rousseau, like David Hume, placed more primacy on instinct, passions, intuitions, emotions, and feelings than Reason. Both men believed these things could provide more insights into what is Good and Evil, and what is real, than can reason. Thus, both Rousseau and Hume

---

491 Augustine. City of God. (New York: penguin Books, 2003.)

492 Jean-Jacques Rosseau. The Social Contract. (Cambridge: Cambridge University Press, 2018.)

493 6. Ibid., p. 74

494 Ibid

495 Ibid., p. 79

minimized the importance of Reason, the great Enlightenment value. But Rousseau appears not to have understood that the concept of Freedom— another Enlightenment value— is meaningless in the absence of Reason.

Thus, in the beliefs of Hobbes and Rousseau we see contrasting views on the issue of basic human nature. One believed humans are flawed, while the others thought that humans are born naturally good. The view of John Locke, in his *Second Treatise on Government*, is a third view on human nature which we will turn to next.[496]

English philosopher, John Locke (1632–1704) discussed his ideas of the state of nature and human nature in his *Second Treatise on Government*. He agreed with both Hobbes and Rousseau that humans are endowed by God with Freedom and Equality by nature. In Locke's view, this caused the state of nature to be a state of sheer freedom and equality in which no one is subordinate to another and there is no supreme authority in the state of nature.[497]

In his *Second Treatise*, Locke appears to rely on natural theology in his depiction of human nature due to his engagement with the Scientific Revolution of the 17th Century. This caused him to believe that in the state of nature humans are governed by Reason, which Locke also calls the "Law of Nature." By this, Locke meant that self-preservation, as well as the preservation of others, are duties that humans owe their Creator.[498]

Locke also believed that Reason intrinsically produces in humans a sense of morality and makes them capable of telling a good man from a bad man. In other words, human beings are capable of discerning which behaviors are permissible in society and which are not. Thus, the English philosopher wrote:

> In a state of perfect Freedom to order their actions and to dispose of their possessions and persons as they see fit, and all of this within the bounds of the Law of Nature.[499]

---

496 John Locke. Second Treatise on Government. (New York: Hackett Books, 1980.)

497 Ibid

498 Ibid. p. 31

499 Ibid., p. 34

This is to say that although humans are equal and free in the state of nature, there are, nevertheless, binding laws in that state, which serve to protect one's self and one's property. Locke also upheld the idea in the *Second Treatise* that human beings are naturally good-natured and that they make intelligent decisions for themselves. For Locke, the purpose of the state became clear because we were reasonable enough to wish to create it.[500]

One element that John Locke in his *Second Treatise* added to Social Contract theory is that subjects, or citizens, have the right to rebel if the Sovereign side of the equation is behaving in an immoral way. Perhaps the most important aspect of Locke's theory of the state, however, is that human nature is defined by rationality and logic Scotsman David Hume took a completely different view of human nature than the other Enlightenment thinkers we have introduced in this Chapter. For one thing, Hume thought that human passions have more effects on human behavior than does reason. In an essay entitled, "Of the Dignity or Meanness of Human Nature," argued against the commonly held view in the 18th Century that self-love or self-interest is the real motivator for human behavior.

Against this views we have indicated above, is the understanding that it is one's passions that are mostly as the motivation of human behavior. The Scottish philosopher essentially argued against what were believed to be two of the most important of the Enlightenment values, which is Reason and Self-Interest.

David Hume argued that all human knowledge is found in experience and passion, as opposed to rationality or reason. For the Scotsman, Reason becomes a slave to the Passions. Indeed, in the third chapter of his *Treatise on Human Nature*, Hume observed, "Reason is and ought to be a slave to reason."[501]

For Hume, in both the essay mentioned above, as well as in his 1739 work, A *Treatise on Human Nature*, the idea of Reason is subordinate to the human passions. The passions make one act and

---

500 David Hume. Treatise on Human Nature. (New York; penguin Books, 2019.)

501 Ibid

then reason justifies those acts. Contrary to Hobbes, Rousseau, and Locke, David Hume was convinced that human passions are the key for understanding human behavior.

This brings us to the Second Section of Chapter of Chapter Eight in which our central focus shall be what the fourth President of the United States, James Madison believed and wrote about the issue of human nature.

James Madison on Human Nature

The major way to understand James Madison's views on human nature is to look at several of the essays he wrote in the *Federalist Papers*, where he specifically addressed the issue at hand. Among the *Federalist* where human nature is a topic of conversation is one essay by Alexander Hamilton, essay number six, and four by Mr. Madison [10, 34, 37, and 51.]

In *Federalist Papers* essay number six, Mr. Hamilton boldly expressed his view of human nature when he wrote:

> Has it not, on the contrary invariably been found that momentary passions and immediate interests, have a more active and imperious control over human conduct that general or remote considerations of policy, utility or justice.[502]

Mr. Hamilton added:

> To presume a want of motives for such contests as an argument against their existence would be to forget that men are ambitious, vindictive, and rapacious.[503]

Alexander Hamilton asserted in essay number six of the *Federalist Papers* that, "In order to have a stable and lasting government, you must first account for the flaws in human beings."[504] Mr. Hamilton recognized that in the past, human nature has been the most fundamental

---

502 Alexander Hamilton. Federalist Papers. essay no 6
503 Ibid
504 Ibid

cause of the deterioration of governments. Mr. Madison added that two other causes have been an inability to change when the ideal state loses balance and a lack of protection and Factions that bring on anarchy.[505]

In these quotes, it appears that Alexander Hamilton was in the camp of Thomas Hobbes when it came to the issue of human nature. We move now to Mr. Madison's understanding of basic human nature, which, interestingly enough, are also connected to his understanding of Democracy in the next Section of Chapter Eight.

In the context of discussing what Mr. Madison referred to as "Factions," James Madison wrote in *Federalist* number ten:

> The latent cause of Factions are thus sown in the nature of men.... and rendered them much more disposed to vex and oppress each other than to cooperate for their common good.[506]

Mr. Madison suggested that Factions are caused by human nature, but what is that natural state like in the fourth President's mind? He tells us in *Federalist* thirty-four:

> To judge from the history of mankind, we shall be compelled to conclude that the fiery and destructive passions of war reign in the human breast with much more powerful a sway than the mild and beneficent sentiments of peace; and that to model our political systems upon speculations on lasting tranquility would be to calculate on the weaker springs of human character.[507]

James Madison at first in this passage appears to assent to the Thomas Hobbes' view concerning human nature and he appears to find little room in human nature for the "weaker springs of human character," that is the view like Rousseau and John Locke.

In essay number ten of the *Federalist Papers*, Mr. Madison also indicated that one goal of government ought to be to "break the

---

505 James Madison. Federalist Papers. essay no. 10
506 Ibid
507 Ibid., essay no. 34

control and violence of Factions," by which he appears to have meant political parties and which he regarded as the greatest danger to popular government. He also indicated that the many causes in the formation of Factions is what he called "human passions," a nod in the direction of the views of David Hume.

In *Federalist* essay number thirty-seven, Mr. Madison returned to this same idea of the evidence from human history. He related:

> The history of almost all great councils and consultations held among mankind for reconciling discordant opinions, assuaging their mutual jealousies and adjusting their respective interests, is a history of factions, contentions, and disappointments, and may be classed among the most dark and degrading pictures which display the infirmities and depravities of the human character.[508]

Clearly, Mr. Madison is throwing his vote into the Thomas Hobbes Camp with respect to the issues of basic human nature. He seems to be taking the same view when he wrote a famous passage in *Federalist Papers*, essay number fifty-one:

> If men were angels, no government would be necessary. If angels were to govern men, neither external nor internal controls on government would be necessary.[509]

By this we may assume that Mr. Madison meant that Angels, since they do not have physical bodies do not suffer from the same passions as human beings. And since their nature is thought to be good, if people were Angels the human race would operate very differently than it does now.

In another section of essay 51, Mr. Madison explained, "Ambition must be made to counteract ambition. Ambition is actually one thing that makes the Constitution work, and there would appear to be no shortage of it in politics."[510] The fourth President also wrote in essay

---

508 Ibid., essay no. 37
509 Ibid., essay no. 51
510 Ibid

51, "It may be a reflection of human nature that such devices should be necessary to control the abuses of human government. But what is the Government itself but the greatest of all reflection of human nature?"[511] And what is it about that human nature that Mr. Madison finds so significant? It is the brutishness and nastiness written about by Thomas Hobbes in his *Leviathan*.

President James Madison realized that human beings need governance due to their sinful nature. At the same time, however, we must remember that the elite politicians are of the same human nature as the rest of us.

In *Federalist Papers* essay number seventy-five, Mr. Madison again turns his attention to the issue of human nature and again he spoke of it by referring to the extensive evidence from human history about the matter. The fourth President observed:

> The history of human conduct does not warrant the exulted opinion of human virtue which would make it wise in a nation to commit to treaty-making... to the sole disposal of a... President...[512]

Again, Mr. Madison appears to side with Augustine, Aquinas, and Thomas Hobbes on the question of basic human nature, and he seems to castigate some for the "exulted opinion that some have of human virtue."[513]

Although Alexander Hamilton appears to have agreed with James Madison's pessimistic view on human nature, but Thomas Jefferson did not. The third President took the view that the nature of man is generally good. Like him, John Locke and Jean Jacques Rousseau

recognized the "dignity of human nature," whereas, Thomas Hobbes, Alexander Hamilton and, James Madison for that matter, distrusted it.

In essay number sixty-two of the *Federalist Papers*, Mr. Madison suggested that human happiness of the people is the common goal

---

511   Ibid
512   Ibid., essay no. 75
513   Ibid

of a modern society and another aim, like in Plato's *Republic*, is the perfectibility of those people. Mr. Madison, however, finds a fallacy in the idea of human perfectibility and uses experiential knowledge as evidence that human nature is indeed flawed. Thus, again we have another example of where the fourth President agreed with the more pessimistic view of human nature like that of Thomas Hobbes, as well as Alexander Hamilton's view in his essays of the *Federalist Papers,* like essay number six, for example.

Finally, we see another hint of James Madison's view on human nature in his *Federalist Papers* essay number fifty-five. In that essay, in the context of speaking about passions and reason, and we should think with Plato's understanding of the Soul in his mind, the great American statesman observed:

> In all the numerous assemblies, of whatever characters it composed, passion never fails to wrest the scepter from reason. Had every Athenian citizen been a Socrates every assembly would have been a mob.[514]

Clearly, Mr. Madison had in mind here the Appetitive function of the soul in Plato's view. But he also have had in mind the role that David Hume thought that the passions play in human behavior. In either case, one of the major causes of human factions, Mr. Madison believed, is the human passions.

Mr. Madison also spoke here of what reason should control the soul in Plato's view and that any society ruled by one's passions, or the Appetitive part of the soul, could easily morph into a mob. And this is chiefly because the main problem of a Democracy, as we shall see in the next Section of Chapter Eight, is what the fourth President of the United States called "Factions.

This brings us to the Third Section of this Chapter Eight in which we will explore what James Madison believed and wrote about Democracy. As we shall see, his views on this matter are intricately related to his understanding of human nature, as well as the idea of Factions being ruled by human passions.

---

514   Ibid., essay no. 55

James Madison on Democracy

One of the most interesting aspects of the founding of the United States is that the word "democracy" is not referred to in either the Declaration of Independence or the U.S. Constitution. How can that be? Our Government is a Democracy, is it not? One of the reasons for this fact is that some of the Founding Fathers actually feared democratic rule. James Madison expressed this attitude in his *Federalist Papers* number ten, where he wrote, "…instability, injustice, and confusion… have in truth been the moral disease under which popular governments everywhere have perished."[515]

The English word "Democracy" comes from two Greek classical terms, *demos*, or 'people," and *kratia*, or "power" or "authority." Thus it means the 'power' or 'authority' is in the people. The notion of a Democracy has evolved over time from the Ancient Greek city-states to the 18th Century Democracy of the United States.

Historically, Democracies and Republics have been rare. Those who have favored the latter have generally suggested that a Republic should remain small, but if it became larger, it should have checks and balances to control the different parts of the Government.

James Madison was very clear throughout his political life that he favored a Federalist form of Government. A Federalist structure calls for a balancing and a protection of both the national and state spheres and, indeed Madison's career reflected a concern about both sides of Federalism—the national dignity and the states' competence. Depending on the issue at the moment, the fourth President would direct his attention to the side needed to bring the system back into balance.

Thus, Mr. Madison's nationalism is evident in his proposal for the Constitution, spurred by his perception of the weaknesses of the Articles of Confederation. But the great statesman was equally concerned about the curbing the possibility of the excessive influence of political power. This was a particular concern that Mr. Madison voiced in his authorship of the Virginia Resolve in 1799.[516]

---

515 Ibid., essay no. 10
516 Ibid

In more modern times, the application of these Federalist ideas of Mr. Madison ought to be the Supreme Court's willingness to police Congress's use of power delegated to it under Article 1 of the U.S. Constitution. And secondly, the Supreme Court's acting as an arbiter of the Federalism—a function of what Mr. Madison called the "balance wheel" of the Federal system.[517]

One of the most peculiar things to learn about Founding Father, James Madison, is his views on the idea of Democracy. The great statesman preferred a republican government over the idea of a democracy. The major reason for this preference had to do with what Mr. Madison called political "Factions." What Mr. Madison meant by a "Faction" was the possibility that popular sovereignty—the will of the people and self-government could easily be changed with the formation of a Faction that could result in a majority of the people.

James Madison referred to this situation as what he called the "Tyranny of the majority." Mr. Madison wrote, "The influence of factious leaders may kindle a flame within their particular states but will be unable to spread a general conflagration through the other states. Mr. Madison voiced his 'special concern,' as he put it in his essay number ten of the *Federalist Papers*. There the great statesman reflected:

> I have a need to break and control the violence of factions. Measures are too often decided not according to the rules of justice and the rights of the minor party, but by the superior force of an interested and overbearing majority."[518]

The fourth President added, "The principal task of modern legislation, therefore, is the regulation of the various and conflicting interests."[519] Mr. Madison tended to dislike both the ideas of political Factions and political parties. In the 20th and 21st Centuries parties actually have served to dilute factions and crass self-interests. Yet, the Supreme Court has contributed to the decline of political parties, for

---

517 Article 1 of U.S. Constitution
518 James Madison. Federalist Papers. essay no. 10
519 Ibid

example, in its ruling against patronage.[520]

It is clear, however, that James Madison—both before, during, and after his presidency— was decidedly against the idea of Factions, while being in favor of a Federalist form for the national Government.

Mr. Madison defined the idea of a Faction in *Federalist* ten, where he worried that a Faction might be an impetuous mob ruled by its passions. He called a Faction, "A group united and actuated by some common impulse of passion, or of interests adverse to the rights of other citizens, or to the permanent and aggregate interests of the community."[521] "Factions arise," James Madison believed, 'when public opinion forms and spreads quickly."[522] But Factions may dissolve if the public is given time and space to consider long-term interests rather than short-term gratification.[523]

To prevent Factions from distorting public policy and threatening liberty, James Madison resolve to exclude the people from a direct role in Government. Mr. Madison railed against "A pure democracy 'by which I mean a society consisting of a small number of citizens who assemble and administer the Government."[524] In other words, the great American statesman was against the idea of the modern sense of Democracy with one man and one vote; he was in

favor of a Federalist form of Government, and against the idea of what he referred to as political "Factions."[525]

In more modern times, in late 20th and 21st Century America, many members of Congress have allowed themselves to be caught up on Factions, and they seem more interested in advancing their Faction's goals than working towards the good of the entire nation. But unlike the Factions that Mr. Madison described in *Federalist* ten, today's Factions are not "tyrannical majorities." Rather, they are tyrannical minorities who shout with voices louder than their numbers would suggest.

---

520 Ibid
521 Ibid
522 Ibid
523 Ibid
524 Ibid
525 Ibid

Still, these modern-times Factions wield political power and frequently use that power to advance what is often very narrow and self-centered crusades. What is worse, these modern Factions are assisted by politicians who are eager to create divisions by engaging in what has come to be called "Identity Politics."

One might ask, of course, if it is naïve to ask about what has happened to James Madison's concern about the dangers of political Factions? There has always been passionate participation in government throughout history. But our ideals should provide a target that we should strive for. The modern, political moment is unique in that our Constitutional form of Government is itself under attack. The constraints of the Constitution are often seen as barriers to the policies of Factions rather than the "bulwark against Tyranny" that Mr. Madison envisioned.[526]

James Madison called on Congressional Representatives to "refine and enlarge" the views of their constituents so that "the public voice… will be more consonant with the public good."[527] Certainly, we wish that more of today's politicians would do just that.

In his analysis of Factions in the *Federalist Papers*, Mr. Madison also wrote about an analogy about Liberty and Factions. He wrote, "Liberty is to a Faction what air is to fire, an aliment without which it instantly expires."[528] Mr. Madison added:

> But it could not be less folly to abolish liberty, which is essential to political life, because it nourishes Faction than it would be to wish annihilation of the air, which is essential to animal life, because it imparts to fire its destructive agency.[529]

In other words, for Mr. Madison there could be no national Union if there was no liberty. The fourth President was very skeptical about political Factions and what he saw as the 'dangers" of them.

---

526 Ibid
527 Ibid
528 Ibid
529 Ibid

Thus, our short answer as to why the fourth President of the United States, James Madison, was against the idea of Democracy was the danger that he saw that we related to his notion of Factions that tend to be ruled by the Passions rather than by Reason.

This brings us to the Fourth and Final Section of Chapter Eight of this Study on James Madison's Religion. In the next Section we will show how Mr. Madison's views on the two topics of this Chapter—human nature and democracy, came together in the mind of the fourth President of the United States.

Madison, Human Nature, and Democracy

In many ways, James Madison was a true son of the Enlightenment. He proclaimed in *Federalist Papers* essay number ten that, "The first act of Government is the protection of human faculties."[530] In his *Memorial and Remonstrance* of 1784, Mr. Madison declared that, "The opinions of men, depending only on the evidence, contemplated by their own minds, cannot follow the dictates of other men."[531]

Mr. Madison's theory of politics was securely anchored in the concepts of natural rights. He espoused notions of classical liberties, and chief among them were the Liberty to Conscience and the Freedom of expression.

In so far as the constitutional language of the First Amendment guarantees freedom of speech and freedom of the press, 18th and 19th Century cases owe much to the language of James Madison's political career. Current cases about first amendment rights, however, go well beyond Mr. Madison's views.

Today's individual liberty cases owe as much to John Stuart Mill and his political theories than to Mr. Madison. The traditional notion or rights has been expanded to reach into many, non-political contexts. Self-expression as a value, for example, has become more important than Civic pride and other Civic Virtues.

The idea from his political philosophy that makes John Stuart Mill one of the foundations of modern Liberty is what he calls the "Principle

---

530 Ibid

531 James Madison. Memorial and Remonstrance [1784.]

of Harm," that one's right to be free only extend as far as the nose of the next man.

We also see the influence of John Stuart Mill's views in new judicial opinions that have established new 'privacy" and "autonomy" rights. James Madison obviously would not have agreed with the Supreme Court opinion of *Griswold v. Connecticut*, where the Court found that citizens have a "privacy" right to use contraceptives.[532] Similarly, in the Court's *Roe V. Wade* decision held that due process protects a woman's right to have an abortion.[533]

These modern applications of the concept of rights may clash with the state's interest in enforcing morals in the community and thus chart ground more familiar to 20th and 21st Century notions about the individual and of the state than to those of the Founders like Mr. Madison.

Still, in examining these new "rights" the specter of basic human nature can still be seen in the background. One of the reasons that the Founders put in check and balances in the American political system is that they understood the view of human nature of Thomas Hobbes, Alexander Hamilton, and James Madison was most likely the proper view. In Saint Augustine's view, the Fall, and its subsequent Original Sin Theory, has resulted in the human's sinful tendency to abuse power.

This was articulated by Lord Acton who was famously quoted by Winston Churchill, "Democracy is the worst of all governments, except for all those others that have been tried."[534] Mr. Acton also observed on the same occasion that, "Power corrupts, but absolute power corrupts absolutely."[535] The more power placed in the hands of an individual, a ruling elite, or even a large central government, the greater the danger of certain kinds of corruption. Government is necessary to uphold the Rule of Law. Yet the more concentrated power that is given to our government, the greater becomes the danger of abuse.

---

532 Griswold v. Connecticut. 381. U.S. 479. [1965.]

533 Roe v Wade. 110 U.S. 113. [1973.]

534 Lord Acton quoted by Winston Churchill. In Gary Galles. "Lord Acton on Liberty and Government." Mises Daily Articles. November 5, 2002

535 Ibid

James Madison believed a limited Government, with a set of checks and balances, is best equipped to handle both the sinful nature of human beings, both of those in government as well as the people they serve.

The fourth President of the United States worried about the possibility of a "Tyranny of the Majority," who might rule by their passions. Now, the idea of Identity Politics is again slowly beginning to form a very new, 'Tyranny of the Majority,' one that President James Madison would not have approved.

In the 13th Century, Thomas Aquinas came to a conclusion similar to Mr. Madison's about the difficulties of human nature and just government. In his book, *On Kingship*, the Italian philosopher argued that the best government would be a Monarchy, provided that the King was a good and just man.[536]

Thomas also reminded us, however, that since the King is human, he also suffers from the same *Peccatum originale*, or Original sin, which can be found in his subjects. Ultimately, both Thomas Aquinas and James Madison realized that no notion of how a government might be constructed should be considered, unless one first also understands the human nature of the leaders and the people be considered first.

In other words, if human beings are basically flawed, as Aquinas and Mr. Madison both believed, then any form of Government would be constructed by human beings with that same nature.

In his *Satires*, the Roman poet Juvenal wondered: *"Quis custodiet Ipsos custodes?"* Or in English translation he asked, 'Who watches the watchers?'"[537] This is a very good question, especially when the Watchers come forth with some big plan ideology, a few henchmen, and a taste for utopian reform.

Alexander Hamilton and James Madison were not the only Founding Fathers that had a pessimistic view of human nature. As a young man in 1763, President John Adams wrote a brief essay entitled, "All men Would be Tyrants if They Could."[538] This essay was never published, but Adams

---

536 Thomas Aquinas. On Kingship. (New York: Hyperion, 1979.)
537 Juvenal. Satire. (New York; penguin Books, 1999.)
538 John Adams. "All Men Would be Tyrants if They Could." [1763; revised

apparently revisited it in 1807 to endorse the essay's conclusion that, "All simple (unmixed) forms of government, including pure democracy, as well as all moral virtues, all intellectual abilities and all powers of wealth, art, and science are no proof against the selfish desire that rage in the hearts of men and issue in cruel and tyrannical Government."[539]

It would appear from lines like 'desire that rage in the hearts' that, as the second President wrote, "All men would be tyrants if they could." In the same essay, Mr. Adams again made his views on human nature very clear when he wrote:

> It means, in my opinion, no more than this plain and simple observations about human nature, which every Man, who has ever read a treatise on Morality, or conversed with the World...must have often made, vis. That selfish Passions are stronger than the Social, and that the former would prevail over the latter in any Man, left to the natural Emotions of his own mind, unrestrained and unchecked by other Power extrinsic to himself.[540]

President Adams appears to have been aware of the views on human Nature of Hobbes, Locke, and Rousseau, but he also gave special credence to the views of Greek historian, Thucydides. In fact, in his Preface to Mr. Adams' *Defense of the Constitution of the United States*, the second President related about Thucydides:

> It is impossible to read in Thucydides his account of the factions and confusions throughout all of Greece, which were introduced by this want of equilibrium without horror.[541]

Mr. Adams then goes on to give a paraphrase of Thucydides' narrative of the Battle and Siege of Coryra in 373 BCE, in which Adams

---

in 1807.]

539 Ibid., p. 25

540 Ibid

541 John Adams. Defense of the Constitution of the United States. (Washington: Liberty Lamp Books, 2015.) p. 27

suggests that death and violence raged in ways that could "only be natural."[542] Thus, we should add the name of President John Adams to our list of American Founding Fathers that had, like Thomas Hobbes, Augustine, and Aquinas, a pessimistic view of human nature.

This brings us to the Major Conclusions of this Chapter Eight, followed directly by the Notes of the same. The subject-matter of Chapter Nine of this Study on James Madison's Religion is what the fourth President of the United States believed, did, and wrote about Religious traditions other than his own Anglican-Episcopal Church background.

Conclusions to Chapter Eight

In the Introduction to Chapter Eight on James Madison on Human Nature and Democracy, we have suggested that the Chapter will unfold in four major Sections. The first of these was an exploration of the many views on human nature among many 17th and 18th Century philosophers in Europe.

Among the figures we have identified and discussed in this Fist Section of Chapter Eight were those of Thomas Hobbes, Jean-Jacques Rousseau, John Locke, and Scottish philosopher, David Hume. Hobbes thought humans are basically flawed, Rousseau that they are basically good and become evil by forming societies. John Locke took a middle of the road view on basic human nature but he based it on the ideas of Reason and Self-Interests.

The view of David Hume on huma nature, as we also have shown in the First Section of Chapter Eight, was mostly a reaction to the views of Hobbes, Rousseau and particularly John Locke. Hume believed that human passions were must more fundamental that the idea of Reason. In fact, he thought that reason was much less basic than passion.

The central focus of the Second Section of Chapter Eight of this Study on James Madison's Religion has been what the fourth President believed and has written about the phenomenon of human nature. The chief evidence for discerning the views of James Madison on the issue at hand was five of the essays in the *Federalist Papers*, one, number six,

---

542 Ibid

written by Alexander Hamilton and four [10, 34, 37, and 55] written by James Madison.

From this evidence in the *Federalist Papers*, we have concluded that both Mr. Hamilton and James Madison, like Augustine, Thomas Aquinas, and Thomas Hobbes, believed that human nature is flawed,

In the Third Section of Chapter Eight, we have shifted the focus to speak of what Mr. Madison believed and wrote about Democracy. In that Section, as we have shown, he was against the idea, chiefly because of what he saw as the "dangers of Factions." For Madison, a Faction can be formed by the melding together of the passions of men. For him, it is what is at the root of a mob.

The danger of a Faction, at least in the mind of Mr. Madison was that if enough people came together to form a Faction, it could well produce what he called a 'Tyranny of the Majority.'[543]

We went on in Section Three of Chapter Eight to discuss the observations that James Madison made on Factions in his essay number ten of the *Federalist Papers*, where he related that a Faction, "is a group united and actuated by some common impulse of passion."[544]

We also have pointed out that in the modern American two party system, we have seen that system devolve into nothing more than what James Madison referred to as two "Factions."

We also have shown in the Third Section of Chapter Eight that Mr. Madison believed that "Liberty is to a Faction what air is to a fire."[545] And the impetus for those Factions is human passions.

In the Fourth and Final Section of Chapter Eight, we have attempted to show what the fourth President of the United States, James Madison, believed was the relationship of human nature to the practice of Democracy. In that Fourth Section we have spoken of the fact that both Mr. Hamilton and Mr. Madison had the more pessimistic understanding of human nature, like Hobbes, and that must be kept in mind in the process of forming a Government.

---

543 James Madison. Federalist Papers. essay no. 10
544 Ibid
545 Adams. Defense

We also have indicated in Section Four of Chapter Eight that the second President of the United States, John Adams, in an essay entitled, "All Men Would be Tyrants if Thy Could," also held a view on human nature that comes close to the Hobbesian perspective.[546] Mr. Adams also set forth the same view on human nature in the introduction of his 1807, *Defense of the Constitution of the United States*, in which he put forth the idea that Greek historian, Thucydides, also held a pessimistic understanding of basic human nature.[547]

Indeed, Mr. Adams gives a short paraphrase of Thucydides' account of the Battle or Siege of Coryra in 373 BCE, where the "rage and violence" could only have been "natural."[548] Thus, as we have shown, we added the names of John Adams and Thucydides to our list of thinkers who had a Hobbesian understanding of human nature.

Other of our Founding Fathers, as well, commented on the problem of basic human nature. Alexander Hamilton, as we have shown earlier in this Chapter Eight, made remarks upon the "folly and wickedness of mankind," and he declared that we should approach human nature as it is without flattering its virtues nor exaggerating its vices.[549] Consequently, Mr. Hamilton thought that, "Men are ambitious, vindictive, and rapacious."[550]

Mr. Hamilton's pessimistic view of human nature was also shared by John Jay, the third author of the *Federalist Papers*. In a letter to Mr. Jay, from August 15, 1786, George Washington told the Judge, "We must take human nature as we find it, perfection falls not to the share of mortals."[551] Given the letters between these two Founding Fathers. Mr. Jay clearly shared the pessimistic view as well.[552]

In his "Newburgh Address," however, given on March 15, 1783, George Washington suggested the loftiness that might be attained by humans when he wrote:

---

546 Ibid
547 Ibid
548 Ibid
549 Alexander Hamilton. Federalist Papers. essay no. 6
550 Ibid
551 George Washington to John Jay. August 15, 1786
552 Ibid

And you will, by the dignity of your Conduct, afford occasion for Posterity to say, when speaking of the glorious example you have exhibited to Mankind, had this day been wanting, the World had never seen the last stage of perfection to which human nature is capable of attaining.[553]

Even Benjamin Franklin, in his 1771 *Autobiography*, referred to the Hobbesian view on human nature where he wrote:

In reality there is perhaps no one of our natural Passions so hard to subdue than Pride. Disguise it, struggle with it, beat it down, stifle it, mortify it as much as one Pleases, it is still alive and will now and then peek out and show itself.[554]

The conclusion of this discussion of the Founding Fathers on basic Human Nature should be clear. George Washington, John Adams, James Madison, Benjamin Franklin, Alexander Hamilton, and John Jay, among many others, were convinced that the Hobbesian account of human nature was the proper one.

This brings us to the Notes of this Chapter Eight, followed by Chapter Nine. The content of Chapter Nine will be what the fourth President of the United States believed and wrote about Religions other than his own Episcopal faith in Orange County, Virginia. Among the other Faiths we shall discuss are the Baptists, the Presbyterians, his relations with Judaism and Catholicism. And we will also answer the question in Chapter Nine, "Was James Madison a Deist?"[555] Our provisional answer to that question, as we shall see in Chapter Nine, is a resounding No!

---

553 George Washington. "Newburgh Address." March 15, 1783

554 Benjamin Franklin. Autobiography. (New York: Norton, 2012.), p. 114

555 As we shall see, James Madison believed that God acted in history by answering prayers and by performing miracles. So the short answer to this question is, "James Madison could not have been a Deist

Chapter Nine:
James Madison on Other Religions

I will insist that the Hebrews have done more to civilize men than any other nation. If I were an atheist and believed in blind and eternal Fate, I would still believe that Fate had ordained the Jews to be the most essential instrument in civilizing nations.

—President John Adams. Letters.

And thus we should be recognizing the religious rights of the Mohamedan, the Jew, and the pagan.

—Thomas Jefferson. Virginia Bill for Religious Toleration.

It is impossible that the man of pious reflection, not to perceive in it [the Constitution] a finger of that Almighty Hand, which has been so frequently and signally extended to our relief in the critical stages of the Revolution.

—James Madison. Federalist Papers.

Introduction

The purpose of the Ninth Chapter of this Study on James Madison's Religion is to review what the fourth President of the United States believed or wrote about religions other than his own Anglican-Episcopal faith in which he was raised in Orange County, Virginia.

Already in this Study we have written much about what Mr. Madison believed about certain Baptist preachers arrested in Virginia and the influences on his religious views from Presbyterians like his teachers Donald Robertson and President John Witherspoon of the College of New Jersey.

To our general theme of James Madison on Comparative Religions, if you will, we will divide Chapter Nine into the following parts:

1. James Madison and Deism.
2. Madison and the Baptists.
3. Madison and the Presbyterians.
4. Madison and Judaism.
5. Madison and the Roman Catholics.
6. Madison on Islam.

James Madison and Deism

Deism was a philosophical movement that arose in Europe and America in the late 17th and 18th Century. The major belief of the Deists were that God created the world, and the rules by which it works, and then allowed it to operate on its own. In this sense, the Deists believed in a *Deus Absconditis*, or a "God Who Absconds; or "Goes away."[556]

Because of the new Scientific Age and the discoveries of thinkers like Sir Isaac Newton, the Deist believed in an ordered Universe constructed by a disengaged God who appears to care little about His creation. In this sense, the Deist believed that God created the Universe in a grand Design and God was the Grand Designer.[557]

Many of the American Founding Fathers have been associated with the philosophy of Deism, including Benjamin Franklin, Thomas Jefferson, and even James Madison by some scholars. The only Founding Father that appears to have admitted to a faith in Deism

---

556 The expression, Deus Absconditis was first used in Europe by Thomas Aquinas in his Summa Theologica

557 For more on Deism in general, See: Beth Houston. Deism. (New York: kindle Editions, 2013.)

was Thomas Paine who published his famous defense of Deism in his *Age of Reason*.[558]

Thomas Paine was born in England and lived only twenty of his seventy-two years in America. The *Age of Reason* was written and first published in Europe. Although it sold reasonably well in the United States, America's civil leaders were almost uniformly negative about the book.[559] Samuel Adams denounced the book;[560] John Adams, John Witherspoon, William Paterson, and John Jay also criticized Paine's text.[561] Benjamin Rush referred to Thomas Paine's book as "absurd and impious."[562] American Catholic Founding Father, Charles Carroll, condemned the *Age of Reason* as a 'blasphemous writing against the Christian Religion.'"[563]

Similar evaluations of Thomas Paine's *Age of Reason* can be found in Connecticut Judge, Zephaniah Swift who wrote, "We cannot sufficiently reprobate the beliefs of Thomas Paine in his attack on Christianity."[564] One of Mr. Madison's mentors, Elias Boudinot, and Patrick Henry, as well, went so far as to write book-length rebuttals of Paine's tract.[565]

When Thomas Paine returned to America from Europe, he immediately became vilified. Indeed, with the exception of Thomas Jefferson and a few others, Mr. Paine was abandoned by all of his old friends. When Paine passed away in 1809, he was buried on his farm because the Quakers refused to have him interred in their Church burial grounds. Only six mourners came to his funeral.[566]

Some of the American Founding Fathers, like Franklin and Jefferson, for examples, may have secretly approved of the *Age of*

---

558 Thomas Paine. Age of Reason. In Collected Writings. (New York; Must Have Books, 2019.)
559 Ibid
560 Ketcham, p. 68
561 Ibid
562 Ibid
563 Ibid., p. 69
564 Ibid., p. 70
565 Ibid
566 Ibid., p. 71

Reason. Nevertheless, if some of the elite were willing to embrace Deism, it was clear that the American public was not. But what about American statesman, James Madison? What did he think about the Philosophy of Deism?

The best evidence for answering our question can be found in some observations of James Madison on God that we saw back in Chapter Two. That evidence came directly from the essay of the *Federalist Papers* written by James Madison discussed in Chapter Two. In *Federalist* 37, Mr. Madison wrote:

> It is impossible that the man of pious reflection, not to perceive in it [the Constitution] a finger of that Almighty Hand, which has been so frequently and signally extended to our relief in the critical stages of the revolution.[567]

Like many of the other Founding Fathers, Mr. Madison demurred from employing the word "God." But he also suggested in this passage that there was a Divine Mind behind the actions of the American Revolution. The God of which Mr. Madison wrote is one that acts in history, something that would have been anathema to the Deists.

We can also see Mr. Madison's belief in a God Who acts in history in another reference in *Federalist* thirty-seven, as well as in three mentions of "Providence" in essay number two of the *Federalist Papers*. In the first reference, Mr. Madison said that "God favored America with a variety of soils and innumerable streams."[568] He added that, "God gave no connected nation to one united people."[569] And in the third reference in *Federalist* essay two, Mr. Madison suggested that this inheritance from God appears to have been designed, contrary to the ideas of Deism.[570]

In *Federalist* 20, Mr. Madison suggests that Americans should praise and have gratitude for the "auspicious amity distinguishing

---

567 James Madison. Federalist Papers. essay no. 37
568 Ibid., essay no. 2
569 Ibid
570 Ibid

political counsels rise to Heaven."[571] In essay 44, Mr. Madison sets forth the idea that there must be safeguards against the misuse of religion, in that no religious test shall be required as a qualification to any "office or public trust, under the United States."[572]

In essay number 51, Mr. Madison related that, "In a free Government, the security for Civil Rights must be the same as that for Religious Rights."[573] And in essay 57 of the *Federalist Papers*, James Madison briefly stated that no qualification related to 'wealth, birth, religious faith, or civil profession is permitted to fetter the judgments or disappoint the inclinations of the people.'[574]

The conclusion of this analysis of James Madison's views on God in the *Federalist Papers* should be clear. The fourth President of the United States was no Deist. In his *Memorial and Remonstrance*, as well, Mr. Madison observed that the rights of individual Conscience and the duties that men owe first to the "Governor of the Universe," before any other human Government.[575] This is further evidence that James Madison believed in a God that acted in history, a repudiation, therefore, of the doctrines of Deism.

There are, however, some scholars who have been convinced that President James Madison was, in fact, a Deist. Irving Brant, for example, pronounced Mr. Madison to be a Deist.[576] James Smylie, who was a Presbyterian Minister and scholar, in a book he published in 1966, claimed that "Madison was nothing less than a "lay theologian," perhaps another nod in the direction of Deism.[577] This conclusion of this analysis should be clear—James Madison was no Deist. For Mr. Madison God acts in history and this is contrary to the philosophy of Deism.

---

571 Ibid., essay no. 20

572 Ibid

573 Ibid., essay no. 51

574 Ibid., essay no. 57

575 James Madison. Memorial and Remonstrance

576 Irving Brandt. Bill of Rights: Origins and Meaning. (New York: New American Library, 1965.), p. 67

577 James Smylie. Brief History of the Presbyterians. (Geneva: Geneva Press, 1996.), p. 100

This brings us to the Second Section of Chapter Nine and an examination of what James Madison thought about the Baptists in America, the subject-matter of the next Section of Chapter Nine.

James Madison on the Baptists

Earlier in this Study on James Madison's Religion we have indicated that sometime between 1772 and 1775, Mr. Madison had heard about a number of Baptist Ministers who were imprisoned for preaching and publishing their religious views in Culpepper County of Virginia.

We also have shown that Mr. Madison's indignation over this matter is evident in a letter to his friend, William Bradford, in which the great, American statesman wrote:

> The diabolical Hell conceived principle of persecution rages among some and to their eternal infamy, the Clergy can furnish their Quota of Imps for such business. This vexes me the most of anything whatever. There are at this time in the adjacent County not less than 5 or 6 well-meaning men in close [jail] for publishing their religious Sentiments which in the main are very orthodox.[578]

It has been suggested that, later in life, Mr. Madison's memory of these men was very much on his mind when a decade later, he wrote the text that has guided so much of America's history. Mr. Madison wrote:

> Congress shall make no law respecting an establishment of Religion or prohibiting the free exercise thereof; or abridging the freedom of speech, or of the press; or of the right of the people peaceably to assemble, and to petition the government for a redress of grievances.[579]

We also have indicated earlier in this Study of James Madison's Religion that Baptist leader, John Leland, was a supporter of Mr. Madison and the Bill of Rights after the great statesman visited Mr. Leland on

---

578 James Madison to William Bradford. January 24, 1774
579 James Madison to Benjamin Rush. September 23, 1800

his Virginia family farm and they thrashed out their differences about the Bill of Rights, eventually coming to a compromise.[580]

In many of Mr. Leland's writing we also can see his affinity to several of the political principles of James Madison. For example, the idea that the "Right of Conscience" is an Inalienable right. The two Virginians also agreed on the moral question of Slavery, was we shall see in Chapter Ten of this Study. The Baptist, John Leland also agreed with Mr. Madison on the idea that humans first have a duty toward God for his Right to Conscience before any duties to the State or national authority.[581]

The two Virginians also shared their views on Religious Toleration and the idea that no faith should be 'preeminent above the rest...whereas all should be equally free, Jews, Turks, Pagans, and Christians," as the Rev. Leland observed in his *A Chronicle of My Time in Virginia*.[582]

In short, our conclusion about James Madison and the Baptists should be obvious. From his early adulthood the fourth President of the United States supported a half a dozen Baptist preachers in Jail in Culpepper Virginia, as was indicated in a letter to his friend William Bradford. Mr. Madison also formed an alliance of sorts with Baptists leaders and chief among them was the Rev. John Leland.

This brings us to the Third Section of Chapter Nine in which we will review what great American statesman, James Madison believed and wrote about the Presbyterian Faith, the next subject matter to be considered in this Chapter Nine.

James Madison and the Presbyterians

In the Fall of 1763, at the age of twelve, James Madison began five years of study at the Robertson Virginia boarding school. His teacher was Presbyterian, Donald Robertson who had emigrated to America from his homeland in Scotland. As we have indicated in Chapter One

---

580 Mr. Madison visited Rev. Leland's farm on January 5, 1788 on the latter's farm in Orange County, Virginia

581 Ibid

582 John Leland. A Chronicle of My Time in Virginia. In The Writings of the Elder John Leland. (New York: Kindle Editions, 2013.) p. 59

of this Study, Mr. Robertson introduced James Madison to the Classical languages of Greek and Latin, as well as the modern tongues of French and Italian.

Donald Robertson also made the soon-to-be great American statesman familiar with the Bible and most likely with a twist from the Church of Scotland's Westminster Confession, a 1647 document that sketched out the beliefs of the Westminster Divines who had assembled to develop the Confession of the beliefs of Church of Scotland, or the Presbyterian Church in America.

Donald Robertson also introduced the adolescent James Madison to Greek and Roman philosophers and historians, as well as more Contemporary political thinkers like Englishman, John Locke and French nobleman and philosopher, the Baron Montesquieu. Later in life, as we have indicated earlier in this Study, Mr. Madison observed about Mr. Robertson, "All that I have
been in life I owe largely to Mr. Robertson."[583]

At the age of seventeen, James Madison was finished with his lessons from Presbyterian, Donald Robertson and the statesman and his father eschewed the College of William and Mary, the normal designation for college study among the Virginia Colony's elite. Thomas Jefferson, for example, attended William and Mary College.

James Madison was sent instead to study under the new President of the College of New Jersey, John Witherspoon and his faculty, most of whom were Presbyterians. Mr. Witherspoon had only been President of the College for several months when Mr. Madison began to matriculate there. The College at the time was known for its training of Presbyterian Ministers. Indeed, Donald Robertson had graduated from the College of New Jersey before he began tutoring Mr. Madison.

Earlier Scottish and Irish immigrants had brought Reform Theology and Presbyterianism to the American Colonies in the early 18th Century. The first Presbytery was established in America In Philadelphia in 1706.

Because of his previous study with Mr. Robertson, James Madison enjoyed an advanced status, being given credit essentially for what

---

583 Madison quoted in Ketcham, p. 48

amounted to two years of College. Consequently, Mr. Madison finished his Bachelor of Arts study in only two years. While at the College, James Madison attended Sunday services at the Presbyterian Church on the square and the entire faculty were members of the Presbyterian Faith. Mr. Madison, while in College also attended daily Presbyterian Chapel service, in which President Witherspoon was often the Preacher.

As we have indicated earlier in this Study, in Chapters One and Two, James Madison stayed on at the College of New Jersey for an additional year as a graduate student, the first graduate student of the College. In that year he studied classical Hebrew with President Witherspoon and he became familiar with the several forms of Hebrew poetry we have described in Chapter Two of this Study. This would have effects on Mr. Madison's writing style for many years to come.

In that year in graduate school, Mr. Madison also studied Moral Philosophy with President Witherspoon, and the subsequent effects on the life of the great American statesman from Presbyterian, John Witherspoon cannot be over-estimated. Witherspoon was a deep theological source for the later religious life of James Madison, as was his Presbyterian Faith and his knowledge of the Biblical languages.

Indeed, one of the most important gifts that John Witherspoon gave to James Madison was the abilities to read the Old Testament in the original Hebrew language, as well as the new Testament in its Koine Greek. These were skills afforded to Mr. Madison that he used for the remainder of his life.

This brings us to the Fourth Section of Chapter Nine in which we will discuss what contacts and beliefs the fourth President of the United States, James Madison had with the Jewish people and the Faith of Judaism.

James Madison on Judaism and the Jews

There are many examples among the American Founding Fathers in the second half of the 18th Century that speak of relations with Judaism and the Jews. John Adams, in challenging the Anti-Semitism of French Enlightenment luminaries like Voltaire, argued that "Jews have influenced the affairs of mankind more and happily than any other nation, ancient or modern."⁵⁸⁴ In a letter he wrote in 1809, John Adams related that God had "ordained the Jews to be the most essential instrument for civilizing nations."⁵⁸⁵

In a letter to F.A. Van Der Kemp on February 16, 1809, Mr. Adams wrote:

> I will insist that the Hebrews have done more to civilize men than any other nation. If I were an Atheist and believed in blind eternal fate, I would still believe that Fate had ordained the Jews to be a most essential instrument for civilizing nations. If I were an Atheist of another Sect...I would still have to believe that Chance had ordered the Jews to preserve and to propagate for all mankind the doctrine of a Supreme, Intelligent, Wise, Almighty Sovereign of the Universe which I believe to be the great essential principle of all Morality and consequently of all civilization.⁵⁸⁶

Thomas Jefferson, on the other hand, had ambivalent views on the Jews and Judaism. In an 1803 letter to Dr. Benjamin Rush of Philadelphia, Mr. Jefferson accused the Jews of having a "degrading and injurious" understanding of God that was 'imperfect' and was devoid of 'sound dictates of reason and morality."⁵⁸⁷ Mr. Jefferson added, "The Jews need reformation in an eminent degree."⁵⁸⁸

On the other hand, Mr. Jefferson's advocacy for the civil liberties of Jews in America can be seen all the way back to 1776, when he sponsored a bill before the Virginia Legislature that was ultimately defeated, but would have allowed the "naturalization of "Jews, Catholics, and other Non-Protestants as Virginia citizens."⁵⁸⁹ During the debate on the bill,

---

584 Voltaire. Treatise on Toleration. (New York: Penguin Books, 2017.), p. 17

585 John Adams. The Works of John Adams. Vol. IX, p. 609

586 John Adams to F.A. Van Der Kemp. February 16, 1809. This letter is also in Works, p. 610

587 Thomas Jefferson to Benjamin Rush. April 21, 1803

588 Ibid

589 Thomas Jefferson. "Bill to Naturalize of Jews, Catholics, and Other non-Protestants." [1776.]

Mr. Jefferson quoted from John Locke who wrote, "Neither Pagan, nor Mohamedan, nor Jew ought to be excluded from the Civil Rights of the Commonwealth because of his Religion."[590]

Four decades later, in 1820, Thomas Jefferson wrote to Charleston Rabbi and physician, Dr. Jacob De la Motta telling him that, "Religious freedom is the most effectual anodyne against religious dissension."[591] Mr. Jefferson also told Dr De la Motta that he was delighted to see American Jews assuming full social rights and hoped they soon, "will be seen as taking their seats on the benches of science as preparatory to their doing the same at the Board of Government."[592]

Mr. Jefferson also complained that the King James Version of the Bible should be read in Virginia public schools. The third President was against the idea because, he said, "It would be a cruel addition to the wrongs Jews have historically suffered by "imposing on them a course of theological reading which their Consciences do not permit them to pursue."[593] In a letter to Jewish man, Joseph Marx of Richmond, Mr. Jefferson expressed regret…at seeing a sect of Jews, the parent and basis of all Christendom, be singled out for persecution and oppression."[594] Joseph Marx (1772–1840) immigrated to America from Hanover, Germany in the 1790s. He and his family attended the Beth Shalom Congregation in Richmond, Virginia.[595]

As mentioned above, however, there were some aspects of traditional Judaism that Mr. Jefferson did not agree. He found the Chosen People of the Old Testament to be a 'blood- thirsty race, as cruel and remorseless as the being whom they represented as the family God of Abraham, of Isaac, and of Jacob, and the local God of Israel."[596]

In general, Mr. Jefferson was against the idea of Revelation in any

---

590 Ibid

591 Thomas Jefferson to Jacob de la Motta. September 1, 1820

592 Ibid

593 Thomas Jefferson. The Life and Morals of Jesus of Nazareth. (Washington: Smithsonian Books, originally published in 1819.], p. 18

594 Thomas Jefferson to Joseph Marx. December 8, 1817

595 Joseph Marx emigrated to America in 1794

596 Jefferson. Life and Moral. P. 20

Religion. In a 1787 letter to his nephew he told the boy to be 'skeptical of those facts in the Bible which contradict the laws of Nature.'[597] One example he gave was Joshua ordering the Sun to stand still for several hours. It bothered Mr. Jefferson that he saw the God of the Old Testament to be, "A being of terrific character, cruel, vindictive, capricious, and unjust."[598]

Earlier in this Study of James Madison's Religion, we have indicated that when Mr. Madison was President he received letters from two prominent American Jews who both had dedicated two Synagogues in the United States. These men were Rabbi Jacob de la Motta (1789–1845) and Rabbi Mordecai Manuel Noah (1785–1851.) Rabbi Noah had served as the U.S. Consul in Tunis. He was now dedicating a Synagogue in New York City on April 17, 1818.[599]

The Synagogue dedicated by Dr. de la Motta was being dedicated in his hometown, Savannah, Georgia. Both Rabbis had sent Mr. Madison letters to announce the two Jewish houses of worship. Mr. Madison replied to Dr. De la Motta, responding to his August 7, 1820 correspondence about the Synagogue. The fourth President's letter back to the Rabbi was written in August of 1820. In his response, the great American statesman observed that, "The history of the Jews must forever be interesting. The modern part of it is…so little generally known, that every ray of light on the subject has its value."[600]

James Madison wrote a similar letter to Rabbi Mordecai Noah in announcing the dedication of a Synagogue in New York City. In that correspondence Mr. Madison again expressed his admiration for the history of the Jews and the "central place that Judaism has enjoyed in the development of human civilization."[601]

The fourth President of the United States was also aware of the leadership of other American Jews, like Rabbi Gershom Mendes Seixas who was the head Rabbi of the Shearith Israel Congregation

---

597 Thomas Jefferson to Peter Carr. August 10, 1787
598 Ibid
599 Rabbi Noah served as U.S. Consul in Tunis from 1813 to 1816
600 James Madison to Jacob de la Motta. August 7, 1820
601 James Madison to Mordecai Noah. May 7, 1820

in New York City was also the first American-born Rabbi in America. Rabbi Seixas was the spiritual leader of American Jews during the Revolutionary War and Mr. Madison knew of his work and greatly admired him.[602]

Along with Thomas Jefferson, James Madison also supported the idea that in the state of Virginia, religious liberty extended to Jews, to Muslims, and even to non-believers, if that is what a citizen believes.

This brings us to the Fifth section of this Chapter Nine in which we will discuss what connections can be discerned of James Madison's attitudes and beliefs about Roman Catholics and Catholicism in America.

James Madison and the Catholics

Although the Stuart kings of England were not haters of the Church of Rome, many of their subjects were with the result that Catholics in England were harassed and persecuted throughout the 17th Century. Driven by the idea of "finding a refuge for his Roman Catholic brethren, George Calvert (1580–1632) a lieutenant of King James I, at least until his religion cost him his job, was given a charter from King Charles I in 1632, for the 'territory between Pennsylvania and Virginia, that is, Maryland.

The Maryland Charter offered no guidelines on religion, but it was assumed that Catholics would not be molested in the Colony. After the Glorious Revolution of 1689 in England, the Church of England was legally established in the Colony of Maryland.

The English Declaration of Rights, enacted by Parliament in 1689, had stated:

> The subjects which are Protestants may have arms for their defense suitable to their conditions allowed by law.[603]

This would seem to suggest that Catholics could not own arms in the British colonies. James Madison during the Queen Anne's War

---

602 Gershom Mendes Seixas (1745–1816.) was the first American born rabbi in America

603 Charter of the Territory of Maryland. Between Pennsylvania and Virginia." The English Declaration of Rights. [1689.]

aimed to make sure that the religious restrictions on the right to bear arms, particularly in regard to Catholics, should not be allowed in America.

In a speech to Congress on the Bill of Rights, Mr. Madison specifically condemns the restrictions of Catholics not being permitted to bear arms. Thus the Second Amendment contains none of the limitations or exceptions found in the English statute.[604]

The Queen Anne's War mentioned above was fought between 1702 and 1713. It was the second in a series of French and Indian Wars, involving the Colonial states of Great Britain, France, and Spain. It is also known as the "Third Indian War" and the "Second Intercolonial War in France.[605]

In addition to Mr. Madison's views on the legal rights of Roman Catholics, the fourth President of the United States had a number of Catholic friends. After Mr. Madison proposed the first draft of the First Amendment, Daniel Carroll of Maryland was the only Congressman to support the measure. In a speech to Congress, Mr. Carroll articulated what the general sentiment concerning the right to religious liberty had been.[606] Mr. Madison was very appreciative of Mr. Carroll's support.

Mr. Carroll's cousin, Daniel Carroll, participated in the Constitutional Convention. He was convinced like his good friend James Madison that a strong central government was needed to regulate commerce among the states in dealing with other nations. Following the Convention, Daniel Carroll emersed himself in state and national affairs. He was a key figure in the Maryland State ratification struggle and he debated well-known Anti-Federalist Samuel Chase, defending the side of James Madison.[607]

Some of these Anti-Federalist warned that abolishing religious tests in the Colony would allow "Jews, Catholics, and Quakers—even

---

604 James Madison. Speech to Congress on Bill of Rights. June 8, 1789

605 The 'Queen Anne's War was one of the French and Indian Wars

606 Michael Breidenbach. 'Catholics and the First Amendment." @starting-pointsjournal.com/catholics-and-the-first [amendment/]

607 Ibid

pagans, Deists, and Mahometans to hold federal office, perhaps even to dominate the new national Government."⁶⁰⁸

Many Evangelical, religious leaders took their concerns to George Washington in 1789, objected that that the Constitution failed to acknowledge the 'only true God and his Son, Jesus Christ."⁶⁰⁹ Through his frequent letters to Mr. Jefferson in Paris, Mr. Madison managed to hold together Mr. Jefferson's vision of Religious Liberty and in a later draft of the First Amendment from 1791, we first see the Madison wording:

> Congress shall make no law respecting an establishment of Religion or prohibiting the free exercise thereof.⁶¹⁰

Mr. Madison's views of Catholics can also be seen in another letter to member of the Carroll family, this time John Carroll, the Bishop of Baltimore. The letter in question was written on November 20, 1806. The fourth President was responding to a missive sent to him by the Bishop of Baltimore asking for some religious provisions in regard to the Catholic Church in New Orleans. Mr. Madison told the Bishop:

> But as the case is entirely Ecclesiastical it is deemed most congenial with the scrupulous policy of the Constitution in guarding against a political interference with religious affairs, to decline the explanations which you have thought might enable you to accommodate the better the execution of our trust, to the public advantage.⁶¹¹

In other words, Mr. Madison denies the request of Bishop Carroll about the Catholic Church in New Orleans, chiefly on the President's concern of violating the doctrine of the Separation of Church and State.

As we have suggested earlier in this Chapter, Daniel Carroll, a signer of the Declaration of Independence and a cousin of the Archbishop of Baltimore, attended the Constitutional Convention as a

---

608 Ibid
609 George Washington. "Prayer Proclamation." October 3, 1789
610 James Madison. Draft if First Amendment. [1791.]
611 James Madison to John Carroll. November 20, 1806

Delegate for the state of Maryland in the Summer of 1787. Mr. Carroll strongly supported the plan of Mr. Madison for a strong centralized Government that, among other things, was needed to regulate the commerce between and among the states.

In July of 1788, debates during the North Carolina Ratifying Convention, Delegate Henry Abbot feared that no Christian, religious test to the U.S. Constitution would lead to "Papists, Deists, and Mahometans taking office."[612] North Carolina Delegate David Caldwell wanted a religious test because, "The Christian religion was best calculated, of all religions, to make good members of Society on account of its Morality."[613]

In general, Anti-Federalist throughout the country had three major reservations for not having a religious test in the Constitution. First, it might result in the electing of the "wrong kind of people." The new federal Government might interfere with the rights of the states. And finally, religious liberty in general would not be protected from invasion by the federal Government.[614]

At any rate, James Madison spoke of the nation in 1785, as an "Asylum to the persecuted and oppressed of every Nation and Religion."[615] Presumably, the fourth President was including the rights of Roman Catholics to worship, as well. But deep religious discord—particularly in relation to Catholicism—had been part of America's DNA since the early 17h Century. And James Madison was fully aware of that fact.

This brings us to the Sixth and Final Section of Chapter Nine in which we will describe and discuss what contact James Madison may have had with Muslims and the Islamic Faith. That Section will be followed by the major Conclusions of the Chapter, as well as the Notes of the same.

---

612 Henry Abbott, quoted at North Carolina Ratifying Convention. July 12, 1788

613 David Caldwell, quoted at North Carolina Ratifying Convention. July 12, 1788

614 Author's analysis

615 James Madison. Ketchem, p. 24

James Madison and Islam

Among the many contacts that the fourth President of the United States, James Madison, had with the Islamic Faith in general and certain Muslims in particular, were the views of other American Founding Fathers of the life of the Prophet Muhammad and his followers and a friend of Mr. Madison's named George Bethune English (1787–1828.) We will deal with these two examples of Madison's dealings with Islam in reverse order, as well as a third incident involving James Madison's grandfather, Ambrose Madison.

George Bethune English (1787–1828) was an American diplomat, adventurer, American soldier, and convert to the Islamic Faith. He was born in Cambridge, Massachusetts. His father was a prominent merchant in Boston. English attended Harvard College and then the Harvard Divinity School from which he received his Master of Divinity degree in 1811.[616]

While a divinity student he began to become disillusioned with Christianity and particularly with many doctrines in the New Testament. Among these doctrines were: the Trinity; the Crucifixion; Original Sin; and the narrative of the Atonement. Mr. English so strongly rejected these ideas that he wrote a book called *The Grounds of Christianity Examined*, which led to his dismissal in 1814 from the Church of Christ, the denomination in which he was raised.[617]

In 1815, Mr. English's friend, James Madison was now President of the United States. The Cambridge-born scholar shared with his Virginian friend some of his misgivings about traditional Christian beliefs. Mr. Madison appointed Mr. English to the United States Marine Corps as a Second Lieutenant.[618]

A short time later, Mr. English sailed to the Mediterranean Sea, where he found the opportunity to study Islam while in Egypt. In fact,

---

616 Mr. English received his MDiv. Degree at Harvard in 1811

617 George Bethune English. "The Grounds of Christianity Examined," appears in Edward Everette. The Grounds of Christianity of George English Examined. (New York: Hard Press Publishing, 2013.)

618 The appointment was made in April of 1815 while Mr. Madison was President

he converted to Islam after a brief period of reflection and took the name Mohammad Afendi. He also resigned his commission from the U.S. Marine Corps, renounced Christianity, and he joined the army of Ismail Pasha.[619] Ismail Pasha (1830–1895) was a Viceroy of Egypt under the Ottoman Suzerainty before the British occupation of Egypt in 1882. Ismail Pasha studied in Paris and undertook various diplomatic missions in Europe before becoming Viceroy in 1863.

Meanwhile, George English embarked on a plan to learn Arabic, al-Qur'an, and Shariah Law. George English also revamped Pasha's Artillery and he was appointed as one of the chief Artillery officers. His account of his voyage on the River Nile was published in 1822, under the title, *Narrative of the Expedition to Dongola and Sennaar*.[620] This text was read by George Washington, James Madison, and Thomas Jefferson.[621]

The other contact that James Madison had with the religion of Islam were some observations that many of the other American Founding Fathers had made about the Islamic Faith. Many of these go back to John Locke's 1689 seminal *Letter on Toleration* in which the English philosopher insisted that Muslims and all other faiths that believed in God should be tolerated in England.[622]

Thomas Jefferson, following his philosophical mentor, John Locke, agreed in the importance of "recognizing the religious rights of the Mohamedan, the Jew, and the Pagan."[623] Supporting the view of Mr. Jefferson was his old Virginia ally, Richard Henry Lee who made a motion to Congress on June 7, 1776 that the American Colonies declare independence. "true Freedom," Mr. Lee said that day that America "embraces the Mohamedan and the Gentoo (Hindu), as well as the Christian Religion."[624]

---

619 Mohammad Afendi joined the Army of Ismail Pasha in 1817

620 George B. English. Narrative of an Expedition to Dongola and Sennaar. (New York: Wentworth Press, 2016.)

621 Ibid

622 John Locke. Essay on Toleration. (Oxford: Clarendon, 2006.)

623 Thomas Jefferson on John Locke. [June 20, 1775.]

624 Richard Henry Lee

In New England, Ezra Stiles, the President of Yale College, cited a study that suggested that, "Mohamedan Morals are far superior to those of the Christian."[625] Sometimes even ordinary citizens shared these views on the Islamic Faith. A petition of a group of citizens of Chesterfield County, Virginia—not far from James Madison's farm—on November 14, 1785, that asked that "Jews, Mohamedan, and Christians of every denomination enjoy their religious liberty.[626]

It is not clear if James Madison was aware of this petition in Chesterfield County. What is clear, however, is that the fourth President of the United States, James Madison, as well as many of the other Founding Fathers of this nation, explicitly meant to include Islam and Muslims in their vision of the future of the Republic. Father of American Jurisprudence, Joseph Story, in clarifying the meaning of the First Amendment, wrote:

> The real object of the First Amendment was not a countenance, much less to advance Mahometanism, or Judaism, or Infidelity by prostrating Christianity but to exclude all rivalry among Christian Sects and to prevent any Ecclesiastical Establishment which should give to a hierarchy the exclusive patronage of the National Government.[627]

There is no doubt that in the views of Jefferson, Judge Joseph Story, Ezra Stiles, George English, and, most importantly, James Madison, were all convinced that the religious liberties guaranteed by the U.S. Constitution were to be extended to Muslims in the exercising of their religious rights. James Hutson, in an essay entitled, "The Founding Fathers and Islam,' summed up what he believed about Islam and the finding of the Unites States when he wrote:

It is clear that the Founding Fathers thought about the relationship of Islam to the new nation and were prepared to make a place for it in

---

625 Ezra Stiles

626 James Madison visited the Rev. Joh Leland' farm in Orange County, Virginia November 14, 1785

627 Joseph Story, quoted in James Hutson. 'The Founding Fathers and Islam." Library of Congress Journal. Vol. 61, no 5. [May 2002.]

the Republic…The Founders explicitly included Islam in their vision of the future of the Republic…and would have incorporated it into the fabric of American life.[628]

One final aspect of James Madison's relations to the Islamic Faith has to do with his paternal grandfather, Ambrose Madison who died under mysterious circumstances when three of his Igbo slaves, who may well have been Muslims as well, were convicted of murdering their Master by allegedly poisoning him.

We know that these three slaves—two men and a woman—were all Igbo, but we cannot be sure whether they were also Muslims or not. We do know that with Ambrose's death, James Madison Sr. became the richest landowner in Orange County, Virginia, owning 5,000 acres tended by many slaves. When Madison Sr. married his new wife, Nelly Conway, she brought another dozen slaves to the Madison household. The fourteen year old, Sawney, discussed earlier in this Chapter, was most likely among them.

This brings us to the major Conclusions we have made in this Chapter Nine on James Madison and Other Religions other than his own Episcopal Faith. These Conclusions will be followed by the Notes to Chapter Nine and then onto Chapter Ten. The principal focus in Chapter Ten will be what the fourth President of the United States, James Madison believed and wrote about the phenomenon of Slavery.

Conclusions to Chapter Nine

The central focus of Chapter Nine has been what James Madison, the fourth President of the United States believed, had to say, and wrote about Religions other than the Episcopal Church in which he was raised. To that end, we have divided the Chapter into six Sections. In the first of these, we began the First Section with a short description of what the philosophical movement known as Deism was in the second half of the 18th Century in Europe and America.

In that description, we pointed out that the Deist believed in a God who created the Universe, and the rules by which it runs, and then has very little contact with His Creation. In that sense, we have indicated

---

628 Ibid

that the Deist believed in a *Deus Absconditis*, or a God Who Absconds or 'Goes Away.'"[629]

Next in the first Section of Chapter Nine, we have pointed our several passages in the *Collected Works* of James Madison that seem to imply that the American statesman believed that God causes miracles to occur on earth, as well as the answering of prayers. From these premises we went on to conclude that James Madison could not have been a Deist

In the Second Section of Chapter Nine, we have indicated what James Madison believed and wrote about the American Baptists. The evidence for ascertaining what the fourth President thought of the Baptists, we have turned to the group of six Baptist preachers who had been confined to Jail for the simple act of expressing their theological beliefs.

The other piece of evidence for what James Madison thought of the Baptists was the President's relation with Baptist Preacher, John Leland and the many theological matters about which the two men shared. We also have indicated in the Second Section of Chapter Nine that Mr. Madison and the Rev, Leland disagreed on the U.S. Bill of Rights, though eventually when the former visited the latter's farmhouse in Virginia they worked out a compromise view on the matter.

James Madison and the Presbyterians was the subject-matter of the Third Section of Chapter Nine. In that Section we mostly relied on Mr. Madison's two Presbyterian teachers, Donald Robertson and President John Witherspoon of the College of New Jersey. In that Third Section of Chapter Nine, we gave a list of the many things that these two Scottish teachers gave to the young James Madison, including the study of Ancient languages, such as Greek, Latin, and Classical Hebrew, as well as Greco-Roman history, poets, and philosophers, modern languages, like French and Italian, as well as a number of Enlightenment figures from the 17th and 18th Centuries, like John Locke, David Hume, and French thinker, the Baron Montesquieu.

In the Fourth Section of Chapter Nine our preoccupation was with the dealings that James Madison had with leading Jewish thinkers of his

---

629 The expression, Deus Absconditis was first used in Europe by Thomas Aquinas in his Summa Theologica

time, including Rabbi Mordecai Manuel Noah, Dr. Jacob de la Motta, and a Richmond Jew named Joseph Marx. We also have indicated in that same Section that Mr. Madison was aware of the work of Rabbi Gershom Mendes Seixas, the most famous American Rabbi in Mr. Madison' time.

In the Fifth Section of Chapter Nine we provided an analysis of what contacts James Madison had with the Roman Catholic Church, as well as a number of prominent members of that same Church. Indeed, we have indicated that many of these prominent members of the Roman Church were members of the same family, the Carroll family from Maryland. In fact, we have shown that the fourth President had dealings with Archbishop John Carroll, as well as his cousin, Daniel Carroll, a member of the U.S. Congress who supported Mr. Madison's wording of the first draft of the First Amendment of the U. S. Constitution. Charles Carroll of Carrollton was another prominent member of the Carroll family and Mr. Madison was fully aware of his accomplishments both in Maryland and in national politics, as well.

The Sixth and Final Section of Chapter Nine was centered on what contact the fourth President of the United States, James Madison had with the Religion of Islam and the Muslims who follow that Faith.

We began Section Six of Chapter Nine buy speaking of James Madison's friend, George Bethune English (1787–1828), who changed his name to Mohammed Afendi after he converted to the Islamic Faith from Christianity. As we have indicated Mr. English studied at the Harvard Divinity School and a short time later began to become disillusioned with the Church of Christ in which he had been raised.

As we have indicated, among the Christian ideas that George English had some doubts were the Trinity, the Crucifixion, Original Sin, and the nature and extent of the Atonement. Mr. English so strongly rejected these central Christian theological ideas that he wrote a book called *The Grounds of Christianity Examined*.[630] As we have shown, this led to his dismissal from the Church of Christ in 1814.

---

630 George Bethune English. "The Grounds of Christianity Examined," appears in Edward Everette. The Grounds of Christianity of George English Examined. (New York: Hard Press Publishing, 2013.)

Mr. English became friendly with President James Madison in 1815, when the latter appointed the former to a post in the U.S. Marines, which Mr. English served in the Mediterranean Sea. We also have indicated that after his conversion to Islam in 1815, he began to learn both Arabic and the Turkish languages. In fact, English served in the Artillery of Ismail Pasha, the Viceroy of Egypt under the Ottoman Empire.

We also have shown in Section Six of Chapter Nine of this Study on James Madison's Religion that George English wrote a book called a *Narrative of the Expedition to Dongola and Sennaar*, his account of a voyage on the Nile from Cairo to Nubia and the Sudan.[631]

In the remainder of Section Six of Chapter Nine, we have examined the contacts that many of Mr. Madison's friends—particularly in American Politics—who had some commerce with Islam and or Muslims. Among these political figures were Thomas Jefferson, Richard Henry Lee, Ezra Stiles, the President of Yale College, and Supreme Court Justice, Joseph Story.

We also have shown that when James Madison wrote the drafts of the First Amendment of the U.S. Constitution he clearly had a view that the right of Muslims, or "Mahometans," as he called them, were among the people in the United States whose religious rights were to be protected; and Mr. Madison made this point many times in the remainder of his life

It is likely that, like George Washington, Mr. Madison owned some Muslim slaves and that Thomas Jefferson did as well for that matter. As we have indicated earlier in this Chapter, the three Igbo slaves who poisoned President Madison's grandfather, Ambrose, may also have been members of the Muslim Faith.

At any rate, this brings us to the Notes of this Chapter Nine on James Madison's views on other faiths other than his own Episcopal tradition at home in Virginia. This will be followed by Chapter Ten, as we shall see, the most controversial of the essays in this Study.

The central focus of Chapter Ten will be what the fourth President of the United States, James Madison, believed, said, and wrote about

---

631 George B. English. Narrative of an Expedition to Dongola and Sennaar. (New York: Wentworth Press, 2016.)

the phenomenon of Slavery from his early childhood to the time of his retirement and death. As we shall see, Mr. Madison had a number of things to say and write about Slavery before his Presidency, during his Presidency, as well as after he was President.

Chapter Ten:
James Madison and Slavery

> One day, seeing a gang of Negroes, some in irons, on their way to the Southern Market, Mr. Coles taunted the President by congratulating him as the Chief of our grand Republic, that he was not then accompanied by a Foreign Minister and thus saved the deep mortification of witnessing such a revolting sight in the presence of the representative of a nation, less boastful, perhaps, of its regards for the rights of man but more observant of them.
>
> —Edward Coles, *Letters*

> He is a young man who astonishes by his eloquence, his wisdom and his genius and has had the humanity and courage, for such a proposition requires no small share of courage to propose a general emancipation of the slaves.
>
> —French visitor quoted in Ralph Ketcham's *James Madison*

> On a view of all the circumstances I have judged it most prudent not to force Billey back to Virginia, even if it could be done; and I have accordingly taken measures for that separation from me.
>
> —James Madison, *Letters*

Introduction

Of the Chapters of this Study on James Madison's Religion, this Chapter on his views on the phenomenon of Slavery is clearly the most controversial This is mostly because, as we shall see in this Chapter Ten because the fourth President of the United States was fundamentally ambivalent about the practice of Slavery.

We will begin Chapter Ten with some general observations about the American Presidency and Slavery, as well as some reflections on the practice of Slavery in the Virginia Colony and State. This opening Section of Chapter Ten will be followed by a discussion of a few prominent slaves owned by James Madison and his family. Among these were slaves named Paul Jennings, Sukey, and Sawney.

These two Sections of Chapter Ten will be followed by the central Section of the Chapter we will call the "Ambivalent Views of James Madison on Slavery." In that Section we will indicate, by looking at evidence from his family records and his letters and other published works, that the fourth President of the United States had profoundly ambivalent perspectives on what James Madison believed about the phenomenon of Slavery

Slavery Among the American Presidents and Early Virginia History

Of the first eighteen presidents of the United States from 1789 until 1877—from George Washington until U.S. Grant, twelve of them owned slaves at some point in their lives. Only John Adams, John Quincy Adams, Millard Fillmore, Franklin Peirce, James Buchanan, and Abraham Lincoln did not own slaves.[632] This means that Washington, Jefferson, Madison, Monroe, Andrew Jackson, Martin Van Buren, William Henry Harrison, John Tyler, James K. Polk, Zachary Taylor, Andrew Johnson, and even U.S. Grant, who was given a slave by his father-in-law, all owned captive human beings.[633]

---

632 Author's historical analysis
633 Ibid

In terms of numbers, George Washington and Thomas Jefferson owned the most slaves, about six hundred apiece.[634] Zachary Taylor was next with nearly three hundred.[635] They were followed by Andrew Jackson, around two hundred[636]; James Madison who owned about a hundred slaves.[637] James Monro3 [75.]; James K. Polk [56.]; John Tyler [29.]; William Henry Harrison [11.]; Andrew Jackson [10.]; and both U. S. Grant and Martin Van Buren owned a single slave.[638]

Of these twelve American Presidents who owned slaves, eight of them owned their captives while in office as President. Washington was the first to own slaves and Zachary Taylor was the last to own slaves during his presidency. Ulysses S. Grant, however, was the last to own a slave at some point in his life.[639] Woodrow Wilson was the final president born into a household with slave labor, though the Civil War ended during Mr. Wilson's childhood.[640]

George Washington was a major slave owner before, during, and after his time as President. His will had a provision that his slaves were to be freed within a year of Martha Washington's, his wife's death.[641]

Thomas Jefferson fathered multiple children with enslaved woman, Sally Hemings, the likely half-sister of his late wife, Martha Wayles Skelton. Despite being a life-long slave owner, Mr. Jefferson routinely and publicly condemned the institution of slavery, attempted to restrict its expansion, and advocated a gradual path to Emancipation, as did James Madison. During his time as President, Mr. Jefferson saw the abolition of the international slave trade in March of 1807.[642]

---

634 Ibid
635 Ibid
636 Ibid
637 Ibid
638 Ibid
639 Ibid
640 Ibid
641 Ibid
642 Ibid

James Monroe supported the idea of sending freed slaves back to the new country of Liberia in Africa.[643] Andrew Jackson was involved in controversy when he was against anti-slavery tracts, and during his campaign for President, he was accused of being a slave trader. Mr. Jackson, however, did not free his slaves in his will.[644]

Martin Van Buren's father owned six slaves. Van Buren himself only owned one slave, a man named Tom who escaped in 1814. When Tom was found in Boston, Mr. Van Buren agreed to sell him to the founder, but the transaction was never completed, so Tom remained free.[645]

William Henry Harrison, the first Governor of Indiana and the owner of a dozen slaves, lobbied the Indiana Legislature to legalize slavery in the state but he was unsuccessful.[646]

President John Tyler never freed any of his thirty slaves. While President, he consistently supporter the rights of the slave-holder and the expansion of slavery into the West in his time in office from 1841 to 1845.[647]

James K. Polk provided for the freeing of his sixty slaves after the death of his wife. But the Emancipation Proclamation (1861) and the 14th Amendment of the U.S. Constitution freed them in 1865. long before Mrs. Polk's death in 1891.[648]

James Buchanan appears to have had an ambivalent attitude toward slavery. Some suggests that he had purchased slaves on a few occasions but those same sources also indicate that he sold them immediately.[649]

President Zachary Taylor owned 300 slaves but he resisted attempts to expand slavery in the Western territories. There were even some rumors that pro-slavery advocates had poisoned Mr. Taylor, but tests of his body a hundred years later were inconclusive.[650]

---

643 Ibid
644 Ibid
645 Ibid
646 Ibid
647 Ibid
648 Ibid
649 Ibid
650 Ibid

Andrew Jackson owned a handful of slaves, but as Governor of Tennessee he convinced Abraham Lincoln to exempt that area from the Emancipation Proclamation of September of 1862.[651]

Although U.S. Grant served as a General in the Union Army, his wife Julia owned four slaves during the American Civil War given to her by her father. As indicated earlier. President Grant owned one slave, a man named William Jones who was given to Mr. Grant by his father-in-law. Mr. Jones was manumitted by Grant on March 29, 1859.[652]

Finally, James Madison, who owned approximately one hundred slaves, did not manumit them in his will. Paul Jennings, one of Mr. Madison's slaves, served him in his Presidency, as we shall see in a later Section of this Chapter Ten. He later published a memoir of his life in the White House.[653]

Meanwhile in terms of Slavery in the Colony and state of Virginia, two dates are very important, 1501 and 1619. The former was shortly after Christopher Columbus had discovered America, Spain, and Portugal began sending slaves to Brazil in South America to work on their plantations there.

The latter date, 1619, refers to the arrival of the African slave ship the *White Lion* that brought twenty-three slaves to the American Colony of Virginia. These slaves were from the area in Africa that would be the present-day nation of Angola. The ship had been seized by a British crew from the Portuguese slave ship, the *Sao Joao Bautista*.[654]

By the year 1661, Virginia has passed its first law that suggested that any free person had the right to own slaves in the Colony. Between 1619 and 1661, Africans were legally deemed to be "Indentured Servants," including one man named John Casor, who was declared an 'Indentured Servant for life' in 1655.[655] Additional laws were

---

651 Ibid

652 Ibid

653 Ketcham. P. 619

654 The White Lion was an English privateer, operating under a Dutch letter of marque which brought the first Africans to Colonial Virginia in 1619, a year before the arrival of the Mayflower

655 Virginia Law on Black Indentured Servants. [1661.]

passed in Virginia in the 17th Century leading to the Colony's first Slave Code in 1705.[656]

One of these Virginia laws, passed in 1662, said that children born in the Virginia Colony would take the social status of their mothers, regardless of who the father might be.[657] This was in direct contradiction of the English Common Law at the time. The passage of this 1662 law in Virginia resulted in generation after generation of enslaved people, including mixed-race children and adults, some of whom were majority White. Among the most notable of these people were the 7/8 White Sally Hemings and her siblings, all fathered by planter John Wayles, as well as the four children Ms. Hemings bore and were fathered by Thomas Jefferson.[658]

In the first decades of the 19th Century, in Virginia, we saw the first two major Slave Revolts in the state. The first of these was called the Gabriel's Rebellion in 1800, and the second was the Nat Turner Rebellion of 1831.

The Gabriel Rebellion is named after a literate Richmond slave by the name of Gabriel. He is usually referred to as Gabriel Prosser (1776–1800). Gabriel was a skilled artisan, a blacksmith who sometimes was hired out by his Master. This afforded Gabriel to have more freedom, autonomy, and mobility that he otherwise would not have had.[659] in the year 1800, along with seven of his slave friends, Gabriel organized what was to be a Slave Rebellion. The small band he organized were all Black artisans, as well. Gabriel also believed that in a rebellion he would enlist the help of White Abolitionists, as well as Quakers, Methodists, and Frenchmen who were "friends of liberty."[660]

The assault was planned for August 30, 1800, just before the election for President. The Rebellion, however, never came together, for Virginia had torrential rain the day the rebels had planned for the

---

656 Virginia Colony Slave Code. [1705.]

657 Ibid

658 For more on Sally Hemings, see: Barbara Chase-Ribould. Sally Hemings. (New York: Ballantine Books, 1994.)

659 Anonymous. 'Gabriel's Rebellion Another View." @ushistory.org/us/205asp

660 Ibid

revolt, and a traitor from the cause warned the White authorities about the impending attack. Thus, the Gabriel Rebellion ended in severe repression of the group, the State of Virginia executing twenty-seven Black men—including Gabriel, by hanging.[661]

One of the repercussions of the Gabriel Revolt and another one planned two years later in 1802, was that the state of Virginia tightened the legal restrictions on slaves.[662] Thirty years later, in 1831, Nathanial "Nat" Turner (1800–1831) led a rebellion of enslaved people in Virginia on August 21, 1831. Mr. Turner's actions set off a massacre of up to 200 Black people, followed by a new wave of legislation prohibiting the education of Blacks and the right to rebel.[663]

Originally, the Nat Turner Rebellion was aborted as well and was rescheduled when Mr. Turner and six other slaves killed a White family, the Travis family that gave Turner and his gang arms and horses. He also enlisted the help of another 75 other enslaved people. In a disorganized insurrection, fifty-five more White people were murdered.[664]

After the rebellion Mr. Turner was in hiding successfully for six weeks until he was found, convicted, and hanged at Jerusalem, Virginia, along with sixteen of his followers. Needless to say, the incident put fear into the hearts of White Virginians, and another result was even harsher laws against enslaved people in the state.

The Emancipation Proclamation and the fourteenth Amendment of the U.S. Constitution, passed on January 31, 1865, of course, made the idea of a Slave Rebellion to be unnecessary. This brings us to the Second Section of Chapter Ten, a discussion of prominent slaves owned by James Madison and his family.

Prominent Slaves Owned by James Madison

Among the hundred or so slaves on the Montpelier Farm of the James Madison family, four of them stand out as prominent. These four are the following:

---

661 Ibid
662 Ibid
663 Nat Turner Rebellion @history.com/topics/black-history/nat-turner
664 Ibid

1. Sawney.

2. Sukey.

3. William 'Billey" Gardner.

4. Paul Jennings.

In the Second Section of Chapter Ten, we will comment on each of these figures in the order we have listed them here. When Mr. Madison traveled to the College of New Jersey 1769 along with the Rev. Thomas Martin and his brother, the statesman' s slave, Sawney went along with them. Mentions of Sawney are also found in many of Mr. Madison's letters from 1769, in a letter back to Rev. Martin, all the way up to 1823 when we find the final reference to the slave in question.

The choice of James Madison Sr. to have Sawney accompany his son to Princeton in 1769, tells us a great deal at the high level of trust the family placed in the enslaved man. A few years later, in 1782, Mr. Madison Sr. made Sawney one of the over-seers of the Montpelier Farm, being responsible for a quarter of the Plantation's land. These over-seers did not live in the slave quarters. Rather, the four over-seers had their own cabin.[665]

Sawney was also allowed to grow his own tobacco which he, in turn, sold to the Madisons. It was labeled "Sawney's Crop."[666] We also know that Mr. Madison Sr. permitted Sawney to buy "special English shoes," the kind worn by English gentlemen.[667] We also know that Madison's slave Sawney regularly made purchases for Montpelier, and there is lots of evidence that James Madison Jr. took great care to make sure that Sawney was being taken care of.

In November of 1790, in a document entitled, *Instructions for the Montpelier Overseer and Laborers*, James Madison provided detail instructions for each of his overseers. Sawney was "to have a patent plow, with L. Collins to do the wood work."[668] Tobacco merchants on the docks at Fredericksburg would look for Sawney's

---

665 Ketcham, pp. 25 and 28

666 Ibid

667 Ibid., p. 374

668 Ibid., p. 614

mark on the hogsheads of tobacco. They knew that these containers held prime leaf.

Sukey, Mr. Madison's second slave on our list, was born at Montpelier. She was part of Mrs. Madison's domestic staff, though in one letter from 1818 Dolley Madison complained of Sukey stealing from her.[669] In retaliation, Mrs. Madison had her banished to a distance portion of the property. Eventually, Dolley took Sukey back for as the Mistress wrote, "I find it terribly difficult to be without her."[670] Later, in another letter. Dolley Madison called Sukey, "My most efficient house servant."[671]

It was probably the case that Sukey was responsible for Dolley's wardrobe, helping her to change several times a day; fixing her hair; and inspecting and repairing her clothes when they needed to be mended. From the available evidence, it appears that Sukey had at least five children. Rebecca born in 1824, followed by Ben, George and William. The youngest, another girl named Ellen, was born in 1833.

Sukey and her family used the surname Stewart and when her children became old enough, they became house servants for the Madisons. Sukey served Mrs. Madison for many years. In late 1847, Dolley tried to sell Sukey's daughter Ellen who by now was fifteen years old, for $400.00. The sale was bungled, however, and Ellen ran away.[672] While on the lam, Ellen may have had help from Sukey and Paul Jennings, another Madison slave.

Ellen Stewart is also significant because on April 15, 1848, Ellen was one of the seventy runaway slaves who boarded the schooner *Pearl* under a cover of darkness that then set sale for Philadelphia. When Dolley Madison heard about this, she sold Sukey on the spot to a local family in Washington, suspecting that Sukey had helped her daughter in her escape.[673]

---

669 Ibid., p. 669
670 Ibid
671 Ibid
672 Ibid
673 The *Pearl Incident*, as it was known was the largest, non-violent escape of 77 Black slaves on the British schooner, the *Pearl*. It took place on April 15, 1848

William "Billey" Gardner, Mr. Madison's third slave on our list, was also born at Montpelier. When James Madison traveled to the Continental Congress, his slave Billey accompanied him. Billey was 24 years old in 1783. Mr. Madison's maternal grandmother had given Billey to her eight year old grandson when Billey was an infant.[674] In 1783, after the Convention, Mr. Madison wrote home to his father to tell him that he had decided to leave Billey in the North. As the fourth President told his father:

> On a view of all of the circumstances I have judged it most prudent not to force Billey back to Virginia, even if it could be done; and I have accordingly taken measures for that separation from me.[675]

Billey was the only slave of Mr. Madison who he ever emancipated, but he did not free him directly. Rather, he sold him into an apprenticeship from which Billey would be free after seven years. After his manumission, Billey took the surname Gardener, or Gardner, and he remained in contact with Mr. Madison for the remainder of his life until his death in 1795.[676]

In a letter to his father about Billey the son asked, "Why should Billey be punished merely for covering that liberty for which we have paid the price of so much blood and have claimed so often to be right and worthy the pursuit of every human being?"[677]

By far, the most prominent of the slaves of James Madison's listed above was Peter Jennings. (1799–1874.). Mr. Jennings, who was born at Montpelier, in addition to being Mr. Madison's servant, before, during, and after his Presidency, Mr. Jennings was prominent for other reasons, as well. For one thing, Peter Jennings bought his freedom from another famous America, Daniel Webster.[678] For another thing, Mr. Jennings

---

674 Ketcham, p. 148

675 James Madison to James Madison Sr., Ketcham, p. 148

676 Ibid

677 Ibid., pp. 668–670

678 Peter Jennings. *A Colored Man's Reminiscences of James Madison.* (Washington: Historical publishing, 2017.)

wrote the first memoir of a White House servant ever published. The book was called *A Colored Man's Reminiscences of James Madison*, which was published in 186 right after the Emancipation Proclamation.[679]

A third reason that Peter Jennings is a significant figure in American history is that three of his sons joined and fought for the Union Army during the American Civil War.[680] And finally, in February of 2019, at a University in Virginia named as his Master, James Madison name a residence Hall after the fourth President of the United States freed slave, Peter Jennings.[681]

This brings us to the Third and Central Section of Chapter Ten in which we will explore The Ambivalent Views of James Madison's on Slavery. This will be followed by a Fourth Section on Slavery in the Letters of the Fourth President.

Ambivalent Views of James Madison on Slavery.

The purpose of this Central Section of Chapter Ten of this Final Chapter of this Study of James Madison's Religion is to show the ambivalence that the fourth President of the United States had on the issue of Slavery. Slavery remained a moral dilemma for James Madison. He denounced the institution of Slavery, while at the same time he lived off the fruits of its labor his entire life. Financial difficulties late in life led Mr. Madison to sell some of his Slaves, and he decided against freeing his slaves in his will in order to provide for his wife Dolley's later years.

Nevertheless, James Madison remained a consistent and persistent critic of the institution of Slavery throughout his public career. The Quaker background of his wife Dolley most likely also helped to strengthened his ultimate Anti-Slavery position. Still, while drafting the U.S. Constitution, James Madison strove to ensure the protection of the rights of minorities, while also proposing that a slave should only be counted as three-fifths of a person.[682]

---

679 Ibid

680 Ibid

681 This dedication took place on February 9, 2019 on the campus of James Madison University

682 This was a proviso of the 13th Amendment that counted each slave as

This contradiction in the life of James Madison and etched into the lines of the Constitution would come to define Mr. Madison and the nation that was irreconcilably founded both on the institution of Slavery and the principles of Liberty and Justice. This tension was at the heart of the fourth president of the United States, as well as the nation as a whole.

In 2017, the Montpelier Mansion sponsored an interactive exhibit entitled, "The Mere Distinction of Color."[683] The title came from the 1787 Constitutional Convention and Mr. Madison's comments there. He said, and wrote, at the time:

> We have never seen the mere distinction of color in a most enlightened period of time, a ground for the most oppressive dominion exercised by man over man.[684]

Over the course of the adult life of James Madison, the great American statesman wrote about the phenomenon of Slavery life in many of his published works. In this analysis we will point to three works to give us a flavor of this comments on Slavery. In the Final Section of Chapter Ten we will continue this same analysis by looking at several of James Madison's letters also to help to discern his perspectives on the matter at hand.

The three published works of James Madison on Slavery about which we will speak are the following:

1. His Memorandum of African Colony of Freed Slaves.

2. James Madison's essay number forty-two of his Federalist Papers.

3. A letter to the Farmer's Register.[685]

---

three-fifths of a person

683 "The Mere Distinction of Color." Interactive exhibit. Montpelier Mansion. [2017.]

684 James Madison, quoted at the Constitutional Convention. Philadelphia, Summer of 1787

685 Ibid

In the first of these written works of James Madison, he discussed the idea of starting an African Colony of Freed Slaves in America in Africa. Mr. Madison found this idea to produce fundamental effects in America. He wrote at the time:

> Without enquiring into the practicability or the most proper means of establishing a Settlement of freed Blacks on the coast of Africa, it may be remarked that one motive to the benevolent experiment that if such an asylum was provided, it might prove to be a great encouragement to manumission in the Southern parts of the U. S. and even afford the best hope presented of putting an end to the Slavery in which not less than 600,000 unhappy negroes are now involved.[686]

In the Autumn of 1789, James Madison met a British physician named William Thorton who was an Abolitionist and who supported a plan to Colonize Sierra Leone as a refuge for Freed British Slaves. This encounter and Mr. Madison's work with the American Colonization Society, made the fourth President interested in the idea of Colonization of American Freed Slaves being resettled in Africa, as well. It should be clear from this passage that James Madison was in favor of establishing the Colony of Freed American slaves in Africa and he believed that, if accomplished, it would help to abolish Slavery in America.

Mr. Madison was ardent about not having any language in the U.S. Constitution about Slavery. In essay number 42 of his *Federalist Papers*, Mr. Madison sketched out a plan for the eradication of Slavery in America. He observed in *Federalist* 42, "It ought to be considered as a great point in favor of humanity, that a period of twenty years may terminate forever, within these states, a traffic which has long and so loudly unbraided the barbarism of modern policy."[687]

Mr. Madison added about that twenty year period:

---

[686] James Madison. memorandum of an African Colony of Freed Slaves. October 20, 1789

[687] James Madison. *Federalist Papers*. essay no 42

> That within that twenty- year period it will have abolished by a concurrence of the few states which continue the unnatural traffic to the prohibition example which has been given by so great a majority of the Union. Happy would it be for the unfortunate Africans if an equal prospect lay before them of being redeemed from the oppression of their European brethren.[688]

Again, it is perfectly clear in this passage from the *Federalist Papers* that James Madison was in favor of a twenty year plan for America to abolish Slavery. This essay of Mr. Madison was published on January 22, 1788. The twenty year estimate was far short of the Emancipation Proclamation in 1863 and the Fourteenth Amendment, which was finally adopted on July 9, 1868.[689]

Nevertheless we see in *Federalist* number 42 another example of James Madison's overall view on the matter at hand. He was in favor of the gradual Abolition of Slavery in America. In 1836, while in retirement, the fourth President of the United States sent a letter to the editors of the *Farmers' Register*. He ended that letter with these words:

> It is most obvious that they [the slaves] themselves are infinitely worsted by the exchange from Slavery to Liberty—if indeed, their condition deserves that name.[690]

Again, in this 1836 letter to the *Farmers' Register*, Mr. Madison is in favor of slaves moving from "Slavery to Liberty," but he questions whether they really would be "worsted" in the process and would be any better off.

Even as early as 1785 when Mr. Madison spoke in the Virginia General Assembly favoring a bill Thomas Jefferson had proposed for the gradual Abolition of Slavery, which was rejected by the Assembly, Madison also helped to defeat a bill designed to outlaw the manumission of individual slaves in the state.

---

688 Ibid

689 14th Amendment of U.S. Constitution was adopted on July 9, 1868, but had been proposed the first time in 1865

690 Ketcham, p. 149

Ralph Ketcham, in his biography of Mr. Madison wrote about a "French visitor" who had seen Mr. Madison's behavior in regard to this bill. The visitor said about the young American statesman, 'He is a young man who astonishes by his eloquence, his wisdom, and his genius, and has had the humanity and the courage, for such a proposition requires no small share of courage to propose a general emancipation of the slaves."[691]

Mr. Ketcham sums up the fourth President's attitudes toward Slavery around the time of Mr. Jefferson's proposal in 1785:

> Finally, though Mr. Madison saw no practical way to fight the system and more and more seems to have acquiesced in it. Nevertheless, he maintained his concern and throughout his life took part in largely futile efforts to rid the country of the moral and economic millstone he thought slavery to be.[692]

Mr. Madison made many other comments about the phenomenon of Slavery in some of his other letters which we will examine in the Fourth and Final Section of Chapter Ten of this Study of James Madison's Religion.

Slavery in James Madison's Letters

Finally, in the adult life of President James Madison he made many other comments regarding the phenomenon of Slavery in his letters besides the one mentioned earlier to the *Farmers' Register*. Among these many letters were missives to:

1. Francis Corbin.
2. The Marquise de Lafayette.
3. Robert Pleasants.
4. Joseph Jones
5. Edmund Randolph.

---

691 Ibid
692 Bios on these men appear in notes 62 to 78

6. Edward Coles.

7. John H. B. Latrobe.[693]

In this Section, we will discuss these correspondences one at a time in the order in which they are listed here. On October 10, 1819, Francis Corbin wrote President Madison to inquire about his current views on Slavery. In Mr. Madison's reply to Mr. Corbin, the President called Slavey, "a dreadful calamity," and a 'sad blot on our free Country."[694] Mr. Madison added:

> **The magnitude of this evil among us is so deeply felt, and so universally acknowledged that no merit could be greater than that of devising a satisfactory remedy for it.**[695]

Yet, at the same time James Madison never freed his own slaves despite a promise he made to do so. As we have shown, he advocated the idea of sending some American slaves back to Africa. James Madison joined the newly formed American Colonization Society which aimed to help Freed American Slaves migrate to Liberia in Africa. He became the President of this organization in 1833. In 1820, writing to the Marquise de Lafayette, who was pressing the President on the question of Slavery, conceded in his return letter that Slavery is "the dreadful fruitfulness of the Original Sin of the African Trade."[696]

James Madison wrote a letter at the same time to Thomas Jefferson, on October 17, 1784 when he told the third President that comments that Lafayette had made about Mr. Jefferson brought "real honor and proof of humanity" to the third President.[697]

Robert Pleasants of Philadelphia also wrote to President Madison about the Abolition of Slavery. In the fourth President's return letter, he observed:

---

693 Francis Corbin to James Madison. October 10, 1819

694 James Madison to Francis Corbin. October 21, 1819

695 James Madison to the Marquise de Lafayette. November 19, 1820

696 James Madison to Thomas Jefferson. October 17, 1784

697 James Madison to Robert Pleasants. October 30, 1791

> I cannot but consider the application as likely to harm rather than to do good. It may be worth your own consideration whether it might not produce successful attempts to withdraw the privilege now allowed to individuals, of giving freedom to slaves. It would at least clog it with the conditions that the persons should be removed from the Country.[698]

James Madison's concerns about Slavey in this period went far beyond his public activities. On one occasion, before leaving his estate, he left a letter to his Overseers, "To treat the Negroes with all the humanity & kindness consistent with their necessary subordination and work."[699]

The very first direct reference to Slavery in the *Papers of James Madison* is in a letter he wrote to Joseph Jones who had written the President asking his opinion of offering a slave as a bonus to those who enlisted in the Continental Army. Mr. Madison wrote back by offering another solution:

> I am glad to find the Legislature persist in their resolution to recruit their line of the Army for the war, though without deciding on the expediency of the mode under their consideration, would it not be as well to liberate and make soldiers at once of the Blacks themselves as to make them instruments for enlisting White soldiers? It would certainly be more consonant to the principles of Liberty which ought never to be lost sight of in the contest for Liberty.[700]

Even very early on in his career, James Madison wrote his friend Edmund Randolph that he "wanted to depend as little as possible on the labor of slaves."[701] But forced to abandon his efforts to live free of

---

698 Ketcham, p. 374

699 James Madison to Joseph Jones. November 28, 1780

700 James Madison to Edmund Randolph. September 30, 1787

701 Edward Coles on Madison and Slavery@encyclopediavirginia.org/entries/colers-slaves-1786-1868

slaves and the Plantation system in the 1790s, Mr. Madison continued to do what he could to lessen the degradation and harshness in the treatment of American Slaves.

Mr. Madison's private secretary for many years, Edward Coles, was a strong believer in

Abolitionism. He constantly prodded his boss to take a tougher approach against the phenomenon of Human Captivity. Mr. Coles once related:

> One day, "Seeing a gang of Negroes, some in irons, on their way to the Southern Market," Mr. Coles taunted the President, "by congratulating him, as the Chief of our great Republic, that he was not then accompanied by a Foreign Minister and thus saved the deep mortification of witnessing such a revolting sight in the presence of the representative of a nation, less boastful perhaps, of its regard for the rights of man but more observant of them.[702]

Edward Coles freed his slaves shortly after James Madison retired from the Presidency in 1817. Mr. Coles prepared his slaves for life after their emancipation by giving each of them some land in Illinois, where he resided. He also helped his slaves get started in farming. In responding to these developments, Mr. Madison wrote to his former secretary in an 1819 letter:

> With the habits of the slave, and without instruction, the property, or the employments of a Freeman, the manumitted Blacks instead of, instead of deriving advantage from the partial benevolence of their Masters, furnish arguments against the general efforts in their behalf.[703]

Mr. Madison also related to Mr. Coles that he wished he could change the color of the skin of his freed slaves. Without that, "they seemed destined to a privation of a moral rank and those social participations which gives to freedom more than half of its value."[704]

---

702 James Madison to Edward Coles. September 3, 1819
703 Ibid
704 Ibid

Mr. Cols said of his former boss, "A certain train of thought lulled Mr. Madison's Conscience, despite his abhorrence of Slavery, shows clearly the root of his lifelong compromise with the peculiar institution."[705]

Mr. Coles' moral ardor, which compelled him to emancipate his own slaves, exposed the fourth President's complacency and ambiguity with regard to James Madison's views on Slavery, as well as the national inconsistencies about the matter.

Finally, while in retirement in 1832, James Madison hosted John H.B. Latrobe (1803–1891), American lawyer and inventor, at Montpelier. Mr. Latrobe recorded some of his conversations with the elder American statesman. The Maryland Attorney related:

> He spoke much of Colonization, took an interests in hearing what Maryland had done; regretted that the interests excited in the Virginia Legislature at its last session seemed in a great degree to have died away, but considered that the scheme must and should go on.[706]

From these seven letters of James Madison's, we may make the following conclusions. First, that even later in life, James Madison was convinced that the Slavery Problem would be solved. Second, that in the meantime, Slavery had been the 'dreadful Original Sin" of America. Third, the fourth President, during the Revolution, was in favor of raising companies of Black soldiers into the Continental Army. Fourth, even early on, he wanted to 'depend as little as possible on the labor of slaves.'"[707] And fifth, and finally, the great American statesman, even in his retirement at Montpelier at the end of his life, James Madison kept alive the idea of the Colonization of Freed American Slaves to Liberia in Africa.

Eleven years after his death, President James Madison, in 1847 finally got his wish when the country of the Republic of Liberia, on the Western Coast of Africa established itself as an independent nation on

---

705 John H.B. Latrobe. "On Visiting Madison." August 3, 1832

706 See note no. 68 of this Chapter

707 The American Colonization Society was formed in 1813 by American clergyman and scholar, Robert Finley. (1772–1817.)

July 26, 1847. Liberia was begun by the organization of which James Madison was once President, the American Colonization Society.[708]

George Mason was another Virginia farmer, following Roman writer Cato, called slavery an "infernal practice." He also spoke of the 'pernicious effects on manners, and he worried about the unavoidable 'Judgment of Heaven."[709] James Madison, for the most part, shared the moral revulsion of Mr. Mason and sought to limit the duration of the institution, while keeping direct references to it out of the U.S. Constitution. Mr. Madison was, however, lukewarm on the insistence of the two-thirds clause.[710]

The "Two-Thirds" clause is a reference to a section of the U.S Constitution, Article II, section 2, clause 2, that reads, 'He [the President] shall have the power, by and with the Advice and Consent of the Senate to make Treaties provided that two-thirds of the Senate present concur."[711] This two-thirds requirement would also have applied to the Abolition of Slavery that Mr. Madison was aware could not be a practical accomplishment.

George Mason was also a very vocal participant at the Constitutional Convention in the Summer of 1787 in Philadelphia, particularly in his vigorous objections to the practice of Slavery. Mr. Mason said at the Convention that Slavery was bad for commerce. Mr. Mason also observed that Slavery made America a "Country dominated by the alliance of slave traders and grasping merchants." The old Virginia Republican could find little in Slavery that "would be good for the nation," even though the state he represented at the Convention was one of the most active in the Slave Trade.

George Mason also inherited thirty-five slaves from his father and at its height the slave population at his Gunston Hall property at Mason Creek on the Potomac River numbered about three hundred, many of whom resided at his estate in Fairfax County, Virginia,

---

[708] George Mason, quoting Cato, the Elder on Slavery. *Freeman's Journal.* September 21, 1778.)

[709] James Madison. *Federalist Papers.* essay no 54

[710] U. S. Constitution Article II, section 2, clause 2

[711] James Madison. *Federalist Papers.* essay no 42

This brings us to the major Conclusions of Chapter Ten of this Study on James Madison's Religion, followed by the Notes of the same. Those will be followed by Chapter Eleven in which we will give a catalogue of the major Conclusions we have made in the other Ten Chapters of this Study.

Conclusions to Chapter Ten

We have begun Chapter Ten with some very general comments about Slavery and the American presidency, as well as some general remarks about the practice of Slavery in the Virginia Colony/State in the 17th and 18th Centuries. In addition to these short summaries of Slavery in the Virginia Colony/State, we also have discussed in the Opening Section of Chapter Ten the two major Slave Rebellions in the area.

The first of these was the Gabriel Rebellion organized by a Black smith in 1800, along with other Black tradesmen. The second was the Nat Turner Rebellion that took place in Virginia in the year 1831.

This opening Section of Chapter Ten was followed by a discussion of several prominent slaves at the Jams Madison family Montpelier plantation home in Virginia. Among these slaves, as we have seen is a man named Sawney who accompanied James Madison to the College of New Jersey in 1769 and another man, Paul Jennings who has recently had a residence hall dedicated in his name in Harrisonburg, Virginia. Additionally, we have identified and discussed the lives of Sukey, a house slave to Dolley Madison, and William "Billey" Gardner, who accompanied James Madison to the Constitutional Convention in Philadelphia in the Summer of 1787.

These two Sections of Chapter Ten were followed by the Central Section of the Chapter in which we have discussed the "Ambivalent Attitudes of James Madison on Slavery."

On the one hand, Mr. Madison grew up in a slave-holding household, he never freed his slaves, even in his will, and he clearly profited from the labor of his slaves for most of his life. On the other hand, he was the author of the language of the First Amendment of the U.S. Constitution that protected the rights of minorities, and he took the Anti-Slavery position throughout much of his adulthood.

In this Third Section of Chapter Ten, we also introduced the comments on Slavery from James Madison that were reflected in three of his published works, his *Memorandum of an African Colony of Freed Slaves*, his essay number forty-two of the *Federalist Papers*, and a letter to the editors of the *Farmers' Register*.

We have shown that in the first of these works, Mr. Madison discussed his desire to establish a Colony of Freed American Slaves in Africa. Unfortunately, as we have indicated, he did not live long enough to see the creation of the Liberian Republic in 1847 when that Colony was, in fact, created.

In *Federalist Papers* essay 42, James Madison sketched out a plan for the gradual eradication of Slavery in the United States, suggesting that the goal of the plan may take twenty years or more. In Essay 42, he also referred to Slavery as the 'Barbarism of modern policy.' **78**

This twenty-year estimate in Essay 42, which was published in January of 1788, was, as we have shown, far short of the arrival of the Emancipation Proclamation and the 14th Amendment in the 1860s.

These Three Sections of Chapter Ten were followed by an introduction and discussion of seven separate letters of James Madison over the course of his adult life that mentioned his views on the practice of Slavery in the United States. These seven letters were written by Mr. Madison to Francis Corbin, the Marquise de Lafayette, Robert Pleasants, Joseph Jones, Edmund Randolph, to his secretary, Edward Coles, and to attorney, John H.B. Latrobe. As we have shown, these letters covered a period in James Madison's life from 1790 until 1832.

From these seven letters we have explored in the Fourth Section of Chapter Ten, we have made five conclusions about James Madison's views on Slavery over the course of the second half of his life.

The first of these was that the fourth President was convinced that the "Slavery Problem" would be solved in America. Secondly, in the meantime, Slavery had been the "dreadful Original Sin" of America. Thirdly, during the Revolution, as well as his Presidency, James Madison was in favor of raising companies of Black soldiers to fight in the American Army. In a fourth conclusion we have made in James Madison's letters is that even early on, he wanted "to depend as little as possible on the labor of slaves," as he told his friend Edmund Randolph in a missive on July 26, 1785. Finally, in a fifth conclusion we have drawn from these seven letters of James Madison is that, even in his retirement at Montpelier at the end of his life, the fourth President of the United States kept alive his idea of the Colonization of Freed American Slaves to the West Coast of Africa in the Republic of Liberia.

Unfortunately, eleven years after the death of James Madison, on July 26, 1847, as we have shown, the Republic of Liberia was established by the organization of which Mr. Madison was one of the first presidents, the American Colonization Society. This organization was formed in 1817 to send Freed African-Americans as an alternative to Emancipation.

In 1822, under the leadership of James Madison and others, the American Colonization established on the West Coast of Africa a Colony that in 1847 eventually became the Republic of Liberia. By the year 1867, the Society had sent more than 13,000 emigrants to Africa.[712]

The Society's work was initiated by a successful Quaker ship owner named Paul Cuffee (1759–1817). Mr. Cuffee gained support from the British Government, Freed Black leaders in the United States, as well as members of the U.S. Congress. Among the American political figures that Mr. Cuffee recruited to help in the cause was James Madison who later became the President of the American Colonization Society in 1833.[713]

James Madison received a letter from Mr. Cuffee inquiring if the statesman was willing to lend his name to the Society's cause. Mr. Madison wrote back, "I am much obliged by your friendly communication…Should the evil still go on it will continue to be in my opinion that the imposition of the General Government ought to be applied as far as it may be constitutional."[714] By this, of course, Mr. Madison was reminding Mr. Cuffee that the enslavement of African-Americans in the 17th, 18th, and 19th Centuries, above all, was a violation of the First Amendment of the U.S. Constitution

---

712 Author's research
713 Paul Cuffee to James Madison. June 16, 1812
714 James Madison to Paul Cuffee. June 27, 1812

and its proviso that "All men are created equal and endowed with inalienable rights."[715]

At the close of Chapter Ten we also have indicated that Virginian statesman, George Mason of Fairfax County was one of the most vociferous voices against Slavery in discussion about the matter during the Constitutional Convention which was ironic indeed given the fact that Mr. Mason inherited Slaves and owned nearly three hundred of them at one time in his adult life.

In fact, if George Mason was one of the Presidents of the United States, he would have been tied for third with Zachary Taylor for the most slaves owned by American Presidents, with Washington and Jefferson in positions number one and two on the matter, in that both owned about 600 slaves.

This brings us to the Notes of this Chapter Ten, followed by Chapter Eleven, in which we will provide a catalogue of sorts of the Major Conclusions we have made in this Study of James Madison's Religion.

---

715 First Amendment of U.S. Constitution

Chapter Eleven:
James Madison's Religion: Some Conclusions

There is no principle in all of Madison's wide range of private opinions and long public career to which he held great vigor and tenacity than this one of Religious Liberty.

—Ralph Ketcham. James Madison.

The Memorial and Remonstrance Against Religious Assessment is the most powerful defense of Religious Liberty ever written in America.

—Irving Brant. Madison.

The Civil Rights of none shall be abridged on account of religious belief or worship...nor shall the full and equal rights of Conscience be in any manner, or on any pretexted, infringed.

—James Madison. Wording of the "Bill of Rights."

Introduction

The purpose of this Eleventh Chapter, and Final Chapter, is to give an account or catalogue, if you will, of the major Conclusions we have made in this Study of James Madison's, the fourth President of the United States, Religion. We will go about this catalogue by dividing Chapter Eleven into three parts. In the First of these three Sections, we review the major conclusions on James Madison's Religion in Chapters one, two, and three.

We will continue our catalogue in Section two of Chapter Eleven by discussing the major conclusions in Chapters four, five, and six of this Study. In the Third and Final Section of Chapter Eleven, we will review and discuss the central Conclusions we have made in Chapters Seven, eight, nine, and ten.

This will be followed by the Notes of Chapter Eleven and then an Appendix on Foreign Words and Phrases in this Study on the Religion of James Madison, the fourth President of the United States.

Section One: Conclusions of Chapters One, Two, and Three

After the Introduction to the Study, we then began Chapter One on James Madison's Religion by suggesting that the overall goal of the Chapter would be to explore the earliest and the most sustaining religious beliefs of James Madison in regard to Religion. Indeed, we have shown that James Madison jr. was born on March 16, 1751 at his maternal grandmother's home, Mrs. John Moore.[716] We also have indicated that James Madison was baptized two weeks later, on March 31, 1751, with the Rector of St. Thomas' Church, the Rev. William Davis, conducting the service.[717]

We also have indicated in the First Section of Chapter One that James Madison Sr. took his family to that same Church for Sunday services, as well as for other events there. We also have listed a number of other sources for the earliest religious life of James Madison at this Episcopal Church. Among these other sources were his parents, his maternal grandmother, the Brick Church at Saint Thomas, as well as many of the books in Madison's father's plantation library, including, for example, Joseph Addison's *Spectator*.[718]

In the Second Section of the Opening Chapter of this Study, we turned our attention to the early education of James Madison, from lessons with his maternal grandmother, to the attendance of classes at the school run by Scotsman, Donald Robertson, to the tutoring that Mr. Madison received from the Rev. Thomas Martin, an Anglican cleric,

---

716 Ketcham, pp, 8–9

717 Ibid., p. 9

718 Ibid., pp. 17–18

at the Madison home of Montpelier. The latter in preparation for the fourth President's study at the College of New Jersey in Princeton, his college experience.

We also have indicated that James Madison's mentor in college was the President of the institution, Scotsman John Witherspoon, who instructed his young charge in classical Hebrew and Moral Philosophy. We also have shown that a major influence of John Witherspoon and James Hamilton was what was called at the time the "Scottish Common Sense School," that held that the "moral sense" in human beings is innate and is tied to what the school called the Conscience.[719]

We also have shown in the Second Section of Chapter One that, while in College, some of Mr. Madison's most important intellectual influences in addition to the mostly Presbyterian faculty, were some of his fellow students, including William "Billy" Bradford and Philip Freneau.[720]

In the Section on Mr. Madison's early education, we also have indicated the long-lasting effects on the life of James Madison that may be seen in the contributions of Donald Robertson and the Rev. Thomas Martin in the early education of James Madison Jr. In fact, as we have shown, the Rev. Martin came to live at Montpelier while tutoring the young "Jemmy" Madison, as he was called by his family and friends. The Rev. Martin and his brother also accompanied Jemmy on his trip to New Jersey to begin college, along with one of the Madison's slaves as we saw in Chapter Ten, a man named Sawney.

In the same Section of Chapter One, we also have indicated the strict, Calvinist schedule that John Witherspoon had outlined for his charges, from the 5;00 a.m. opening bell to the 9:00 p.m. lights out.[721]

In the Third Section of Chapter One, we have explored and discussed the phenomenon of Religion in the life of James Madison after college. In this Section we made two major conclusions. First, while Mr. Madison was President he attended Sunday services at the Saint John's Episcopal

---

719   For more on the Scottish Common Sense School, See: Rosaleen Keefe. *Scottish Philosophy of Rhetoric*. (Edinburgh: Imprint Academic, 2013)

720   Ketcham, pp, 35–36

721   Ibid., pp. 19–20

Church in Washington, D.C. And secondly, that the fourth President of the United States rarely said, or wrote, anything about Religion.

In the Fourth and Final Section of Chapter One of this Study on James Madison's Religion, we have described some of the ways that the subject of Religion may be found in the letters of James Madison, mostly from the 1770s and 1780s. Among these letters we have analyzed were missives to Mr. William Bradford, one to Rabbi Jacob de la Motta, and one to Mr. Madison's friend and judge, Edward Livingston.[722]

In each of these several letters, we had seen the following conclusions. First, that James Madison believed in God as the Architect of the Universe. Second, that he preferred a Republican Government overruled by a monarch and ruling, upper class. Third, that James Madison was dedicated to the idea of the free expression of Religion, 'according to one's Conscience.' Fourth, that Madison was persuaded by the Scottish Common Sense School of Philosophy in regard to the nature and extent of moral principles.

Fifth, we have indicated James Madison's penchant for utilizing expressions like 'equal rights under the law,' and the 'security of those rights.' And lastly, we have shown that the emphasis in the words and speeches of James Madison, were sometimes influenced by the cadences of Hebrew poetry he learned from Mr. Witherspoon, as well as the Enlightenment's dedication to Reason with little reference to Revelation, much like his friend, Thomas Jefferson.

Indeed, as we have shown many of the American Founding Fathers put little emphasis on the idea of Revelation as a source for truth. Among these figures were also: Benjamin Franklin, Alexander Hamilton, and Thomas Paine, among many others.

In the Introduction to Chapter Two, on Madison on God of this Study on James Madison'sReligion, we have indicated that the Chapter would consist of four separate Sections. Mr. Madison's General Comments about God; the substitute words for 'God' in his works; what the fourth President had to say and write about the Christian Faith; and finally, what James Madison believed about Jesus Christ.

---

722 Edward Livingston was one of Mr. Madison's oldest friends, as was Mr. Bradford with whom the great statesman attended college together

In the first of these Sections of Chapter Two, we have introduced and discussed several observations that James Madison made about God, including comments about the Virginia Declaration of Rights from 1776, from letters to Frederick Beasley, one comment from Mr. Madison's 'Essay on Property," and in a letter to his friend, William Bradford, among other material. We also have shown in the First Section of Chapter Two that James Madison held a view in his college Senior Theses much like that of English philosopher, John Stuart Mill in his 1859 work, *On Liberty*, on the issue of Religious Toleration.[723]

In the Second Section of Chapter Two of this Study, we began by introducing the penchant among many of the American Founding Fathers to avoid the actual word 'God' in their discourses, while at the same time using instead various synonyms for the Deity. In fact, of the 120 uses of these synonyms in the works of James Madison, we have found fourteen separate names for God.[724]

Indeed, of the 156 total references to the Divine in the works of James Madison in his *Collected Works* only thirty of them employed the word 'God,' or 'Almighty God,' while in the ninety others, he used 'Governor of the Universe,' 'Universal Sovereign,' 'Supreme Law-Giver,' the Annals of Heaven,' 'Nature's God,' 'Creator,' the 'Patronage of the Author,' and many other substitutes for the Deity.[725]

At the end of the Second Section of Chapter Two, we also raised the question of why Mr. Madison, as well as many of the other Founding Fathers in America, engaged in this process of circumlocution about God, but with little definitive answer to that question. Most scholars from the period, however, point to a propensity among many of the Founding Fathers to avoid the use of the word God in deference to the new Enlightenment ideas of the 17th and 18th Centuries that had begun to occupy the many of minds European philosophical thinkers. In this view, the Americans were simply following suit, while avoiding any traditional Biblical language in their documents.

---

723 John Stuart Mill. *On Liberty*. (New York: Dover Books, 2002)
724 Author's research on *Collected Works* of James Madison
725 Ibid., Vol. III, pp. 200–219

In the Enlightenment's mind, 'Nature's God' was tied to the modern, natural rights philosophy developed by Thomas Hobbes, Baruch Spinoza, John Locke, and others as part of a larger project to supplant the traditional Judeo-Christian language about the Divine. The use of 'Nature's God' was tantamount to belief in a rational, organized principle of the Universe, and thus is radically different from the Providential, moralistic Creator, or Father, of the Universe.[726]

At any rate, in the Third Section of Chapter Two we have explored the phenomenon of what the fourth president of the United States, James Madison, had to say and wrote about the Christian Faith. Through the use of Mr. Madison's letters, his comments on the Virginia Bill of Rights, as well as other material, we then made eight conclusions in regard to President Madison's views on Christianity. These conclusions may be summarized this way:

1. Madison wanted Christianity to spread in America.
2. He was against the idea of an Established Church.
3. He believed that Christianity was the foundation of Civil, Legal, and Political institutions in America.
4. He feared that Religious Wars would come to America.
5. He thought that Christian charity and love should be extended among all Americans.
6. He thought Christianity was the greatest Religion in human history.
7. He believed that Jesus was the greatest moral teacher in the world.
8. He said very little about the idea of Religious Diversity.

In the Fourth and Final Section of Chapter Two, we have shown what James Madison believed and wrote about the person of Jesus Christ of Nazareth. We began Section Four by pointing out another tendency among the American Founding Fathers that the most primitive

---

726　Ibid., pp. 211–212

teachings of Jesus have been corrupted by the history of the Church, particularly by Roman Catholicism and the Calvinists. Indeed, we have suggested in Section Four that both Thomas Jefferson and James Madison held this view.

In the remainder of Chapter Two, we have catalogued a series of remarks that James Madison had made about the person of Jesus Christ. In that analysis, we have quoted from the fourth President's remarks on the Virginia Bill of Religious Liberties, a 1795 comment on Anti-Catholicism, a number of remarks from the great American statesman's *Memorial and Remonstrance*, as well as some observations made in a letter to the Rec. Jasper Adams, in which Mr. Madison wrote of cursing all that is 'contrary to the Cross of Christ.'[727]

We also have introduced in the Final Section of Chapter Two a work of James Madison's entitled, *A Syllabus of the Merits on the Doctrines of Jesus Christ Compared with Those of Others*, in which the fourth President compares and contrasts the teachings of Jesus with those of prominent Greco-Roman philosophers. We also have indicated that in the opinion of James Madison, the Ethical views of Jesus are far superior to those of Socrates, Plato, Aristotle, and others.[728]

At the very end of Chapter Two of this Study on James Madison's Religion, we have provided a summary of ten propositions that the great American statesman held about Jesus Christ and his teachings. These ten propositions may be summarized this way:

1. Jesus was the greatest moral teacher who ever lived and Christianity is the greatest human Religion.

2. The most primitive form of Christianity has been corrupted over the years.

3. If not for the followers of Platonism, there would have been no Christian Infidels.

4. The history of the Roman Catholic Church and Calvinism have been responsible for the corruption.

---

727 James Madison to Rev. Jasper Adams. September 10, 1833

728 James Madison. *A Syllabus on the Merits of the Doctrines of Jesus Christ Compared with Those of others. In Collected Works*. Vol. III, p. 222–228

5. That Jesus Christ is Savior and Redeemer of human beings.

6. That too many Sects and denominations of the Christian Religion believe that they are the only true faith.

7. That James Madison was against the idea of adding the words "Jesus Christ" to the amended preamble of the U.S. Constitution.

8. That the competing Christian Sects all claim the same authorities—Jesus and the New Testament.

9. That many beliefs in Mr. Madison's day should be curses because they run counter to the Cross of Christ.

10. That there is no contradiction between Republican Government and the genuine, primitive teachings of Jesus Christ.

In the introduction of Chapter Three of this Study on James Madison's Religion, we have indicated that the Chapter will deal with the views of the great American statesman on Holy Scripture. We also related in the Introduction that Chapter three was to have three Sections.

In the first of those Sections, we provided an account of the major sources of Mr. Madison's views on the Bible. Among those sources we have identified eight. These included: the great statesman's knowledge of ancient languages, including classical Hebrew, classical Greek, Medieval Latin. Additionally, we have indicated the influences from Donald Robertson, the Rev. Thomas Martin, and President John Witherspoon of the College of New Jersey.[729]

At the end of the First Section of Chapter Three, we have pointed out a number of Biblical allusions that can be found in Mr. Madison's written works and speeches, and that these should be considered in the context of other Founding Fathers such as John Adams and Thomas Jefferson.

The Second Section of Chapter Three has been devoted to what James Madison said, wrote, and directly quoted from in regard to the

---

729 Ketcham, p. 51

Old Testament or Hebrew Bible. We also indicated in Chapter Three that the Madison family Bible was a copy of William Burkitt's *Expository Notes on the Bible,* and that many of Mr. Madison's observations about the Old Testament were consistent with the Anglican Vicar, Mr. Burkitt (1650–1703.)[730] We also have indicated that another source in understanding Mr. Madison's views on the Old Testament was his college mentor, John Witherspoon (1723–1794), noted Bible scholar and signer of the Declaration of Independence.

Indeed, in the Second Section of Chapter Three, we have examined Mr. Witherspoon's treatment of five Old Testament passages in his *Collected Sermons* and the possible influences there may have been on the fourth President of the United States.[731] To that end, we have discussed many of the notes that James Madison had written into the family Bible. Among these notes, we have discussed passages from the Book of Job, Psalms, the Prophet Isaiah, the Book of Daniel, and many other Hebrew Bible, or Old Testament selections.

We also have shown in the Second Section of Chapter Three that among the books of the Old Testament on which Mr. Madison has commented, he provided a more extensive treatment of the Book of Proverbs than any other book. In fact, we have shown that the fourth President's remarks on Proverbs contain assents to many of Mr. Madison's central theological tenets such as the Divinity of Jesus, the existence of angels and devils, as well as belief in both Resurrection of the Body and Immortality of the Soul.

Mr. Madison's views and uses of the New Testament were the central focus in the Third Section of Chapter Three of this Study. Again, we have suggested that the two main sources for his views on the New Testament were the Rev. William Burkitt's *Expository Notes on the Bible* and the notes that the fourth President took in John Witherspoon's course on the New Testament while in college and graduate school.

---

730 William Burkitt. *Expository Notes on the Bible.* (London: Wentworth Press, 2016)

731 John Witherspoon. *Collected Sermons.* (Philadelphia: Franklin Classics, 2018)

In the remainder of the Third Section of Chapter Three, we have examined many of the notes on the New Testament that Mr. Madison referred to as his "Notes on the Commentary on the Bible," which were completed from 1770 to 1773 when the fourth President was in college and in graduate school.

We also have indicated that in these New Testament notes, Mr. Madison gave a much more thorough account on the Acts of the Apostles than he did the other books of the New Testament. Indeed, we have shown that many of the great American statesman's key theological ideas can be seen in his remarks on Acts.

Among these theological ideas we have indicated that the fourth President believed were most central were his views on Conscience, his views on the Soul and Survival After Death, and the idea that God does not cause Evil but He does sometimes Permit it.

We also have indicated in the Third Section of Chapter Three that Mr. Madison only made cursory comments on the four Gospels, and far more on the Synoptic Gospels, Matthew, Mark, and Luke, than on the Gospel of John.

Along the way in Chapter Three, we also have indicated many of the central ideas of the New Testament to which it appears that the fourth President had assented. Among these theological ideas we have mentioned seven in particular. These may be summarized this way:

1. The belief in the Virgin Mary.
2. The meaning of the word Bethlehem.
3. Madison's understanding of Papists and Confession.
4. His idea of Adoption.
5. His view of Forgiveness.
6. The difference between a 'Gift' and a 'Grace.'
7. Madison's understanding of marriage for Ministers of Faith.

We also have cautioned, however, that James Madison made these remarks on the New Testament at a youthful time in his life and there are many gaps in the document where the great American statesman made no comment at all. There is nothing, for example, about the first eight chapters of the Gospel of Matthew, nor anything after chapter twenty-one of the text. The only chapter of the Gospel of John, to cite another example, on which Mr. Madison made some comments was chapter twenty of the fourth Gospel.[732]

In regard to Mr. Madison's comments on Mark, he only supplied commentaries for the first eight chapters of the Gospel and only chapter two of the Gospel of Luke. In fact, we even indicated that the fourth President appears to have mentioned the shrine of the Ka'baa, the cube-shaped shrine in Mecca in Saudi Arabia.[733]

In short, as we have indicated, Mr. Madison's treatment of the New Testament falls far short of a thorough analysis of the twenty-seven books of the New Testament. Indeed, of those 27 books, Mr. Madison only comments on five of them—the four Gospels and the Acts of the Apostles.

Section Two: Conclusions to Chapters Four, Five, and Six.

The two main goals of Chapter Four of this Study, as we have maintained in the Introduction to the chapter was to give a thorough account of what James Madison believed and wrote about the phenomena of Ethics and Conscience. We attempted to meet these two goals by dividing the chapter into three main Sections.

In the first of these Sections, we put forth an account of the major sources that went into the development of the fourth President of the United States's ethical views. Among those intellectual sources we have mentioned the following:

1. The Scottish Common Sense School of Philosophy.
2. John Witherspoon's Sermons and Lectures on Moral Philosophy.
3. Aristotle's Nicomachean Ethics.

---

732 Madison. *Syllabus*. Pp. 7–29
733 Ibid., p. 19

4. Seneca's Letters on Virtue.

5. Cicero's essay, On Virtue.[734]

After discussing the contributions that each of these five sources may have made in the early intellectual life of James Madison, we moved to a Second Section of Chapter Four in which we identified and discussed the ideas of Morality and Conscience in thirteen of the other American Founding Fathers.

Of the other Founding Fathers who commented upon the idea of Conscience, we have identified, and commented upon, the views of the following American Founding Fathers:

1. Roger Williams.
2. George Washington.
3. John Adams.
4. Thomas Jefferson.
5. John Jay.
6. John Witherspoon.
7. Benjamin Rush.
8. Patrick Henry.
9. Samuel Adams.
10. William Livingston.
11. Charles Grandison Finney.
12. John Quincy Adams.

After indicating what each of this dozen of Founding Fathers said or wrote about the idea of Conscience, we turned our attention to the Third Section of Chapter Four, in which we discussed the views of James Madison on Ethics and Conscience. One thing we may point out, however, about the other twelve Founding Fathers is how many of them appear to be cognizant of, or have positively assented to, the

---

734 Ketcham. Pp. 21–24

Scottish Common Sense view on Morality and Conscience. Among these figures, as we have shown, were John Adams, Thomas Jefferson, Benjamin Rush, and, of course, John Witherspoon who taught the theory of James Madison.

The major belief of the Common Sense School in the 17th and 18th century was the notion that the idea of moral goodness is an innate trait in human beings, and the Scottish School usually referred to this innate ability as the Conscience. We also have indicated that the main figures in the Common Sense School of Philosophy were Thomas Reid (1710–1795.), George Campbell (1719–1796), and James Oswald and his *An Appeal to Common Sense in Behalf of Religion*, a popular vindication of Religion and the Conscience.[735]

The main focus of the Third Section of Chapter Four has been what James Madison said and wrote about the phenomena of Ethics and Conscience. We began the Third Section by pointing out that many of the most important things that James Madison related about the idea of Conscience can be found in a work of his entitled, "An Essay on Property," in which the fourth President maintained that the "Conscience is the most sacred of all property."[736]

In the remainder of Section Three of Chapter Four, we have quoted Mr. Madison in a variety of his works where he said or wrote something about the phenomenon of Conscience. These quotations came from his letters, his 1785, *Memorial and Remonstrance*, as well as in his various drafts of the First Amendment of the U.S. Constitution.

A number of conclusions can be made, as we have suggested in Chapter Four, about James Madison's beliefs about Conscience. First, he believed that Conscience was an innate and universal sense of the Good. Second, he believed it was a gift, or a grace, from God. Third, Mr. Madison believed that no man has the right to interfere in any way with the Conscience of another. And finally, like the Common Sense School and his mentor, John Witherspoon, the fourth President of the United States thought that the right to

---

735 Thomas Reid. *An Appeal to Common Sense on Behalf of Religion*. (London: Garland Publishing, 1978

736 Ketcham, pp. 85–87

Conscience than any of a person's Civil Rights, because Conscience came first, both in terms of time and space.[737]

As we have indicated in the Introduction to Chapter Five, the two central issues to be discussed in the Chapter were James Madison's views on Religious Freedom, or what was called "Religious Liberty" at the time, and what he believed about Religious Toleration. This latter issue, as we have seen, is a central one in the thought of the fourth President.

Chapter Five of this Study was divided into three main Sections. In the first of those we have set forth what Jams Madison believed and had to say about the phenomenon of Religious Liberty. In the Second Section of Chapter Five, our main focus has been on what Mr. Madison believed and wrote about Religious Toleration; and the Third and Final Section of Chapter Five, we have explored what great, American statesman, James Madison thought and wrote about Religious traditions other than his own, the Episcopal Church."[738] These traditions included Catholicism, Judaism, the Baptists, the Presbyterians, as well as other points of view, including the Faith of Islam.

We began the First Section of Chapter Five by pointing out Mr. Madison's reaction to the jailing of six Baptist ministers in Culpepper, Virginia, who appear to have done nothing more than expressing their religious views.

Next, in Chapter Five, we wrote about Mr. Madison's amending of George Mason's formulation of a clause on religious liberty that, "All men should enjoy the fullest toleration in the full exercise of Religion."[739] As we have indicated in Chapter Five, Mr. Madison's reformulation of Mr. Mason's draft was a radical shift, from toleration to human nature, as we will discuss in our summary of Section Two of Chapter Five.

In the First Section of Chapter Five, we also have explored an attempt by Patrick Henry before the Virginia state legislature to replace the established church in the state with "multiple established

---

737 James Madison. *Federalist Papers*. essay no. 51
738 Ketcham, p. 237
739 George Mason. Formulation of Preamble to Bill of Rights

churches," all to be supported with Virginia taxpayers. James Madison's work, *Memorial and Remonstrance*, written in 1785, was principally a negative response to Mr. Henry's proposal. Indeed, in the *Memorial*, Mr. Madison ushered fifteen separate arguments against Mr. Henry's bill.[740]

In the Section on Religious Toleration in Chapter Five, we began by giving a summary of how religious toleration had been dealt with from the beginning of the colonies. We also have pointed out that with the passing of a statute for Religious Freedom, drafted by Thomas Jefferson, that statute began to serve as a model for other states, as well as for the First Amendment of the U.S. Constitution.[741]

After sketching out the various views about established churches in the thirteen colonies, we returned to the idea of Mr. Madison's reformulation of George Mason that, "All men should enjoy the fullest Toleration in the exercise of their religion. As we have indicated, the fourth President amended the line to say, "All men are equally entitled to the full and free exercise of religion."[742]

We also have shown that Mr. Madison's change was a radical shift from one view about religious freedom to another entirely different perspective. More specifically, we have suggested that it was a shift from what we have called the "Toleration View," to a perspective that the right to Conscience is far more fundamental and prior than any of our Civil Rights. This new perspective we will call the "Human Nature View." This view essentially says that God gave every human being a Conscience and an innate desire to do the good. Mr. Madison believed that this innate desire is built into human nature. So, at least in his view, the issues of religious freedom and toleration should be shifted from the 'Toleration View,' to the 'Human Nature View.[743]

In the Second Section of Chapter Five, we also have indicated the indebtedness of James Madison to the philosophical views of English

---

740   Ketcham, p. 237

741   James Madison. Memorial and Remonstrance. [1785]

742   Thomas Jefferson. Virginia Bill for the Establishment of Religious Freedom. [1779]

743   James Madison. Formulation of Preamble to Bill of Rights

philosopher, John Locke, particularly in regard to the Englishman's *Letter Concerning Toleration*, as well as how far Mr. Locke believed that religious rights extend. In fact, as we have shown, Mr. Locke and Pierre Bayle, among others, disagreed with Mr. Madison on whether Catholics have a right to the free exercise of their religion. Locke and Bayle said no, while Mr. Madison said yes.[744]

At the close of Section Two of Chapter Five, we have introduced the scholarly work of Kevin Vance who suggests that all that Mr. Madison said and wrote about religious liberty and religious toleration can first be found in the works of John Locke, and we heartily agree with Mr. Vance's conclusion.[745]

The Third Section of Chapter Five, as we indicated in the Introduction to the Chapter, was taken up with what the fourth President believed and wrote about other religions other that his own Episcopal Faith. We began that Section Three, by reiterating Mr. Madison's reaction to the jailing of six Baptist ministers in Culpepper Virginia in 1773, when those ministers had complained about their treatment from the Episcopal Church in Virginia.[746]

Next, in the Third Section of Chapter Five we turned our attention to James Madison's treatment of Catholics, using an article written for the *Washington Post* by David Kopel who argued that the English *Declaration of Rights* enacted by Parliament in 1689, only granted religious rights to "Protestant subjects of the Crown."[747] Mr. Kopel concluded that the Second Amendment of the U.S. Constitution was a by-product of the English statute that denied the "right to bear arms" to Catholics.[748]

We also have indicated that when James Madison proposed the first draft of the First Amendment of the U.S. Constitution the

---

744 James Madison. *Federalist Papers*. essays 10 and 51

745 John Locke. *Letter Concerning Toleration*. (New York: Crete Space, 2014)

746 Kevil Vance. "Golden Thread of Religious Liberty." *Oxford Journal of law and Religion*. Vol. 6, no. 2. [2017.], pp. 227–252

747 James Madison to William Bradford. January 24, 1774

748 David Kopel. Op-Ed on Anti-Catholics. *Washington Post*. November 20, 2015

Catholic, Daniel Carroll, was the only member of Congress to support Mr. Madison's first draft of the Amendment. Indeed, we have supplied a summary of Mr. Carroll remarks to Congress on August 15, 1789, supplied by Thomas Lloyd.[749]

In addition to the support of Baptists and Catholics in Section Two of Chapter Five by Mr. Madison, we also went on in that Section to speak of the admiration that the fourth President had of the Jews and Judaism. In fact, in that portion of Chapter Five we spoke of letters between Thomas Jefferson and James Madison, back and forth, to two prominent 18th Century, American Rabbis, Mordecai Manuel Noah and Dr. Jacob De la Motta. In fact, we have shown that Mr. Madison's two return letters, gave him an opportunity to express his dedication and admiration for the Jewish Faith, as well as his commitment to the Religious Toleration that he thought should be extended to the faith in America.[750]

Next in Chapter Five, still in Section Three, we went on to speak of the many relationships that James Madison had to the American Presbyterian Church, including his time as a student of Donald Robertson and his college mentor, President John Witherspoon of the College of New Jersey.

We also have indicated at the end of Chapter Five that James Madison's *Federalist* essay number fifty-one, the great American statesman voiced his displeasure at the growing number of religious Sects that were proliferating in his day and that he was concerned that this would turn America into "too many tribes'" and factions, while giving up on what they have in common.[751]

Indeed, we have argued at the close of Chapter Five that Mr. Madison's fear in *Federalist* 51 is precisely what is occurring in American political life of the 21st Century. Too many factions, too many interests groups, Mr. Madison related, "destroys unity," and he was entirely correct about that.[752] As Mr. Madison put the matter at the time:

---

749   Ibid

750   Daniel Carroll. 'Remarks to Congress." August 15, 1789

751   James Madison. *Federalist papers*. essay no 51

752   Ibid

The Society would be broken into many parts, interests, and classes of citizens that the rights of individuals, or of the minority, will be in little danger from interested combinations of the majority.[753]

Mr. Jefferson disagreed with Mr. Madison on the meaning of the idea of the "Consent of the People." Mr. Madison saw the idea as related to the problem of Factions, while Mr. Jefferson believed in "one man, one vote, majority rules." James Madison's talent for negotiation also helped in the passage of the Bill of Rights that included the guarantee of religious liberty to be found in the First Amendment. Ultimately, then, Mr. Madison and Mr. Jefferson were on the same page when it came to religious freedom, religious toleration, and the separation of Church and State, as we shall see in the summary of Chapter Six of this Study on James Madison's Religion.

As we have indicated in the Introduction to Chapter Six of this Study, the major focus of the Chapter was to be the idea of the Separation of Church and State in America, as well as what Thomas Jefferson and James Madison believed and wrote about that phenomenon.

We began the First Section of Chapter Six by supplying a catalogue of sorts of views on the idea of Separation of Church and State. Among the sources we have pointed to in Section One were: the religious clause of the First Amendment; Mr. Madison's original proposal for the Bill of Rights; Judge Joseph Story's remarks on Church-State Separation; and two U.S. Supreme Courts cases, *Everson v. Board of Education* [1947.] and *Lemon v. Kurtzman* [1971.][754]

The main focus of the Second Section of Chapter Six has been to give a short history of Western Views on Church and State. Among the views we have introduced and then discussed were Bishop Augustine of Hippo's idea of "Two Cities."; Martin Luther's idea of "Two Kingdoms," and Jean Calvin's adoption of that idea.; Roger Williams and his *The Bloody Tenant of Persecution*, in which he called for the Separation of Church and State; the Rev. James Burgh who also put forth a claim of total Separation in his *Political Disquisitions*; and

---

753 Ibid

754 Everson v, Board of Education [1947.] Lemon v. Kurtzman, [1971]

Thomas Jefferson and his letter to the Danbury Baptists in which the third President sketches out the idea of Separation of Church and State in America.[755]

We also have shown in the Second Section of Chapter Six that other early evidence for American views on Church and State may be found in Article 11 of the "Treaty of Tripoli," in the writings of Baptist preacher, John Leland, and in George Washington's 1790 letter to the Jewish Community of Newport, Rhode Island.[756]

In the Third and Central Section of Chapter Six, we have sketched out the views of the fourth President of the United States on the phenomenon of the Separation of Church and State. Many of Mr. Madison's comments about the matter can be found is his letters to Christian organizations, like the Baptist Churches of North Carolina, for example, or letters to Mr. Madison's friends and acquaintances like Rev. Jasper Adams, Edward Livingston, and to Edward Everett, among many others.[757]

What this evidence showed in Chapter Six is Mr. Madison's clear assent to his belief in the idea of Separation. We also have suggested that the great American statesman endorsed the phenomenon of the Separation of Church and State in his *Detached Memorandum*, as well as two bills he vetoed about the matter when he was President, one in 1814 and the other in 1815.[758]

In Section Four of Chapter Six, we turned our attention to some matters in Mr. Madison's retirement where he appeared to have expressed some reservations about some issues related to Church and State Separation. Among these issues were the use of government

---

755 Roger Williams. *The Bloody Tenant of Persecution*. (New York: Palala Books, 2016)

756 Rev. James Burgh. *Political Disquisitions*. (Washington: Applewood Books, 2009

757 James Madison to the Christian Churches of North Carolina. August 20, 1787

758 James Madison. *Detached Memorandum*. One of these bills h vetoed was in Alexandria, Virginia on February 21, 1814. The other veto was a bill from March 4, 1815

funds for institutions like the American Baptists in the American West, the making of Prayer and Thanksgiving Proclamations, of which Mr. Madison made two as President, and the idea of having Chaplains in both the U.S. military and the U.S. Congress.

About each of these issues, as we have shown, Mr. Madison appears to have changed his mind in his retirement, because the Mr. Madison, in retirement, believed that each of these ideas was a violation of his long-held belief in the Separation of Church and State.[759]

Section Three: Conclusions to Chapters Seven, Eight, Nine & Ten

We have begun Chapter Seven of this Study on James Madison's Religion by pointing out that the Chapter would be about what the fourth President of the United States believed and wrote about Survival After Death. We have completed that aim by dividing Chapter Seven into four principal Sections. In the first of those, we have compared and contrasted the views called Resurrection of the Body and Immortality of the Soul in the history of the Judeo-Christian Tradition.

As we have shown, the former view is an Old Testament and thus an ancient Hebraic idea, while the latter idea has been gleaned from Greek Philosophy, or, more specifically, from the works of Athenian philosopher, Plato.[760]

In order to explicate the differences between these two perspectives, we have employed the grave markers of a 19th Century Presbyterian couple, one of whom is now "sleeping in the dust," while the other has "gone to her eternal reward."[761]

We also have indicated in the First Section of Chapter Seven that James Madison was fully aware of the arguments of the Greek philosopher Plato on survival after death, but we have no indication of what the fourth President of the United States thought about that series of Platonic arguments that establishes, at least in the mind of Plato and his followers, that the soul survives bodily death and is immortal. There

---

759 James Madison on Separation of Church and State. In Robert Alley. *James Madison on Religious Liberty*, pp. 142–151

760 Plato. *The Republic*. (New York: Penguin Books, 2007)

761 Grove Street Cemetery. New Haven, Connecticut

is no evidence, however, that Mr. Madison employed these Platonic arguments in any way.[762]

In the Second Section of Chapter Seven, we have introduced the two major views on survival after death that existed at the time of James Madison's birth in 1751. One of these views was that of David Hume who was skeptical about the matter, while the other perspective, held by German philosopher, Immanuel Kant, who proposed that Immortality of the Soul may be proven through a series of complicated philosophical arguments by what Kant called "Practical Reason."[763]

Indeed, of the 17th and 18th Century philosophers who believed that Immortality can be proved were the following: Rene Descartes and Bishop Joseph Butler in addition to Immanuel Kant. Among those who denied the Immortality of the Soul were the Baron D'Holbach and French philosopher, Voltaire.[764] James Madison, as we have shown, would have been aware of this philosophical literature on Immortality of the Soul going all the way back to Plato and his student, Aristotle.

In the Third Section of Chapter Seven, we have explored what we have called the "Sources for James Madison's Views on Survival After Death." In that Section we have pointed to six principal sources. These were: Plato, Aristotle, John Witherspoon, the Thomas Jefferson Bible, other American Founding Fathers, and Enlightenment ideas from people like Rene Descartes, David Hume, Immanuel Kant, Bishop Joseph Butler, the Barons Montesquieu, and D'Holbach, and many other figures that Mr. Madison became familiar with through the teachings of Donald Robertson and John Witherspoon.

Of these sources, as we have indicated, Thomas Jefferson's project to eliminate with a razor all the traces of miracles and survival after death in the 'Jefferson Bible,' may have been the major source behind

---

762 Ibid

763 Immanuel Kant. *Critique of Practical Reason*. (Cambridge: Cambridge University Press, 2016)

764 Voltaire's view on the soul can be seen in his article on "Death," in his *Philosophical Dictionary*. (London: penguin Books, 1984)

the lack of information about what the fourth President believed about these philosophical issues.[765]

If the Jefferson Bible was not the principle source of James Madison's views on Immortality, then it could also have been the many sermons of his College mentor, President John Witherspoon, in which the Scotsman indicated his assents to both Resurrection of the Body and to Immortality of the Soul.[766]

In the Fourth and Final Section of Chapter Seven, we have sketched out the few places in the *Collected Works* of James Madison, where the fourth President of the United States said or wrote anything about Immortality and Resurrection. As we have indicated in Section Four of Chapter Seven these few references all came from Mr. Madison's essays of the *Federalist Papers*.

Indeed, as we have shown the meager references to Survival After Death in the work of James Madison may be found in essays numbers 10, 17, 18, 46, 51, and 55 of the *Federalist Papers*. And in each of these examples, Mr. Madison used the words 'Spirit' and 'Soul,' but not in a metaphysical or theological context. The overall pieces of evidence, however, in regard to James Madison's understanding on Survival After Death are few and far between, and there is little evidence to assert that James Madison was an active believer in either Resurrection of the Body or Immortality of the Soul.

In the Introduction to Chapter Eight on James Madison on Human Nature and Democracy, we have suggested that the chapter would unfold in four, separate Sections. The first of these was an exploration of the many views on human nature among many 17th and 18th Century philosophical thinkers in Europe.

Among the figures we have identified and discussed in this First Section of Chapter Eight were the views of Thomas Hobbes, Jean-Jacques Rousseau, John Locke, and Scottish philosopher, David Hume. Hobbes believed that human beings are basically flawed, Rousseau that they are basically good and became evil by forming societies. John

---

765 Thomas Jefferson. *The Bible*. (London: A & D Books, 2009

766 John Witherspoon. 'Sermons," in *The Works of John Witherspoon*. (Philadelphia: Franklin Classics, 2016.), pp, 93 to 147

Locke took a middle of the road on basic human nature but he based his view on the ideas of Reason and Self- Interest.[767]

The views of David Hume on human nature, as we have shown in the First Section of Chapter Eight, were mostly reactions to the views of Hobbes, Rousseau, and, particularly John Locke, in that Hume believed that human passions were much more fundamental to human behavior than the idea of Reason. In fact, he thought that Reason was much less basic to human nature than is Passion.[768]

In the Second Section of Chapter Eight our central focus has been on what James Madison believed and said about basic human nature. The chief evidence for discerning the views of the fourth President on this matter is five essays of the *Federalist Papers*, one by Alexander Hamilton [number six] and four written by James Madison [10, 34, 37, and 55.]

From this evidence in the *Federalist Papers*, we have concluded that both Mr. Hamilton and Mr. Madison—like Augustine, Thomas Aquinas, and Thomas Hobbes—believe that human nature is flawed. Both of these American Founding Fathers were advocates of a pessimistic view on basic human nature.

In the Third Section of Chapter Eight, we have shifted our focus to speak of what Mr. Madison believed and wrote about Democracy. In that Section, as we have shown, we have shown that James Madison was against the idea of one man one vote and majority rules, chiefly because of what he called as the "dangers of Factions." For the fourth President a Faction may be formed by the melding together of the passions of disparate people. For him, it is the forming of Factions that is responsible for a mob.

The danger of a Faction, at least in the mind of James Madison, was that if enough people came together to form a Faction, it could well produce what he called a "Tyranny of the Majority." **52** We went on in Section Three of Chapter Eight to discuss observations that James Madison made on Factions in his essay number ten of the *Federalist*

---

767 See note 30 of this Chapter

768 David Hume *A Treatise on Human Nature*. (Edinburgh: Hackett Books, 1993)

Papers, where he related that a Faction, "is a group united and actuated by some common impulse of passion."⁷⁶⁹

We also have pointed out that in the American two party system, we have seen that system devolve into nothing more than what James Madison referred to as two competing "Factions." We also have shown that Mr. Madison related that, "Liberty is to a Faction, Air is to a Fire." And the impetus for those Factions is human passions.⁷⁷⁰

In the Fourth and Final Section of Chapter Eight, we have attempted to bring the two topics of Chapter Eight together by speaking of what James Madison saw as the relationships and connections of human nature to the practice of democracy. In that Fourth Section we have reiterated the fact that both Mr. Hamilton and Mr. Madison has assented to the more pessimistic view of human nature, like Thomas Hobbes, and that must be kept in mind in the process of forming a government.

We also have indicated in Section Four of Chapter Eight that the second President of the United States, John Adams, in an essay entitled, "All Men Would be Tyrants if They Could," also held a view of human nature that comes close to the Hobbesian perspective.⁷⁷¹ Mr. Adams also set forth the same view on human nature in the introduction of his 1807 *Defense of the Constitution of the United States*, in which he put forth the idea that Greek historian, Thucydides also held a pessimistic understanding of basic human nature.⁷⁷²

Indeed, in that work Mr. Adams gave a short paraphrase of Thucydides' account of the Battle or siege of Coryra in 373 BCE, where the "rage of violence could only have been natural."⁷⁷³ Thus, as we have shown, we may add the names of John Adams and Thucydides to our list of thinkers in the West who had a Hobbesian understanding of human nature. Other American Founding Fathers, as we have shown,

---

769 James Madison. *Federalist papers*. essay no. 10

770 Ibid

771 John Adams. A Defense of the Constitution of the United States. (Boston, N.P.1807)

772 Ibid

773 Ibid

also commented upon the question of basic human nature. Alexander Hamilton, as we had shown earlier in Chapter Eight, made remarks about what he called "the folly and wickedness of mankind," and he suggested that we should approach the question of human nature without 'flattering its virtues, nor exaggerating its vices."[774] Consequently, Mr. Hamilton declared that, "Men are ambitious, vindictive, and rapacious."[775]

Mr. Madison's pessimistic view on human nature was also shared by John Jay, the third author of some of the *Federalist Papers*. In a return letter to Mr. Jay, Georg Washington on March 15, 1786 told the judge of his assenting to a pessimistic view of human nature. General Washington wrote to Mr. Jay, "We must take human nature as we find it, perfection falls not to the share of mortals."[776] Given the correspondence between these two Founding Fathers, Mr. Jay clearly shared this pessimistic view as well.

In his "Newburgh Address," however, that was given on March 15, 1783, General Washington suggested the loftiness that might be attained by humans when he wrote: And you will, by the dignity of your Conduct, afford occasion for Posterity to say, when speaking of the glorious example you have exhibited to Mankind, had this day been wanting, the World have never seen the last stage of perfection to which human nature is capable of attaining.[777]

Even Benjamin Franklin, in his 1771 *Autobiography*, referred to the Hobbesian view of human nature when he wrote:

> In reality, there is perhaps no one of our natural Passions so hard to subdue than Pride. Disguise it, struggle with it, beat it down, stifle it, modify it as much as one pleases, but it is still alive and will now and then peek out and show itself.[778]

Mr. Franklin appears here to make the connection between the passions of humans and basic human nature. This is connected, of

---

774 Alexander Hamilton. *Federalist Papers*. essay no. 6
775 Ibid
776 John Jay. *Federalist Papers*. essay no 44
777 George Washington. "Newburgh Address." Match 15, 1783
778 Benjamin Franklin. A*utobiography*. (New York: Norton, 2012.) p. 139

course, to the view of Mr. Madison that the root of what he called "factions" is nothing more than the Passions of Men. Ultimately, at least for James Madison, following David Hume, the Passions are the best explanations for interpreting human behavior.

The conclusion, therefore, of this discussion of the American Founding Fathers on basic human nature should be clear. George Washington, John Adams, James Madison, Benjamin Franklin, Alexander Hamilton, and John Jay, among many others, were all convinced that the Hobbesian view of human nature was the proper one. And this must be kept in mind during the proofs of forming a Government.

Another way to put this matter, the problem with Democracy, according to James Madison, is nothing more than the effects of human nature and more particularly on the human Passions. Thus, the Enlightenment ideas of Reason and Equality, must be used as tools to combat the passions of men. In this sense, Mr. Madison would appear to be assenting to the views of Thomas Hobbes and John Locke on human nature and the forming of government, at the same time.

The central focus of Chapter Nine has been what James Madison, the fourth President of the United States, believed, said, and wrote about religions other than the Episcopal Church in which he was raised in Virginia. To that end, we have divided the Chapter into six sections In the first of these, we began the first Section of Chapter Nine with a description of the philosophical movement known as Deism in the second half of the 18th Century in Europe and America.[779]

In that description, we pointed out that the Deist believed in a God Who created the Universe, and the rules by which it runs, and then has little contact with His creation. In that sense, we have suggested that the Deist believed in a *Deus Absconditis,* that is a "God Who absconds," or "goes away."[780]

Next, and still in the First Section of Chapter Nine, we have pointed out several passages in the *Collected Works* of James Madison

---

[779] For more on Deism, See: Bob Johnson. *Deism.* (London: World Union of Deists, 2009)

[780] The expression "Deus absconditis" was first employed by Thomas Aquinas in his *Summa Theologica*

that seem to imply that the great American statesman believed that God causes miracles to occur on Earth, as well as His answering of prayers of human beings. From these two premises, we went on to conclude that James Madison could not have been a Deist.

In the Second Section of Chapter Nine, we have indicated what James Madison believed and wrote about the American Baptists. For the evidence of what the fourth President believed about the Baptists we have turned to the six Baptist Preachers who had been confined in jail for the simple act of expressing their religious views in 1771 in Culpepper County, Virginia.[781]

The other piece of evidence for what James Madison thought of the Baptist was his interaction with Baptist preacher, John Leland and the many theological matters about which the two men shared. We also have indicated in the Second Section of Chapter Nine that Mr. Madison and the Rev. Leland disagreed on the U.S. Bill of Rights, though eventually when the former visited the family farm of the latter in Virginia, they worked out a compromise view on the matter.[782]

Janes Madison and the Presbyterians was the subject matter of the Third Section of Chapter Nine In that Section we mostly relied on Mr. Madison's two Presbyterian teachers, Donald Robertson and President John Witherspoon of the College of New Jersey. In that Third Section of Chapter Nine, we gave a list of the many things that these two Scottish teachers gave to the young charge, James Madison. Among these things were the study of Ancient languages such as Greek, Latin, and Classical Hebrew, as well as Greco-Roman history, poets, and philosophers, modern languages like French and Italian, as well as a number of Enlightenment figures from the 17th and 18th Century, like John Locke, David Hume, and French philosopher and nobleman, the Baron Montesquieu, among many others.

In the Fourth Section of Chapter Nine, our preoccupation was the dealings that James Madison had with leading Jewish thinkers of his time, including Rabbi Mordecai Manuel Noah, Dr. Jacob De la Motta,

---

781 This event took place in November of 1773

782 James Madison to John Leland. February 29, 1789. This letter came as a response to John Leland to Madison's letter on February 15, 1789

and a Richmond, Virginia Jew named Joseph Marx. We also have shown that Mr. Madison was aware of, and respected greatly, the work of Rabbi Gershom Mendes Seixas.[783]

In the Fifth Section of Chapter Nine, we provided an analysis of what contacts James Madison had with the Roman Catholic Church, as well as a number of prominent American members of that same Church. Indeed, we have indicated that many of these prominent Catholics were members of the same family, the Carroll family in Maryland.

In fact, we have shown that the fourth President had dealings with Archbishop John Carroll of Baltimore, as well as his cousin, Daniel Carroll, a member of the U.S. Congress who supported Mr. Maison's original proposal for the wording of the First Amendment of the US Constitution. Charles Carroll of Carrollton was another prominent member of the Carroll family and American Catholicism in the late 18th Century. Mr. Madison was fully aware of Mr. Carroll's accomplishments, both in Maryland and in national politics, as well.[784]

The Sixth and Final Section of Chapter Nine was centered on what contact and relations the fourth President of the United States had with the Religion of Islam and with Muslims. We began Section Six of Chapter Nine by speaking of James Madison's friendship with George Bethune (1787–1828), who changed his name to Muhammad Afendi after he converted to the Muslim Faith from Christianity.[785]

As we have indicated, Mr. English studied at the Harvard Divinity School and a short time later he began becoming disillusioned with the Church of Christ in which he was raised. As we have shown, among the Christian ideas that George English began to have doubts were the Trinity, the Crucifixion, Original Sin, and the nature and extent of the Atonement. Mr. English so strongly rejected these ideas that he wrote

---

783 Rabbi Gershom Mendes Seixas was the most famous Jew in American in James Madison's time

784 Ketcham, pp. 194 and 318

785 George English changed his name to Mohammad Afendi in 1815, shortly after his conversion

a book he called *The Grounds of Christianity Examined*.[786] As we have shown, this led to his dismissal from the Church of Christ in 1814.

Mr. English became friendly with James Madison in 1815, when the latter appointed the former to a post in the U.S. Marines, which Mr. English served in the Mediterranean Sea. We also have indicated that after the conversion of Mr. English to Islam in 1815, he began to learn Arabic and the Turkish languages. In fact, Mr. English served in the Artillery of Ismail Pasha, the Viceroy of Egypt under the Ottoman Empire.[787]

We also have shown in Section Six of Chapter Nine of this Study on James Madison's Religion that George English wrote a book entitled *A Narrative of an Expedition to Dongola and Sennaar*, his account of his voyage up the Nile from Cairo to Nubia and the Sudan.[788]

In the remainder of Section Six of Chapter Nine, we have examined the contacts that many of Mr. Madison's friends—particularly American politicians—who had some contact with Islam in the second half of the 18th Century. Among these political figures were Thomas Jefferson, William Henry Lee, Ezra Stiles, the President of Yale College, and Supreme Court Justice, Joseph Story.[789]

We also have shown that when James Madison wrote the drafts of the First Amendment of the U.S. Constitution, he clearly had a view that the rights of Muslims, or "Mahometans," as he called them, were among the people in the United States whose religious rights were to be protected. And Mr. Madison made this point other Islam, as well as other Religious minorities, in the remainder of his life.

We have begun Chapter Ten of this Study on James Madison's Religion with some very general comments about Slavery and the American Presidency, as well as some general remarks about the

---

786 George English. *The Grounds of Christianity Examined*. (London: Wentworth Press, 2019)

787 George English. A Narrative of an Expedition to Dongola and Sennaar. (London: Wentworth Press, 2016

788 Ibid

789 All of these figures are discussed in James H. Hutson. "Islam in the Founding Fathers." *Library of Congress Journal*. Vol. 61, no. 5. [May, 2002]

practice of Slavery in the Virginia Colony-State in the 17th and 18th Centuries.

In the opening Section of Chapter Ten, we have also identified and discussed the two major Slave Rebellions in Virginia in Colonial Times. Th first of these Rebellions, as we have shown, was known as the Gabriel Rebellion because it was named after and organized by a Black blacksmith in 1800 who, along with other Black tradesmen, participated in the Rebellion.[790] The second Slave Rebellion was the Nat Turner Rebellion that also took place in Virginia in the year 1831.[791]

This Opening Section of Chapter Ten was followed by an identification and discussion of several prominent slaves at the James Madison family home, Montpelier in Virginia. Among these prominent slaves, as we have shown were a man named Sawney who accompanied James Madison to the College of New Jersey in 1769 and worked as an Overseer at the Montpelier Farm.[792]

Another of Mr. Madison's slaves, Paul Jennings, who served Mr. Madison in the White House and has recently had a college residence hall named after him on the campus of James Madison University in Harrisonburg, Virginia. Additionally, we have also identified and discussed the lives of Sukey, a house slave to Dolley Madison and William 'Billey' Gardner, who accompanied James Madison to the Constitutional Convention in Philadelphia in the Summer of 1787.[793]

These two Sections of Chapter Ten were followed by the Central Section of the Chapter that we have labeled the "Ambivalent Attitudes of James Madison on Slavery." In fact, on the one hand, Mr. Madison grew up in a slave-holding household, he never freed his slaves, even in his will, and he clearly profited from the labor of his slaves for most of his life. On the other hand, he was the author of the language of the

---

790 Gabriel Rebellion

791 Nat Turner Rebellion

792 For more on Sawney, See pp. 25–28 and 668–670 of Ketcham

793 For more on Sukey, See: Ketcham, p. 669. William 'Billey "Gardner accompanied James Madison to the Constitutional Convention in Philadelphia in the Summer of 1787

First Amendment of the U.S. Constitution that protected the rights of minorities, and he expressed his Anti-Slavery and Abolitionist views throughout much of his adult life.

In this Third Section of Chapter Ten, we also have introduced the comments on Slavery from James Madison that were reflected in three of his published works, his *Memorandum od an African Colony of Freed Slaves*, his essay number 42 of the *Federalist Papers*, and a letter to the editor of the *Farmer's Register*.[794]

We have shown that in the first of these three works, Mr. Madison discussed his desire to establish a Colony of Freed American Slaves in Africa. Unfortunately, as we have indicated, Mr. Madison did not live long enough to see the establishment of the Republic of Liberia in 1847, when the proposed Colony was created.[795]

In *Federalist Papers* essay number forty-two, James Madison sketched out a plan for the gradual eradication of Slavery in the Unites States, suggesting that the goal may take as long as twenty years or more to compete. In essay 42, the fourth President also referred to Slavery as the "Barbarism of modern policy."[796] Mr. Madison's essay 42 was published in January of 1788, far short of the arrival of the Emancipation Proclamation and the Thirteenth Amendment of the U.S. Constitution in the 1860s.[797]

These three Sections of Chapter Ten were followed by an Introduction and discussion of seven separate letters of James Madison over the course of his adult life, where he mentioned his views on Slavery. These seven letters were written by Mr. Madison to Francis Corbin, the Marquise Lafayette, Robert Pleasants, Joseph Jones, Edmund Randolph, to his Secretary, Edward Coles, and to attorney John H.B. Latrobe. As we have shown, these letters covered a period in James Madison's life from 1790 until 1832.[798]

---

794 James Madison. Federalist Papers. essay no. 42

795 The Republic of Liberia celebrated their independence on July 26, 1847

796 James Madison. Federalist Papers. essay no. 42

797 Ibid

798 John Latrobe visited Montpelier on August 3, 1832. Also see: Ketcham, pp. 427–429

From these seven letters, we have made five conclusions about James Madison's views on Slavery over the last forty years of his life. First, the fourth President was convinced that the Slavery Problem would be solved in America. Second, in the meantime, Slavery had become the "Original Sin" of America. Third, during the Revolution and his Presidency, James Madison was in favor of raising companies of Black soldiers to fight in the American Army.

Fourth, even early on, Mr. Madison wanted "to depend as little as possible on the labor of slaves," as he told his friend Edmund Randolph in a missive on July 26, 1785. And fifth, even in his retirement at Montpelier at the end of his life, the fourth President of the United States kept alive his idea of the Colonization of Freed American Slaves to the West Coast of Africa in the Republic of Liberia.

Unfortunately, eleven years after the fourth president's death, on July 26, 1847, as we have shown, the Republic of Liberia was established by the organization of which Mr. Madison was one of the founders, the American Colonization Society. Mr. Madison would have been happy indeed.

This brings us to the Notes of the Chapter Eleven followed by an Appendix on Foreign Words and Phrases in this Study of James Madison's Religion.

Appendix A:
Foreign Words and Expressions

Over the course of this Study on James Madison's Religion, we have employed several foreign words and expressions that have been translated by the Author. Altogether, we have employed words and expressions in six other languages besides English. These languages are:

1. Classical Hebrew.
2. Classical Greek.
3. Koine or New Testament Greek
4. Classical Latin.
5. Medieval Latin.
6. Classical Arabic.

Accordingly, we will divide this Appendix into Six Parts, beginning with Classical Hebrew

Classical Hebrew

1. *Beth Shalom.* The House of Peace.
2. *Leviathan.* Great Sea Monster and a book by Thomas Hobbes.
3. *'Ra.* Evil.
4. *Shearith Israel.* The "Remnant of Israel." And the name of a Synagogue.

Classical Greek

1. *Demos.* People.
2. *Deus Absconditis.* A God Who Absconds.
3. *Kallipolos.* Republic.
4. *Kratia.* Power or Rule.
5. *Nicomachean.* Name of Aristotle's Son.
6. *Sophia.* Wisdom.
7. *Sophrosyne.* Temperance.

Koine or New Testament Greek

1. *Koine.* Name for New Testament Greek.
2. *Psycchikol.* Spiritual Body.

Classical Latin.

1. *De Oficiis.* On Duty.
2. *Peccatum Originale.* Original Sin.
3. *Quis custodiet Ipsos custodes.* Who Guards the Guardians?
4. *Virtus.* Courage.

Medieval Latin.

1. *Ad Lucilium Epistulae.* The Moral Epistles and Letters, book by Seneca.
2. *Cogito ergo Sum.* I Think, Therefore, I Am.
3. *Imitation Christi.* Imitation of Christ.

4. *Sapiential.* Wisdom.

5. *Sensus Communis.* Common sense.

Classical Arabic

1. *Al-Qur'an.* Muslim Holy Book.

2. *Ka'baa.* Cube Shrine in Mecca.

3. *Dongola.* City in North Africa.

4. *Sennaar.* City in North Africa.

5. *Shariah.* Islamic Law.

Appendix B: Madison and the Scottish Philosophy of Common Sense

> Such beliefs belong to the common sense and reason of mankind. In matters of common sense, the learned and the unlearned, the philosopher and the day-laborer, are upon the same level.
>
> —Thomas Reid, *An inquiry into the Human Mind*

> The Common Sense School developed as a reaction against the Skepticism of David Hume and the subjective Idealism of Bishop George Berkeley.
>
> —Anonymous. Editors of the *Encyclopedia Britannica*

> His [Madison's] exposure to the teachings of Presbyterian ministers, both at Robertson's school and at the College of New Jersey under the Reverend John Witherspoon, left him deeply impressed by the Common Sense Philosophy of the Scottish Enlightenment.
>
> —Anonymous "James Madison," *Encyclopedia of Virginia*

Introduction

The purpose of this Appendix B on the Scottish philosophical school known as the Scottish Sense Philosophy is ultimately to speak of what influence the school may have had on the religious views of the fourth President of the United States, James Madison. We will begin Appendix B with some comments of the nature and origins of the Common Sense School. This will be followed by a second Section of the Appendix on the influences the Scottish Common Sense Philosophy had on both European and American philosophy. This will be followed by a third and conclusive Section on what James Madison said, wrote, and believed in regard to the Scottish School of Common Sense and how it was incorporated into his overall philosophy.

The Origins and Nature of the Philosophy of Common Sense

In this first section of Appendix B, we will sketch out the origins and the fundamental beliefs of the Scottish Common Sense School of Philosophy. The period of that school was from around 1720 until about 1828. The origins of the school are attributed by some scholars to the teachings of George Turnbull (1698–1748) and his fellow regents at Marischal College of Aberdeen University in Scotland.[799]

The philosophical work of George Turnbull is important for a number of reasons in regard to our purposes in this Appendix. For one, his two college and graduate school theses in 1723 and 1726 indicate that he was the first Scottish thinker to publish writings that argued against many philosophical theories that were current in Scotland and in Europe.

Among the figures and philosophical movements Turnbull was against were David Hume and his movement known as Skepticism; Rene Descartes and his school of Rationalism; and George Berkeley and his philosophical position known as Subjected Idealism.[800]

A second reason that the philosophical work of George Turnbull is important is that in 1742, the publication of his work, *Principles of Moral and Christian Philosophy*, is the first work with the words "Common Sense" in its content.[801]

Perhaps the most important reason that the philosophy of George Turnbull was of significance is that he was a great influence on the man who most scholars identify with the Scottish Common Sense School, Thomas Reid (1710–1796.) In several places of his published works, Reid articulated the basic sense of his philosophical school:

---

799 For more on George Turnbull, see his On the Principles of Moral and Christian Philosophy. (Washington: Liberty Fund, 2005.) two volumes

800 Ibid., vol. I, pp. 39–47

801 Ibid

> If there are certain principles, as I think these are, which the constitution of our nature leads us to believe and which we are under a necessity to take for granted in the common concerns of life, without being able to give a reason for them—these are what we call the principles of common sense; and what is manifestly contrary to them, is what we call absurd.[802]

The Common Sense School taught that every person had "ordinary experiences" that provide intuitively certain assurance of: The Existence of the Self; the existence of real objects that can be seen and felt; and certain first principles upon which sound morality and religious beliefs could be established.

Nicholas Wolterstorff of Yale Divinity School suggests that Thomas Reid's theory of perception can be reduced to four basic precepts. These may be summarized this way:

1. The objects of perception are external objects. "That is, mind-independent spatially-located entities."

2. The necessary and sufficient conditions for perceiving an external object is that the object causes in one a conception thereof and an immediate (non-inferential) belief about it.

3. We human beings are so made that, in perception, the external object causes a conception of, and an immediate belief about, itself, by way of causing a sensation which in turn causes "suggests" the conception and immediate belief.

4. The sensation may cause, and often in fact does cause, the conception and belief without one's being sufficiently attentive to the sensations for a belief about it to be formed in one.[803]

---

802 Thomas Reid, quoted in Cuneo and Woudenberg. The Cambridge Companion to Thomas Reid. (Cambridge: Cambridge University Press, 2004.), p. 85

803 Ibid., pp. 87–88. Nicholas Woltersdorff. "What Sort of Epistemological Realist Was Thomas Reid?" Journal of Scottish Philosophy. [Autumn, 2006.] vol. IV, no 2, pp. 111–112

Thus, Professor Wolterstorff brings together Thomas Reid's views on the Self, the external world. The existence of other minds, and the idea of universal human experience and a sense of the Moral Good.

This brings us to the Second Section of this Appendix B in which we will discuss the influence that the Scottish Common Sense School of Philosophy had in the 18th Century in Europe, as well as in America.

The Influence of the Scottish Common Sense School

Not only did the Common Sense School dominated Scottish philosophy in the late 18th and early 19th Centuries, but it also had a major philosophical influence in France, as well as in the United States. The most important proponent of Thomas Reid's thought in France was Victor Cousin (1792–1867.)[804]

Cousin was probably the best known exponent of what was called Eclecticism, maintaining that schools of philosophical thought, which for him exists in four main categories, all of which have psychological elements involving observation and experimentation. Cousin believed that human nature consists of three distinct but complementary faculties that he called sensibility, will, and reason.[805]

Professor Cousin believed that various schools of philosophical thought should be chided for their neglect of one or more of these three fundamental capacities of human nature. Thus, for example, Cousin thought that the Materialist epistemology of Etienne de Condillac (1714–1780) mistakenly reduced human experience to the passive faculty of sensation.[806]

The psychology of Cousin is expressed in a common sense, or "universal experience" of humanity. The purpose of Philosophy, for Professor Cousin, was to explain the universal convictions or beliefs, but common sense is for him the material by which philosophy works.

---

804 For more on Victor Cousin and his assent to Common Sense, see: Edward H. Madden. "Victor Cousin and the Common Sense Tradition." History of Philosophy Quarterly. Vol. I, no. 1. ['1984.], pp. 93–109

805 Ibid., pp. 95–96

806 Ibid., pp. 97–98

And Philosophy's conclusions must be in accordance and harmony with common sense and universal human experience.[807]

Scottish Common Sense Realism also ca be found in 18th Century American intellectual circles as well. Physician Benjamin Rush spent time being tutored in Edinburgh and was imbued with strong Realist tendencies that informed most of his scientific work, including his moral opposition to slavery.[808] For him, slavery was wrong because it violated the intuitive understanding of natural rights that God has endowed us.

Evidence of the Scottish Common Sense School of philosophy also can be seen in the philosophies of both John Adams and Thomas Jefferson. President Adams, for example, compared the contributions of Common Sense philosopher, Dugald Stewart (1753-1828) favorably to works of Aristotle and opposed to thinkers like Rene Descartes and David Hume.[809]

Scottish Common Sense Realism also greatly influenced Conservative Religious thought in the United States. Princeton Seminary, for example, built its elaborate theological system on the basis of the Common Sense Philosophy in Scotland. The Seminary's three-prong emphases were on Realism, Biblical Literalism, and Confessionalism under the direction of President John Witherspoon.[810] As we will see in the Third Section of this Appendix B, which is how James Madison was introduced to the Scottish Common Sense School, as well.

James McCosh (1811-1894), was brought from Queens College, Belfast to become the Chair of Princeton College's department of Moral Philosophy. Professor McCosh, in his scientific work, wrote

---

807 Ibid., p. 100

808 For more on Dr. Benjamin Rush, see: Stephen Fried. Rush: Revolution, Madness, and Benjamin Rush, the Visionary Doctor Who Became a Founding Father. (Washington; Crown Books, 2018.)

809 For more on Dugald Stewart, see: Charles Bradford Bow. Dugald Stewart's Empire of the Mind. (Oxford: Oxford University Press, 2022.)

810 James McCosh. The Method of Divine Government (London: HardPress, 2018.)

'The Method of Divine Government," a Christian Philosophy that was a precursor to Charles Darwin's 1859, the *Origins of Species*.[811]

Mr. McCosh's most original work concerned an attempt to reconcile the theory of evolution with Christian theology. In 1874, Charles Hodge, an eminent theologian and philosopher at the Presbyterian Seminary at Princeton University, published a book called *What is Darwinism?* His answer was that it is a form of Atheism. For Professor Hodge, Darwinism was at odds with the Argument From Design, or Teleological Argument employed by many Enlightenment thinkers to prove the existence of God.

James McCosh offered the first public endorsement of evolution by an American religious leader. His chief concern in his *Supernatural in Relation to the Natural*, published in 1862, was to show that Darwinism and in his case, Presbyterianism, were perfectly consistent with each other.

In the 1860s and 70s, McCosh's movement was known as "Theistic Evolution." Several of his faculty members of his department took up McCosh's scientific views. New Testament scholar, Grant Osbourne concludes that Scottish Common Sense Realism influenced Biblical hermeneutics, that "at the surface level became popular and individualistic interpretations at the time abounded."[812]

This brings us to the third and final Section of Appendix B, in which we will make some observations about what roles the Scottish Common Sense School of Philosophy may have played in the life of the fourth President of the United States, James Madison.

James Madison and the Scottish Common Sense School

As we have indicated in Chapter One of this study on James Madison's Religion, young "Jemmy" Madison had his first encounter with the Scottish Enlightenment Common Sense School though the teachings of his tutor, Donald Robertson (1717–1783.) Robertson was born and educated in Scotland and established a boarding school on his farm in Virginia.

---

811 Charles Darwin. The Origins of Species. (New York: Signet Books, 2003.)

812 Grant R. Osborne. The Hermeneutic Spiral. (Downers Grove: InterVarsity press, 2006.), p. 27

Mr. Madison attended the Donald Robertson School from the age of eleven until just after his sixteenth birthday. Later, he described Robertson as "a man od extensive learning and a distinguished teacher."[813] The curriculum at the Donald Robertson's school was heavy on the Classics, languages, including French and Italian, and sprinklings of the Scottish Common Sense School of Philosophy that Mr. Robertson had learned at the Divinity College of Edinburgh University in Scotland, whose Moral Philosophy department was based on the philosophy of Common Sense thinker, Thomas Reid.[814]

Perhaps the most important idea that James Madison derived from Thomas Reid, through Donald Robertson, was Reid's views on the nature of morality and its relationship to human nature. Reid believed that the sense of the Moral Good is intrinsic in all human beings placed there by God Himself. In terms of what is called the Nature-Nurture conflict, Thomas Reid was decidedly on the Nature side and against the idea that the "sense of the Good" is something that is learned by human beings.[815]

A similar view about morality and human nature also was held by President Madison's college and graduate school mentor, President John Witherspoon of the College of New Jersey. In fact, among the lectures of Witherspoon that Madison attended was his "Lectures on Moral Philosophy."[816] Dr. Witherspoon began these lectures with this description:

> **Moral Philosophy is the branch of Science that treats the principles and laws of Duty or Morals.**[817]

---

813   King & Queen County, Virginia in 2018, erected a plaque honoring Donald Robertson's School. Mr. Robertson operated his school on his farm in that County for 15 years

814   Mr. Madison spoke of Mr. Robertson's School in a letter to Isaac Donaldson, the son of Donald Robertson, dated April 17, 1804. Isaac Robertson had sent a missive to Mr. Madison on March 17, 1804, and this is the fourth President's response. See microfilm Reel 27. The Madison Papers at the Library of Congress

815   Ibid

816   John Witherspoon. Lectures on Moral Philosophy. (New York: HardPress, 2013.)

817   Ibid., p. 11

Next, President Witherspoon suggested that the 'Duty' to which he refers is a Duty to God, and that this duty had been placed by the Almighty in the human nature of all people. This Duty to God in human nature—in Witherspoon's view—is tied to another idea that we saw in the philosophy of Thomas Reid, that is, that God has endowed in all human beings a sense of Moral Goodness.

Indeed, we find these two ideas—a Duty to worship God and an inherent understanding of Moral Goodness—to be at the heart of John Witherspoon's *Lectures on Moral Philosophy*. Witherspoon also believed that these two ideas are part of what he understood as "plain, common sense."

Even without Witherspoon, the Scottish Common Sense School would have found a ready welcome in the New World, particularly in Philadelphia, when Benjamin Franklin, the first great American statesman, personified this quality of utility and common sense. Moreover, Franklin had deep Scottish roots. His *Proposal for the Education of Youth*, that Franklin published in 1749, drew on the works of two University of Aberdeen professors.[818] In fact, when he established the College of Philadelphia, which would become the University of Pennsylvania, he chose Scot, William Smith, also of Aberdeen, to run it.

Benjamin Franklin also visited Scotland twice, meeting most of the important philosophical and theological thinkers there, and the great American statesman received an honorary doctorate from the University of Saint Andrews in Fife, Scotland, in 1759. This was mostly for his scientific work in electricity. This is also how Franklin came to be called "Dr. Franklin."[819]

Another idea that President Madison inherited from John Witherspoon is the latter's understanding of the soul, or the nature of the self. On this matter, Witherspoon relied a great deal on ancient

---

818 Benjamin Franklin. Proposal for the Education of Youth. (New York: Generic Books, 1927.)

819 The honorary doctorate from St. Andrews in Fife, Scotland was an honorary Doctor of Laws bestowed in 1759, his citation said he was "granted freedom of the burgh."

Greek philosopher Plato and his view of the soul in his classic works the *Republic* and the *Phaedrus*.

In his *Lectures on Moral Philosophy* Witherspoon sketched out a view of the soul or self where human nature consists of what he calls "faculties," with Reason and Conscience at the top of those qualities and emotional and instinctive impulses near the bottom. Witherspoon calls these faculties "passions," and they include pride, greed, arrogance, and lust, and many others.[820]

Plato in his analysis of the soul suggests the self has three elements, or faculties, if you will, that he calls "Rational, Spirited, and Appetitive." Indeed, Plato provides a metaphor for understanding the soul. He suggests it is like a Chariot, a Charioteer, and two horses, a lighter and a darker horse.[821]

The Charioteer is the rational element of the soul. He holds the reins and keeps the chariot on the road and in order. The Spirited element of the soul for Plato is the lighter horse. This element is principally known for its courage and is tied to the rules of society and religion. The darker horse symbolizes the appetitive element of the soul. It consists of emotions, passions, and impulses.[822]

It is very obvious that John Witherspoon's descriptions of the soul in his *Lectures on Moral Philosophy*, or his description of what he calls "faculties" in those lectures was modeled after Plato's understanding of the nature of the Self. Plato's work called the *Phaedrus* is where the chariot, charioteer, and two horses may be found.

But another idea that John Witherspoon borrowed from Plato—an idea that Witherspoon taught Madison in his *Lectures on Moral Philosophy*—is the idea that Justice in the state is related to the idea of justice in the human soul, where one's passions ought to be held in check.

The three parts of the Soul, for Plato, are like three parts of the state. These correspond to the Rational element of the state whose principal virtue is justice, the Spirited element symbolized by the lighter horse

---

820 Lectures on Moral Philosophy, pp. 79–86
821 Plato. The Phaedrus. (New York: Penguin Classics, 2005.)
822 Ibid. Sections 257C to 274A

and in society consists of the army and the police. The virtue identified with the Spirited part of the self is Courage.

For Plato, the third element of the soul, the Appetitive part consists of emotions and passions. Plato believed this is the common people in the just society. This element in society must be controlled by the other two elements, or the dark horse will cause serios damage to the society achieving Justice.

In his *Lectures on Moral Philosophy*, Mr. Witherspoon implies, but does not state outright, that Plato's three parts of the soul are like the three parts of government in the United States. The Executive Branch is the Rational element of society and should rule by Justice. The Legislative Branch is like the Spirited element of the Soul that is connected to the rules of society; and the Judicial element of American society is symbolized by the Appetitive element of the soul.

Now is order for a soul, or a society or state to survive, its three elements must work together to achieve Justice in that society. In the mind of John Witherspoon, which unfolds in the *Lectures on Moral Philosophy*, he comes very close to suggesting that the three branches of Government could best operate together in a Just Society, by taking a page or two from the Platonic dialogue known as the *Phaedrus*. If this were true, then this might have been the greatest gift that John Witherspoon had given to the fourth President of the United States, James Madison.

Appendix C:
James Madison and the Federalist Papers

> There was an estate nearby that belonged to Publius, the chief official of the island. He welcomed us to his home and showed us generous hospitality for a period of three days.
>
> —Acts of the Apostles, 28; 7. [Author's translation.]

> It has frequently been remarked that it seems to have been reserved to the people of this country, by their conduct and example, to decide the important question whether societies of men are really capable or not of establishing good Government.
>
> —Alexander Hamilton. *Federalist Papers* [Essay no. 1.]

> If men were angels no government would be necessary. If Angels were to govern Men neither external nor internal controls of Government would be necessary.
>
> —James Madison. *Federalist Papers.* [Essay no. 51.]

Introduction

The main purpose of this Appendix C is to make some general remarks about the nature of the Federalist Papers, as well as some more specific thoughts on the roles that James Madison played in the construction and writing of the eighty-five essays contained in the *Federalist Papers*, particularly how they are related to the fourth President of the United States, James Madison's views on Religion.

Nature and Extent of the Federalist Papers

The *Federalist Papers* is a collection of essays written by John Jay, Alexander Hamilton, and James Madison in 1788. These essays sought the ratification of the United States Constitution, which had been debated, and then drafted, at the Constitutional Convention in Philadelphia, the year prior, in 1787.

The *Federalist Papers* is considered one of the most significant American contributions to the field of Political Philosophy and Political Theory in the Enlightenment Period of the 18th Century and it is still widely considered to be the most authoritative source for determining the original intents of the framers of the U.S. Constitution.

The three authors of the *Federalist Papers*—John Jay, Alexander Hamilton, and James Madison—worked under the collected pseudonym, "Publius," in order to promote the ratification of the Constitution of the U.S.A. Originally, the collection was known as the *Federalist*, until the name *Federalist Papers* emerged in the early 20th Century.

Publius was the pseudonym employed by New Yorkers, Alexander Hamilton, the first U.S. Secretary of the Treasury; John Jay who became the first Chief justice of the U.S. Supreme Court; and the subject of this Study, James Madison of Virginia, who became the fourth President of the United States, to write the eighty-five essays that make up the *Federalist Papers*.

'Publius' was a common first, or *praenomen*, name in ancient Rome. In fact, the Acts of the Apostles, at 28:7, praises a man name Publius, where the New International Version or NIV of the text tells us:

> There was an estate nearby that belonged to Publius, the chief official of the island. He welcomed us to his home and showed us generous hospitality for a period of three days.[823]

The island mentioned in the text is most likely Malta, which received Paul and his ship-wrecked companions for three days. Many New Testament scholars recognize Publius to be Publius Valerius Publicola, a Roman patriot, statesman, and general, who lived in the

---

823 The edition of the Federalist Papers we have used in this Appendix C is the 2014 Dover Books Thrift Edition published in New York

Sixth Century BCE and who, according to Plutarch in his *Lives*, saved the early Roman Republic several times from tyranny and military subjugation.[824]

It is probably the case that Publius. Republican reputation was regarded by Jay, Hamilton, and Madison as superior to the republican *bona fides* of Brutus and Cato. Another reason for settling on Publius is that prominent Anti-Federalists already had appropriated the pseudonyms of Brutus (Robert Yates) and Cato (George Clinton.)[825]

The Anti-Federalists were a loose political coalition of popular American politicians that included Patrick Henry, Robert Yates, and George Clinton. The Anti-Federalists strongly opposed the vision of a centralized U.S. government as outlined in the U.S. Constitution and the Bill of Rights. The Anti-Federalist in 1791 became the nucleus for Thomas Jefferson's Republican Party, that later became the Democratic-Republican party, and then finally, simply the Democratic Party. Of some interests is that the original Democratic Party were strict Constructionists when it came to the Constitution, something at great odds with the current Democratic Party in the United States.[826]

At any rate, the authors of the *Federalist Papers* intended to influence the American voters to ratify the proposed Constitution. In *Federalist Papers* essay number one, it explicitly sets the debate over the Constitution in political terms when it said:

> It has been frequently remarked that it seems to have been reserved to the people of this country, by their conduct and example, to decide the important question, whether societies of men are really capable or not, of establishing good government from reflection and choice, or whether they are forever destined to depend for their political constitutions on accident and force.[827]

---

824 Acts of the Apostles 28: 7. [Author's translation from the Koine Greek.] Plutarch. Lives. (New York: Penguin Books, 1993.) p. 111

825 For more on the Anti-Federalists, see: Patrick Henry. The Anti-Federalist Papers. (New York: Dover Thrift Editions, 2020.)

826 Ibid., the Introduction, pp. 11–19

827 Alexander Hamilton. Federalist Papers. [Essay no one.]

Because of the uses of pseudonyms, the authorship of the eighty-five essays of the *Federalist Papers* is not always clear. After Alexander Hamilton's death at the hands of the pistol of Aaron Burr in 1804, a list emerged claiming that he alone had written sixty percent of the essays. The scholarly detective work of Douglass Adair in 1944, made the following corrections in regard to assigning authorship of the *Federalist Papers*:

1. Alexander Hamilton. [fifty-one essays.] Nos. 1, 6–9, 11–13, 15–17, 21–36, 59–61 and 65–85.
2. James Madison. [twenty-nine essays.] Nos. 10, 14, 18–20, 37–58, and 62 and 63.
3. John Jay. [five essays.] Nos. 2 to 5 and 64.[828]

The *Federalist Papers* originally appeared in three New York newspapers: the *Independent Journal*, the *New York Packet*, and the *Daily Advertiser*, beginning on October 27, 1787 and continuing for six months until all eighty-five essays had been published. The three writers worked at a great pace, sometimes producing three or four pieces in a single week. Remarking about this fast pace, Garry Wills has written:

> This fast pace of production overwhelmed any possible response. Who, given ample time could have answered such a battery of arguments? And no time was given.[829]

In the first essay of the *Federalist Papers,* written by Alexander Hamilton, he sketches out what he saw as the major six topics to be explored in the subsequent essays. Mr. Hamilton tells us:

1. The Utility of the Union and its relation to Political Prosperity. [Nos. 2–14.]

---

828 Douglass Adair. Fame and the Founding Fathers. (Washington: Liberty Fund, 1998.)

829 Garry Wills. Explaining America: The Federalist. (New York: Continuum International Books, 1981.), p. xii

2. The Insufficiency of the current Confederation so that the Union may be preserved. [No. 22.]

3. The necessity of a Government at least equally energetic to the one proposed to the attainment of this object. [Nos. 23–36.]

4. The Conformity of the proposed Constitution to the true principles of Republican Government. [Nos. 37–40.]

5. The analogy to state constitutions. [No. 85.]

6. Th additional security which its adoption will afford to the preservation of that species of Government, to Liberty and to Prosperity. [No. 85.][830]

This brings us to the second and central Section of this Appendix C on James Madison and his roles and participation in the writing of the *Federalist Papers*. As indicated above, the fourth President was responsible for twenty-nine of the total of eighty-five essays.

Madison's Authorship / Contributions to the *Federalist Papers*

Nearly all 18th Century, American historians agree that the five most important of the *Federalist Papers* are numbers ten, thirty-nine, fifty-one, sixty-eight, and seventy-eight. The final pair, most agree, were authored by Alexander Hamilton. But the three remaining essays in our list—numbers 10, 39, and 51—will be the central concerns in this Second Section of the Appendix C on James Madison and the Federalist Papers.

The focus that Mr. Madison wished to address in essay number ten as to address the question of how to reconcile citizens with interests contrary to the rights of others or are inimical to the interests of the community as a whole. In essay ten, Mr. Madison gives these citizens the name "Factions."

For the fourth President of the United States, a Faction is a small group unconcerned about the interests of citizens as a whole and concentrate instead on the interest of like-minded individuals who came together to form Factions. One aspect of Mr. Madison's concerns

---

830 Hamilton. Federalist Papers. [Essay no. one.]

about Factions is the contemporary ramifications his view may now have for what has come to be called "Identity Politics," by many in the current United States.

By the label "Identity Politics," we mean attitudes and opinions about the self and others is based fundamentally by a particular identity such as race, nationality, religion, sexual orientation, gender, social background, and social class, among other identities. Thus, in Madison's terms there is an African-American Faction; a LGBTQ Faction; a Transgender Faction; and many other possibilities in contemporary American life. Mr. Madison warned in Federalist number ten that the biggest danger to Government is not foreign enemies, nor disease or natural disasters, but rather the forming of factions that care little or nothing about the interests of American citizens as a whole. To show the importance of this point of the fourth President of the United States asks yourself this question. When was the last time those who are members of a group in Identity politics express any concern about the general interest of the American people? The answer is you never have because they are solely self-interested in their own identity.[831]

This brings us to a discussion of *Federalist Papers* essay number thirty-nine also written by James Madison and also considered one of the five most important essays of the collected *Federalist Papers*. Federalist thirty-nine is entitled, "The Conformity of the Plan for Republican Principles."[832] It was published in the *Independent Journal*, on January 16, 1788. In it Mr. Madison defines a republican form of government, and he also considers whether the United States is federal or national and thus a confederacy or a consolidation of states.[833]

As indicated earlier in this Section of Appendix C, in Federalist ten, Madison decided why factions cannot be controlled by a pure democracy. The fourth President wrote:

> A common passion or interest will, in almost every case be felt by a majority of the whole, a communication and concert result from the form of government itself; and there

---

831 Madison. Federalist Papers. [Essay no. ten.], pp. 41–47

832 Ibid., Essay thirty-nine, pp. 182–187

833 Ibid

is nothing to check the inducements to sacrifice the weaker party or an obnoxious individual.⁸³⁴

Mr. Madison argued in Federalist 39 that the Roman Republic was not really a genuine republic because at the top an aristocratic cadre elite cared only about the rich, and the common people were treated as outcastes and not as member of society. Madison suggested that in the Roman Republic the common folk were treated as being politically immature in the fourth President's version of an American Republic everyone is treated equally and has a say in government.⁸³⁵

This, of course, is not all that different from the current Executive Branch of the United States Government, with President Joe Biden at the helm who care far more about the ruling Elite than they do about the common folk who they consider to be politically immature and contribute little to the Government.

In the *Federalist Papers* essay number thirty-nine. Mr. Madison sketches out three rules that must apply to be considered an American Republic. These can be summarized this way:

1. The establishment of an America Republic should be by the Rule of the People.

2. The person chosen to rule the Republic must not break any rules or abuse their power.

3. The rulers in an American Republic should be temporary.⁸³⁶

Finally, most American Enlightenment scholars agree that *Federalist Papers* essay number fifty-one is also one the five most important missive of the total of eighty-five essays. This is chiefly because Mr. Madison introduced the idea of "proper checks and balances between the different departments, or branches, of Government."⁸³⁷ In fact, the fourth President gave Federalist fifty-one the title:

---

834 Ibid., essay ten, pp. 41–42
835 Ibid
836 Ibid., essay thirty-nine, pp. 182–183
837 Ibid., essay fifty-one, pp. 253–256

"The Structure of the Government Must Furnish the Proper Checks and Balances Between the Different Departments.[838]

The essay was first published by Mr. Madison in the *New York Packet* on February 8, 1788, as usual, under the pseudonym, Publius. The idea of checks and balances in the Federal Government is a crucial part of the government of the United States. One of the most important aspects of Federalist 51 is the often-quoted phrase, "Ambition must be made to counteract ambition."[839]

One way to interpret that phrase is to suggest that Mr. Madison had harkened back to the Platonic view of the Soul that the fourth President, as well as his college mentor, john Witherspoon, saw ambition as one of the Appetitive parts of the soul, along with greed, pride, and many other aspects of the personality that have self-interest as its key element.[840]

In Federalist essay 51, Mr. Madison also stressed the idea that the three branches of Government—Executive, Legislative, and Judicial—must operate independently of the other two branches. Essay number fifty-one of the *Federalist Papers* is also the origin, of the James Madison lines:

> If men were angels, no government would be necessary. If angels were to govern Men, neither external nor internal controls of Government would be necessary.[841]

It is not entirely clear what Mr. Madison meant by these lines that appear on both essays 10 and 51 of the *Federalist Papers*. We suspect it had something to do with the High Middle Ages idea of the Great Chain of Being, where existent entities are ranked according to how much of Aristotle's function of the Soul a being possesses, God is pure Reason and has one function. Humans have three, Rational, Sensitive, and Vegetative.[842] Angels, according to thinkers like Thomas Aquinas,

---

838 Ibid., p. 253
839 Ibid., p. 255
840 Plato. The Phaedrus. (New York: Penguin Books, 2005.) 434d–439e
841 James Madison. Federalist Papers. Essay fifty-one, pp. 255–256
842 Ibid., p. 253

have no physical bodies, so they do not eat, excrete, reproduce and grow. If human beings were ruled by Angels in Mr. Madison's view, then they would be ruled by a class of beings devoid of human passions.

This brings us to the Third, and Final Section of this Appendix on James Madison and the Federalist Papers, in which we will make some judgments about the place of Religion in the essays of the *Federalist Papers* written by the fourth President of the United States, James Madison.

Madison and Religion in His Federalist Papers.

In this Final Section of this Appendix on Madison and the Federalist Papers, we will make some general, as well as specific observations about what role the phenomenon of Religion played in the essays of the *Federalist Papers* written by James Madison.

The two main areas where Mr. Madison mentioned Religion in his essays of the *Federalist Papers* are Religious Freedom and the Separation of Church and State. As we have shown earlier in this Study, the fourth President's views about the former can be found in Chapter V and the latter issue in Chapter VI of this Study of James Madison's Religion.

Madison's essay number 51 is the best source in the Federalist Papers for his views on Religious Freedom, where he specifically mentions the Establishment clause of the Constitution and what he called the Right of Conscience. For Madison, as we have shown earlier in this Study, the Conscience is the most valued part of human nature, chiefly because the fourth President believed that God inherently endowed every soul with a sense of the Moral Good. In *Federalist Papers* fifty-one, Madison made the claim that "property is a natural right," and "the most sacred of all property is Conscience," and the fourth President gave Conscience the title of "Intangible Property."[843] Mr. Madison also mentioned the issue of the Separation of Church and State in *Federalist*, essay number ten where he warns that:

---

843 For more on Aristotle's Great Chain of Being, see Arthur Lovejoy. The Great Chain of Being: A Study of the History of an Idea. (Cambridge; Harvard University Press, 1976.), particularly pp. 67–98

> The latent causes of Factions are thus sown in the nature of man... A zeal for different opinions concerning Religion and Government and may other points ambitiously contending for pre-eminence and power.[844]

The fourth President goes on to add more about the dangers of Factions. He related in *Federalist* ten that Factions:

> Divide mankind into parties, inflamed then with mutual animosity, and render them much more disposed to vex and oppose each other than to cooperate for the idea of the Common Good.[845]

For Mr. Madison Church and State were distinct in that the Federal Government could not elevate one religious denomination, or Religious Faction if you will, over all others. Nor did the fourth president think that the Government and its flawed inhabitants, usurp Divine authority by harnessing politics to the Church. As Mr. Madison related in *Federalist* ten, "Faith is no civil contract, but a personal matter not to be profaned by politics."[846]

This brings us to the Notes of Appendix C on James Madison and his contributions to the *Federalist Papers* in which his comments on Religion, as we have shown, come mostly from his three most important essays of the *Federalist Papers,* which is Numbers, ten, thirty-nine and fifty-one.

---

844 Madison. Federalist Papers. Essay fifty-one, pp. 255–256
845 Madison. Federalist Papers Essay ten, pp. 41–42
846 Ibid., p. 42

Appendix D:
Madison's Philosophical Foundations

1. Education.
2. Rev. Robert Innes.
3. Rev. Donald Robertson.
4. Rev. Thomas Martin.
5. Rev. John Witherspoon.
6. Reading.
7. Classical Contributions.
8. Plato. [nature of Soul.]
9. Aristotle [nature of Soul and Ethics.]
10. Thomas Aquinas. [Great Chain of Being.]
11. Enlightenment Sources.
12. John Locke.
13. Thomas Reid.
14. John Witherspoon.
15. Figures with whom he disagreed: Hume, Descartes, Skeptics, Rationalists and Empiricists.

Appendix E
Madison as Father of the Constitution

The meaning of the Constitution should be fixed and known.
—John Marshall

The Constitution only gives people the right to pursue happiness. You have to go out and catch it yourself.
—Benjamin Franklin

The diversity in the faculties of men, from which the rights of property originate... the protection of these faculties is the first object of Government.
—James Madison

Introduction

The aims of this Fifth Appendix, or Appendix E of this Study on James Madison's Religion is to accomplish two major tasks. The first of these is to comment and to discuss the nature and elements of the Constitution of the United States. Thus, the Appendix will open with the First Section in regard to this task.

The other aim of this Appendix E is to discuss how and why the fourth President of the United States, James Madison, is often referred to as the "Father of the U.S. Constitution," in his own time and since.

The Nature and Extent of the U.S. Constitution

The Constitution of the United States established the national government and its fundamental laws. It also guaranteed certain basic human rights for its citizens, rights that were 'endowed' by their Creator, that is, God. The Constitution was signed on September 17, 1787 by delegates of the Constitutional Convention in Philadelphia.

Under what was called the "Articles of Confederation," the national government was weak and the thirteen colonies or states operated as their own fiefdoms, or as independent countries.

At the 1787 Convention, delegates devised a plan for a stronger federal government that would include three separate branches—the Executive, the Legislative, and the judicial, along with a system of "checks and balances" to ensure that none of the branches became too powerful.

In this First Section of Appendix E, we will discuss seven different aspects of the U.S. Constitution. We will list these here and then discuss each aspect individually. These aspects we have in mind are the following:

1. The Preamble.
2. The Articles of Confederation.
3. Forming a More Perfect Union.
4. Debating the Constitution.
5. Ratifying the Constitution.
6. The Bill of Rights.
7. Contemporary Uses and Views on the Constitution.[847]

---

[847] The main source for this Appendix E has been the article by Cary Hardy entitled, "Why James Madison is known A the Father of the Constitution." We also have consulted the following U.S. Federal documents and sources:
  A. British "Petition of Rights." [1628.]
  B. The Bill of Rights. [1791.]
  C. The U.S. Constitution. [1787.]
  D. The Federalist Papers. [1787.]
  E. The 1689 English Bill of Rights. [1689.]
  F. Governor Morris Final Draft of the Constitution. [1787.]
  G. James Madison's First Draft of the Constitution. [1787.]
  H. The Articles of Confederation. [1777.]

The first of these aspects, the Preamble to the U.S. Constitution, outlines the purposes and guiding principles that underlay the document. The Preamble tells us this:

> We the People of the United States, in Order to form a more perfect Union, establish Justice, insure domestic Tranquility, provide for the common defense, promote the general Liberty and secure the Blessings of Liberty to ourselves and our Posterity, do ordain and establish this Constitution for the United States of America.[848]

The Preamble was added to the Constitution in the final days of the Constitutional Convention. It was constructed by a committee known as "the Committee of Style," that was led by Governor Morris of New York. For this work, Morris is known as the "Pen man" of the Preamble.[849]

Our second aspect of the U.S. Constitution, what we have labeled the "Articles of Confederation," was ratified in 1781, a time when the nation was still a loose confederation of states, each operating independently on its own. The national government was comprised of a single legislature, the Congress of the Confederation. There was not yet a President, nor a judicial system. The Articles of Confederation gave Congress the power to govern foreign affairs, to conduct war, and to regulate its own currency, independent from that of the British Government.

Soon after the United States won its independence from Great Britain with its 1783 victory in the American Revolution, it became increasingly evident that the young American Republic needed a stronger, central, if for no other reason, in order to remain stable.

---

848 'Preamble' to U.S. Constitution. It was also written, with Mr. Madison doing the first draft, in July of 1787. Governor Morris refined the fourth President's first draft of the Preamble

849 The 'Committee on Style' was formed in September and consisted of five members. These were Alexander Hamilton of New York; William Johnson [Ct.]; Rufus King of Massachusetts; James Madison [Virginia.]; and Governor Morris of Pennsylvania

Alexander Hamilton, a lawyer and politician in New York was the first to call for a Constitutional Convention to discuss the matter. And so, in February of 1787, the Confederate Congress endorsed the idea and all thirteen states were invited to send delegates to the meeting in Philadelphia.[850]

On May 25, 1787, the Constitutional Convention opened in Philadelphia in what is now known as Independence Hall, and where the Declaration of Independence had been approved eleven years earlier. There were fifty-five delegates in attendance, representing the thirteen states, with the exception of Rhode Island that refused to send any representative because it was reluctant to endorse a powerful, central government. It was also at this time that George Washington was unanimously selected as first President of the nascent United States of America.[851]

Later, these delegates will become known as the "Framers of the U.S. Constitution." They were a well-educated group of mostly merchants, farmers, bankers, and lawyers. Many had served in the Continental Army. Most were Protestant. Eight were signers of the Declaration of Independence and six were signer to the Articles of Confederation.[852]

At the age of eighty-one, Benjamin Franklin was the oldest of the delegates, but the majority of the representatives were in their thirties and forties. Several prominent American politicians were not present at the Constitutional Convention, including Thomas Jefferson and John Adams who were serving in Europe as Ambassadors, and John Jay, Samul Adams, and John Hancock who also were absent.

Virginia's Patrick Henry refused to attend because he did not want to give credence to the idea of a central government possessing too much power, and fearing the "Federalists" would endanger the rights of both states and individuals. Thus, Patrick Henry would become the leader of the 'Anti-Federalists."

---

850 The ratification occurred in February of 1787. The thirteen states sent 54 delegates to the Convention

851 The Constitutional Convention lasted from May 25, 1787 until September 17, 1787

852 Cary Hardy

Throughout the summer of 1787, the delegates debated various issues related to the proposed Constitution. Among the most contentious questions was the role of the states in the federal government. Another controversial issue was Slavery, as well as how the slaves were to be counted, with a general agreement that it would be as three-fifths of a person. Finally, it was also agreed that Slavery was to be outlawed after 1808. This provision, of course, did not come to fruition and slavery continued until the end of the Civil War.[853]

By September of 1787, the five member "Committee of Style, Hamilton, Madison, William Johnson of Connecticut, Governor Morris of New York, and Rufus King of Massachusetts, drafted the final text of the U.S. Constitution that consisted of some 4,200 hundred words.[854]

On September 17, 1787, George Washington was the first to sign the document. Of the fifty-five delegates, only thirty-nine signed. Some already had left Philadelphia and three important figures—George Mason, Edmond Randolph, and Elbridge Gerry of Massachusetts, boldly refused to sign. In order for the Constitution to become law, it had to be ratified the thirteen states.[855]

What followed next was the formation of the *Federalist Papers* by Alexander Hamilton, James Madison and some assistance from John Jay. The purpose of these essays was to garner support for the U.S. Constitution and what came to be known as the Federalist Party, as we have seen in Appendix C of this work. This brings us to aspect six on our list, the Bill of Rights.

In 1789, James Madison, who was now a member of the newly formed U.S. House of Representatives, introduced nineteen amendments to the U.S. Constitution. On September 25, 1789, Congress adopted twelve of Mr., Madison' nineteen and then sent them to the states for ratification. Ten of these amendments became collectively known as the "Bill of Rights." They became part of the Constitution officially on December 10, 1791.[856]

---

853   Ibid
854   See note three.
855   Cary Hardy.
856   Ibid

Since that time, there have been hundreds of proposed amendments to the Constitution, but only seventeen have been ratified in addition to the Bill of Rights. The most recent amendment to the U.S. Constitution—Article XXVII, which deals with Congressional pay raises, was proposed in 1789, but not ratified until 1992.[857]

This brings us to the most controversial aspect of the U.S. Constitution on our list, how the document is now employed and understood in Contemporary America. As we shall see, there are two major schools of thought about the nature and the uses of the U.S. Constitution.

The first of these two camps, we shall call the "Originalists." These are people who wish to ascertain what the "original intentions" of the framers were. The Originalists tend to be particular and exact about their claims on the Constitution. This group is to be distinguished from the other School that we will call the "Constitution as a living Document" School. That argues that this great founding document should be forever growing, often ostensibly to discover "new rights," such as pertaining to Abortion, LGBTQ rights, as well as the rights of Transgender people.[858]

For the most part, those who are proponents of the Originalist School often tend to be Libertarians and Republicans. At the same time, those of the Living Document School tend to be Liberals and Democrats.

This brings us to the Second Section of this Appendix E in which we will attempt to answer the question, "Why is James Madison called the Father of the U.S. Constitution?" As we will see in the Second Section the answer to that question is much more complicated than it might first appear to be.

Why is James Madison Called the Father of the US Constitution?

Much of the material already mention in this Appendix E has given us some hints about why the fourth President of the United States, James Madison

---

857 Ibid

858 These names Originalists and the Living Document view are the inventions of the author. Similar names have been proposed by many contemporary scholars in the late 20th and early 21st Centuries.

began to be known as the Father of the U.S. Constitution. Mr. Madison was generally a good historian in understanding the past documents on human rights like the *Magna Carta* and the English *Petition of Rights* of 1628, a petition sent by Parliament to King Charles I.[859]

As we have shown in this study, Mr. Madison also had been trained in the philosophies of Plato and Aristotle and he was fully aware, as well, of the Enlightenment thinkers like John Locke and the Baron Montesquieu. Thus, Mr. Madison knew most of the major works on natural rights in the English and French speaking worlds, as well as reading the Greeks philosophers in their original language, that Mr. Madison had learned Rev. Robertson and Rev. Martin.[860]

In order to create the Constitution and the Bill of Rights, as well as arguments in the *Federalist Papers*, the fourth President drew on these predecessors. These predecessors had repercussions of the U.S. Constitution the Bill of Rights, as well as the state constitutions of the original thirteen colonies/state, and especially for Mr. Madison's role in the making of the Virginia Constitution of 1776.[861]

Thus, we not only have the Separation of Powers in the U.S. Constitution, but also the natural human rights that it ensures, that, of which, we have Mr. Madison to thank. We have him to thank for adapting the great political philosophies and imbuing them into the structure and philosophical backbone of America.

---

859   English Petition of Rights. [1628.] It was passed on June 7, 1628. It was an English Constitutional document that set out specific individual protections against the government. The Petition, at the time, was purported to be equal to the 'Magna Carta" Later, the 1689 Bill of Rights would follow later in the same century in 1689. The Magna Carta, or properly known as the magna Carta Libertatum, was medieval Latin for the "Great Charter of Rights." It was a document approved by King john of England at the Runnymede near Windsor on June 15, 1215, The first draft of the document is said to have been written by the Archbishop of Canterbury, Cardinal Stephen Langton, in order to make peace between the King and a group of rebel barons.

860   James Madison learned Greek from the age of eleven to sixteen.

861   Federalist Papers. [1787.]

Mr. Madison also was also active in defending the Constitution and the Bill of Rights, working with the Federalists, even though later the fourth President became an anti-Federalist, during his time as leader of the House of Representatives in 1789. At that time, he also supported the Bill of Rights, which he also drafted, and then was a Democrat-Republican seeing as his close friend, Thomas Jefferson, as Secretary of State, and then followed him as the fourth President of the U.S., serving for two terms.

As a backdrop for this period, it is important to remember that the Federalists supported the Constitution but not the Bill of Rights. The Anti-Federalists supported the Articles of Confederation and the Bill of Rights, so we see how vital James Madison centered perspectives were.

Unlike many other of the founding father placed in contemporary America on the Right or the Left. James Madison was an entirely different kind of politician in that he had a more balanced view and it would make more sense to say he today would be better placed in the middle of the American political scene.

The fourth president of the United States, James Madison was skillful in the art of political compromise. In many ways, we owe the balanced nature of our government and rights to Mr. Madison. He realized the elusive nature of political compromise and he understood that sometimes many different arguments may have merit. And thus, in Madison's view, if competing Factions arose, he believed that they could be resolved through the system of checks and balances, as well as the Separation of Powers, another contribution of Mr. Madison.[862]

Although Governor Morris of New York wrote the final wording of the U.S. Constitution, but Madison provided to Governor Morris an earlier draft.[863] Thus, in light of all of these facts, it makes perfectly good sense to say that in addition to be the chief author of the Bill of Rights, an author of the *Federalist Papers*, and the fourth President of the United States, James Madison was also the "Father of the U.S. Constitution."

---

862 Ibid., essays 10, 39, and 51.

863 This earlier draft written by James Madison and sent to Governor Morris of Pennsylvania was completed in July of 1787.

About the Author

Stephen J. Vicchio was born and raised in Baltimore, Maryland, in a working-class neighborhood. He was educated at the University of Maryland; Yale Divinity School; Hertford College, Oxford; and acquired a Ph.D. from St. Andrews University in Fife, Scotland. He has authored more than forty books, including essays, stories, plays, and books about the Bible, slavery, ethics, histories, and many other topics. His writing awards include the Frank Muir Prize for fiction, the A.D. Emmart Award for outstanding writing in the humanities, and the Thomas Grey Prize for Best PhD Thesis in the British Universities for the year 1986.